Recasting History

Recasting History

How CBC Television
Has Shaped Canada's Past

Monica MacDonald

McGill-Queen's University Press

Montreal & Kingston • London • Chicago

ISBN 978-0-7735-5631-7 (cloth)
ISBN 978-0-7735-5632-4 (paper)
ISBN 978-0-7735-5808-3 (ePDF)
ISBN 978-0-7735-5809-0 (ePUB)

Legal deposit second quarter 2019
Bibliothèque nationale du Québec

Printed in Canada on acid-free paper that is 100% ancient forest free
(100% post-consumer recycled), processed chlorine free

Funded by the Government of Canada   Financé par le gouvernement du Canada | Canada Council for the Arts   Conseil des arts du Canada

We acknowledge the support of the Canada Council for the Arts,
which last year invested $153 million to bring the arts to Canadians
throughout the country.

Nous remercions le Conseil des arts du Canada de son soutien. L'an
dernier, le Conseil a investi 153 millions de dollars pour mettre de
l'art dans la vie des Canadiennes et des Canadiens de tout le pays.

Library and Archives Canada Cataloguing in Publication

Title: Recasting history : how CBC Television has shaped Canada's
   past / Monica MacDonald.
Names: MacDonald, Monica, 1965– author.
Description: Includes bibliographical references and index.
Identifiers: Canadiana (print) 20189067179 | Canadiana (ebook)
   20189067187 | ISBN 9780773556317 (hardcover) | ISBN
   9780773556324 (softcover) | ISBN 9780773558083 (PDF) | ISBN
   9780773558090 (EPUB)
Subjects: LCSH: Canadian Broadcasting Corporation. English Televi-
   sion Network–Influence. | LCSH: Television–Social aspects–Canada.
   | LCSH: History on television. | LCSH: Television and history–
   Canada. | LCSH: Television broadcasting policy–Canada–History. |
   LCSH: Historical television programs–Canada–History and criti-
   cism. | LCSH: Documentary television programs–Canada–History
   and criticism.

Classification: LCC PN1992.6 .M33 2019 | DDC 302.23/450971—dc23

Dedicated to the memory of my parents,
Pat and James MacDonald, and Terry Ruddel

Contents

Preface

The idea for this book emerged from my experience twenty years ago as the archival research coordinator at Library and Archives Canada for the CBC/Radio-Canada television series *Canada: A People's History*. Working with the Toronto- and Montreal-based teams on this series exposed me to the many challenges in translating history to television. It led me to explore the origins and development of Canadian history on CBC television as the subject of my PhD dissertation at York University.

History provides us with a means to understand the present and to make informed decisions about the future. This book builds on my discovery that CBC television, from the arrival of television in Canada in 1952, has played an important interpretive role as the primary mass media purveyor of Canadian history. I hope this book encourages television producers to interpret and present history not just as single, uncontested narratives but, rather, as complex accounts arising from multiple perspectives. I hope it also encourages viewers to engage in a critical reading of history on television.

Acknowledgments

This book builds on the work of many scholars, primarily in the fields of Canadian history, public history, communications, and media and journalism studies. Because it is concerned with the relatively recent past, I was fortunate to have been able to conduct interviews with a number of people who have played key roles in producing CBC television documentaries and docudramas on Canadian history. Here I am indebted to the late Eric Koch, the late Vincent Tovell, the late Jack Saywell, the late Knowlton Nash, the late Ramsay Cook, George Robertson, Gene Allen, and Hubert Gendron. Professor Cook and Mr Gendron also graciously allowed me access to some of their private papers.

I would not have undertaken or continued to pursue this work without the encouragement and advice of numerous scholars and colleagues, beginning with the members of my York University supervisory and examination committees: Fred Fletcher, Joy Cohnstaedt, Craig Heron, Ian McKay, Seth Feldman, and Mary Jane Miller, who together made many helpful suggestions. I am also grateful to those who read and commented on whole drafts or chapters of the manuscript: the late Terry Ruddel, Brian Young, and Jerry Bannister. The three anonymous scholars who reviewed the manuscript and provided constructive and detailed criticism helped me to shape and greatly improve the book.

Many thanks to the team at McGill-Queen's University Press, particularly my editor, Kyla Madden, and copy editor, Joanne Richardson. François Trahan prepared the index. Any factual or grammatical errors in the book are mine alone.

Finally, I am so fortunate to have had the support, encouragement, and patience of many loved ones, especially Terry Ruddel and Gerald Walsh, which has been invaluable throughout the long and difficult process of research and writing.

Monica MacDonald

Donald Creighton poses for a photograph during his interview for
A Long View of Canadian History.
Library and Archives Canada/Robert Ragsdale/Henry Fox Fonds/e011202377.

Trial scene in *A War for Survival*. Jack Saywell is third from right.
CBC Still Photo Collection.

Eric Koch, 1960s.
CBC Still Photo Collection.

Barry Morse, as Lord Durham, holding the "press conference"
in *Durham's Canada*.
CBC Still Photo Collection.

Vincent Tovell, c. 1971.
CBC Still Photo Collection.

Pierre Berton in a publicity photograph for *The National Dream*.
CBC Still Photo Collection.

Top Timothy Findley, Louis Applebaum, and William Whitehead during production of *The National Dream*.
CBC Still Photo Collection.

Bottom A scene from *The National Dream*.
CBC Still Photo Collection.

John Colicos, as William Van Horne, and director Eric Till in a
break during filming of *The National Dream*.
CBC Still Photo Collection.

Graham Campbell, as Air Chief Marshal Arthur Harris,
in *The Valour and the Horror*.
CBC Still Photo Collection.

Editorial artwork reproduced in the *Toronto Star* depicting the controversy over *The Valour and the Horror*, 9 March 1993.
Courtesy of Charles Weiss, charlesweissart.com.

Mark Starowicz during filming of the Battle of the Plains of Abraham sequence in *Canada: A People's History*.
CBC Still Photo Collection.

Director Serge Turbide providing instruction for a dramatized scene in
Canada: A People's History.
CBC Still Photo Collection.

Recasting History

Introduction

In the spring of 2017 the CBC faced an angry public reaction to the first episodes of *Canada: The Story of Us*, a television series created to commemorate the 150th anniversary of Confederation. The series was the third attempt of CBC television since its inception to interpret the entire span of Canadian history. *The Story of Us* claimed Quebec City over Port Royal, Nova Scotia, as the beginning of permanent European settlement in what is now Canada, portrayed the French in New France in scenes biased in favour of the English, and featured a slew of celebrities speaking as authorities on historic events. It was one of only a handful of Canadian television programs ever to provoke such a backlash, yet it prompted debates rooted in a long tradition of Canadian history programming on CBC television.

Television: ubiquitous, immediate, and intimate, it greatly influences our understanding of both current and past events. History in books or museum exhibitions does not capture mass audiences like history on television. And the CBC is the only television broadcaster, indeed the only form of electronic mass media, that has regularly produced and broadcast Canadian history. For a time the exception was CBC radio, but CBC radio has long since abandoned the prominent role it once played in this regard. And, unlike the American past, which has been translated into films like *The Post* (2017), *Selma* (2014), and *12 Years a Slave* (2013), the Canadian past has rarely made it to the movie screens.

This book offers an alternate perspective on public history by investigating Canadian history documentary programming on CBC television since television began in 1952. First, it reveals the consistency of the program themes, subjects, and interpretations. Why did producers choose them over others, and what did they leave out? From the early anthology series *Explorations* to the blockbuster mega-series *Canada: A People's History*, producers promoted ideas about national identity and national unity through programs on war, national politics, relations between French and English Canada, and conflict between Canada and the United States. Central Canada was the focus. Even with the great shift in the writing of history beginning in the late 1960s, at which time scholars turned away from nationalist themes, subjects, and interpretations, the television histories barely changed. Clearly, Canadian history on television is about something other than the work of historians.

Second, this book dissects the presentation strategies producers used and how they led audiences to think about history in certain ways. The result was not always the desired one. The conventions were established at the beginning of television; the changes were in the specific techniques, particularly evident in dramatization, first-person testimony, and expert commentary. In later years the elaborate and computer-enhanced dramatization, first-person testimony delivered by actors, and the absence of professional historians onscreen marked a clear departure from earlier works. It was part of the trajectory from an era of experimentation, when staff tried a variety of presentation techniques in an attempt to convey some of the complexities of history, to a time when a more rigid set of ideas determined what should and should not be done. While the content remained distinctively Canadian, it ended up being presented as linear narratives in compelling though standardized formats. It was history only as a story, with little hint of how the story was arrived at.

The producers themselves provide the main clue to these changes, as this book brings to light the role of professional historians in the television productions and the assuming of their role by professional journalists. Historiography covers the written work of historians, but in the early days of the CBC, scholars like Donald Creighton, Charles Stacey, Jack Saywell, and Ramsay Cook, along with senior CBC production staff like Eric Koch, Vincent Tovell, and George Robertson, brought Canadian history to television audiences as well. They were all members of a Canadian intelligentsia who worked together based on mutual respect and a commitment to the educational and nation-building mandate of the CBC. This relationship broke down upon the emergence of professional journalists not only as the new producers of Canadian history programs on CBC television but also as the new content authorities. Journalism had developed a set of professional codes and standards so that, by the 1970s, some journalists producing Canadian history on television believed their work to be at odds with the work of professional historians. Earlier CBC staff, like Koch, Tovell, and Robertson, were program organizers, producers, and directors. They did not consider themselves to be journalists.[1]

History on television is less about history than it is about the production of history for television in its political, economic, and social contexts. Broadcasting regulation and policy, the imperatives of the television industry and television as a medium, and the professional circumstances of television producers were key to shaping these programs.[2] In over sixty years of CBC television, Canadian history programs changed remarkably in some ways and in some ways not at all. These changes and consistencies were a result of attempts by producers to fulfill Canadian government and CBC directives (like those connected to the mandate); of concerns affecting the television industry overall (like those connected to ratings, technological change, and job creation); and of the preconceived ideas of television producers about Canadian history and what they believed to be their own role in interpreting it for television. These factors did not entirely determine program content and presentation. But they had a critical and observable impact on what the final programs looked like as well as on what went to air in the first place – and what did not.[3]

Exploring the major works of Canadian history on CBC television in relation to each other reveals patterns and developments in content, interpretation, and presentation that are invisible if viewing the works in isolation. These patterns and developments emerge most clearly from five series: *Explorations* (1956–64), *Images of Canada* (1972–76), *The National Dream* (1974), *The Valour and the Horror* (1992), and *Canada: A People's History* (2000–02). *Explorations*, an anthology series broadcast over a period of eight years, featured a further five representative works of distinct content and presentation styles. Two of them, "The Fall of Quebec: A Battle for Historians," and

"Winnipeg General Strike 1919," were one-off pieces. Three of them were three- to four-part limited series: *A Long View of Canadian History*, *Durham's Canada*, and *A War for Survival*. Considering these programs in their international contexts is also important. *Images of Canada*, *The Valour and the Horror*, and *Canada: A People's History* all owe something to the popularity (and notoriety) of similar works from Britain, France, and the United States.

This book is about documentary programs, or those featuring a documentary element (docudrama), on the CBC English television network. Documentary has been defined in various ways. At its basic level, the "creative treatment of actuality," from former National Film Board (NFB) founder, John Grierson, is still current.[4] The Canadian Media Fund defines it as "an original work of non-fiction, primarily designed to inform but that may also educate and entertain, providing an in-depth critical analysis of a specific subject or point of view." This includes "auteur point-of-view/creative" works but not instructional, lifestyle, or reality shows.[5] Film scholar Bill Nichols has suggested that documentary can be understood in terms of the following four factors: (1) that a particular institution will produce a type of work recognized as a documentary; (2) that the makers of documentaries share a set of professional codes and assumptions about what they do; (3) that a documentary will exhibit certain conventions, like voice-of-God commentary or first-person testimony, and be categorized into periods and modes; and (4) that audiences have certain expectations for a documentary – namely, that it represents historical reality and real people.[6]

Docudrama is a hybrid of documentary and drama. It combines documentary elements like first-person testimony, expert commentary, and moving or still images with dramatic elements like actors in silent roles or actors speaking words based on the historical record. While documentaries are made for both television and film, docudramas are more typically produced for television. Like the creators of a fictional film, the creators of a documentary or docudrama must select, edit, and shape the content. Yet documentaries and docudramas are still perceived as reliable representations of what actually happened, based on known facts.[7]

The Broadcasting Act, 1991, identifies the Canadian Broadcasting Corporation (CBC) as Canada's national public broadcaster.[8] Public service broadcasting is central to democracy because it provides universal access to diverse educational, informational, or high-quality programming that serves all audiences, including niche audiences. It aims to serve the public good, not commercial ends or those of the nation-state. Yet nation building has always been the foundation of the CBC mandate.[9] From the beginning, officials viewed CBC television as a tool to help instill in Canadians a common set of symbols and stories as a means of building national unity and creating a national identity. The current act states that the CBC is to "contribute to shared national consciousness and identity," and "reflect Canada and its regions to national and regional audiences." Thus it exists to serve not only the public interest but also the national interest.

All public service broadcasting is publicly owned, and the CBC is likewise funded by taxpayers through an annual parliamentary appropriation. Yet it is compromised in this respect as well, because it also generates a portion of its funding through commercial means. In the first decades of CBC television in particular, there were many discussions about how to strike a balance between what was deemed to be entertainment values, which were more often connected with commercial programs, and what was deemed to be public service or educational values, more often connected with documentaries, docudramas, and other informational or non-commercial programs. In the very early years the CBC was the only national television broadcaster in English, so these debates arose more from these different interpretations of the mandate than from fear of market competition.

Commercial content most often meant American content. Indeed, despite the perceived threat to Canada from the impact of American culture, identified long before the beginning of television, the CBC ran American programs because they were often cheaper to buy than domestic programs or producing in house. American content appealed to advertisers because it was already popular in the United States and so was likely to attract Canadian audiences as well. Once committed to the CBC lineup, American programs competed with Canadian programs for promotional resources and good time slots, thus affecting the content and scheduling of Canadian content. And, upon the arrival of Canadian commercial television broadcasters, these programs put the CBC in competition with them too.

It was largely in response to the early Americanization of the Canadian (radio) airwaves that this nation-building component of the CBC mandate began to take shape. In the early 1920s, radio broadcasting in Canada began to develop a strong commercialized and American element. Many Canadians, depending on where they lived, were soon able to receive these American programs either directly or, by the 1930s, via Canadian affiliated stations.[10] In response, in 1932 the government of R.B. Bennett created a national public service radio broadcaster: the Canadian Radio Broadcasting Commission (CRBC). The CRBC closely emulated the British Broadcasting Corporation (BBC) in the two main tenets of public service broadcasting: universal accessibility and education. For the CRBC, however, nation building was also key. In introducing the Radio Broadcasting Act, 1932, to the House of Commons, Bennett laid the foundation for the new public service by describing it as necessary to fill the "national need": a means to foster "national consciousness" and strengthen "national unity."[11]

The Bennett government funded the new broadcasting service (renamed the CBC in 1936) through a licence fee charged to each radio receiver. In order to better support the service and provide opportunities for Canadian business, especially since Canada was in the middle of the Depression, the rest of the funding came from advertising. Commercial entities preferred American programs because they were already created for mass audiences and popular with listeners, so while the government seemingly positioned the CRBC as a BBC-style national public service, in practice it was a mix of public and private elements, heavy on American programming.[12]

For television, the government determined that the public sector would dominate and that the system as a whole would be better regulated than it had been with radio. The first move in that direction was the creation in 1949 of the Royal Commission on National Development in the Arts, Letters and Sciences (the Massey Commission). The mandate of the commission, chaired by chancellor of the University of Toronto and former diplomat Vincent Massey, was to assess the operations of the CBC, the NFB, the national museums, and other national institutions in order to make recommendations on "their most effective conduct in the national interest."[13] Television broadcasting was a particular concern. Although Canadian television had not yet begun, households with a television set and located close enough to the United States were able to receive American programs. Officials worried that Canadians would develop a liking for American works on television, as they had with radio. Yet, despite the Massey Commission's characterizing the American influence on Canadian broadcasting as a menace – detrimental to Canadian national identity, overall good taste, and education – American programs came to prevail on television too.[14]

The nation-building purpose of the CBC, though not specifically spelled out in the mandate until 1968, was always expressed in terms of strengthening national unity and national identity. Over the years CBC staff were often pressed to demonstrate how the television service was fulfilling this requirement. In response, they cited any Canadian history program then in production or on air. For example, in 2002, three of the four primary television contributions that the CBC highlighted as vehicles to build "Canadian awareness and identity through innovative, nation-binding programming" were Canadian history programs: *Random Passage*, a fictional series about life in an early nineteenth-century small outport in Newfoundland; *Trudeau*, a dramatic miniseries about the late prime minister; and *Canada: A People's History*, a two-season, thirty-two-hour series on the history of Canada.[15]

History has long been recognized as "the backbone of nationalism."[16] Stories like these about the hardscrabble lives of our colonial ancestors, the past achievements of great leaders, and the inspirational histories of national progress help define national identity by establishing a uniqueness that sets Canada apart from other nations and that sets Canadians apart from non-Canadians. These stories are promoted as elements of a larger narrative meant to be accepted by anyone who professes to be a member of the national community, or what political scientist and historian Benedict Anderson has referred to as the "fraternity."[17] History – or, rather, popular ideas about history – is central to the naturalization of nations and nationality as the way to think about the world, a pervasive framework of reference represented in all forms of cultural production, including television.[18]

Nationalism is widely seen as a modern development, as something that occurred when the nation-state began to prevail over ethnocultural or religious distinctions as a means of identity. Nationalism scholar Anthony D. Smith has suggested, however, that definitions of the national self arose from a nation's existing dominant ethnic groups and the reinterpretation and politicization of those of their collective memories, traditions, and myths that already had the most resonance: "The shared memories of golden ages, ancestors and great heroes and heroines, the communal values that they embody, the myths of ethnic origins, migration and divine election, the symbols of community, territory, history and destiny that distinguish them."[19] With the rise of nationalism these collective memories, traditions, and myths were not always created anew but recast in new ways. They are binding agents that hold a community together, and the more rooted in the past they are thought to be the better it is, because this allows them to be considered inherent to the national community. While nationalism as an ideology may be modern, nations themselves are imagined as old.[20]

How does this work for a relatively young nation like Canada, officially founded as a union of just four provinces in 1867 and first colonized by Europeans only some 260 years before that? The French and the British, the first Europeans to settle permanently in what is now Canada, initially located in areas they understood only as French or British colonies or territories. Samuel de Champlain, David Thompson, and Isaac Brock, all of whom have been depicted more than once in CBC television histories as national heroes instrumental in some way to the development of Canada, had no comprehension of Acadia or New France in the seventeenth century, or Rupert's Land or Upper Canada in the eighteenth and nineteenth centuries, as part of the much larger nation that is Canada today.

Yet CBC television producers embedded the stories of these men and their exploits into an existing conceptual framework – "colony to nation" – that blurred distinctions between time periods and frontiers, and allowed the dominant Canadian ideologies and values of the television era to be superimposed on the historical characters. Thus the CBC stories of Champlain, Thompson, and Brock, as well as many other men (and they were all men) depicted as heroes on CBC television, like Pierre-Esprit Radisson, James Wolfe, and Lord Durham, helped to establish an idea of national continuity and identity from the earliest days of European exploration and colonization up to the present day.[21] Producers tended to downplay or resolve disruptions to that continuity, especially in connection to the ideas about national identity they wanted to promote, like those connected to borders, mindsets, loyalties, and language.

Governments around the world invoke aspects of a shared past as a way to help instill in citizens a sense of national identity. Scholars see this "national appropriation of the past" as a complex and nuanced process – an act of remembering and forgetting that involves regular people as much as it does elites.[22] Yet, while regular citizens help to create and maintain these historical narratives, powerful cultural producers play an important role. They include television producers of history programs, whose own acceptance of these narratives may be unconscious, but their reinterpretation of them on television reinforces them as the most relevant. It also includes historians who, in the early days of CBC television especially, were key to constructing a public sense of national identity through their written work and their work for television. They helped to strengthen these nationalist narratives and, conversely, to sustain the absence, or "silence," of other versions of history.[23] Historian John (Jack) Saywell, featured here in chapter 1 as the writer and host of a four-part series on the War of 1812, referred to a similar problem with the historical accounts of his predecessors and contemporaries. Saywell's reason for proposing the series was that historians themselves had "built a formidable wall of myths" around the war, and this got in the way of knowing what really took place.[24]

Historians of Canada undoubtedly contributed to myth making about Canada, yet there is a difference between the creation of myth and the current professional practice of history. Myths are idealized accounts that are useful to nationalism because they provide the elements by which a nation can define itself as such. They make sense of complex events through simplified narratives, rendering them easy to understand and to remember. They may contain some fact and plausibility, but they distort what actually happened, as far as that can be known. Modern historians aim to untangle and elucidate the complexities of the past. They interpret events by placing them in their multiple contexts, evaluating the available evidence, and noting continuity and change over time. While historians strive for objectivity, they understand that total objectivity is not fully possible – not only because of their own values and biases but also because of those inherent in their historical sources, which never provide a complete record of the past. Historians must also select, assume, and use their imagination. Historical explanation is therefore always tentative, so, although a necessity, it is an "impossible necessity," as historian Ged Martin has put it.[25]

When CBC television began in 1952, ideas about what was important about the Canadian past were already everywhere, manifest in a wide array of commemorative practices and cultural products such as monuments, novels and plays, and radio broadcasts. These were the stories about European explorers and their "discovery" and mapping of what became known as Canada; the politicians and industrialists, and what was seen as the political, constitutional, and economic events that led to responsible government and the creation of the nation-state; the wars and the heroes who defended the colonies against enemies like the Americans. Americans in particular were important as the national "other," the "them," who made it easier to define what Canadians were not.

These ideas, advanced by the work of historians like Donald Creighton, William Morton, Arthur Lower, and Charles Stacey, provided the bases for the first television programs on Canadian history. Canadian history was then still a relatively small field – those teaching and writing about it had themselves been schooled in Classical, British, and European history. There were few existing studies upon which to build in terms of the national past, so the preoccupation of these scholars was first to create foundational works to explain the growth of Canada as a nation. In attempting to help create a national identity independent of the British and American narratives, they were aware of their part in building Canadian nationalism. Many saw it as a duty, and cultural producers in other fields shared this sentiment. CBC television producers reinterpreted these works to suit the CBC mandate and policies, the visual and other requirements of television, and their own beliefs about what television audiences wanted to see.

This story begins with the launch of CBC television in 1952 and the creation in 1956 of *Explorations,* an educational anthology series featuring documentaries, docudramas, and dramas on a wide variety of subjects, including Canadian history. It was also a vehicle that provided the regional offices with an opportunity to engage in national broadcasting, though the centralization of CBC production in Toronto emerges as a controlling factor. *Explorations* is the earliest attempt by the CBC to produce a sustained schedule of Canadian history programming for television. Eric Koch, its program organizer, relied to a certain extent for content and presentation ideas on his CBC radio experience, but the new and unique requirements of television landed him in unfamiliar territory. Among those he consulted for help were professional historians. Thus began a fruitful relationship between CBC television producers and professional historians of Canada. It was based on their joint desire to educate Canadians and to build good citizens through knowledge of a common national history. *Explorations* also initiated a pattern of themes, subject matter, and interpretation, and introduced a variety of conventions in presentation that lasted throughout the years.

Chapters 2 and 3 take us to the 1970s with *Images of Canada* and *The National Dream*, two in a range of Canadian history programs created under journalist and director of information programming Knowlton Nash. This era of Canadian broadcasting began with the Broadcasting Act, 1968, an act that was revised and created for an increasingly populated industrial landscape. A rival national commercial broadcaster (the CTV) was gaining momentum, cable and satellite distribution was spreading, and newly created provincial broadcasters were beginning to air the type of educational programs that were once the exclusive purview of the CBC. With the continued reliance on American commercial programs, the CBC needed ammunition with which to prove it was fulfilling its mandate as Canada's national public service broadcaster.

Canadian history programs helped, particularly on the heels of the 1967 centennial celebrations. The documentary series *Images of Canada* was the first television series intended to interpret the entire Canadian past. Like *Explorations*, *Images* was an educational project, created along the lines of the internationally acclaimed BBC television series *Civilisation* (1969). *Images* also responded to a revision in the Broadcasting Act, arising from long-standing criticisms about centralization, that the CBC needed to better serve the needs of the Canadian regions. It created a challenge for Eric Koch and executive producer

Vincent Tovell: how to create a national narrative and still pay homage to regional history. The answer was *The Whitecomers*, a subseries of five episodes, each of which dealt with the history of a Canadian region. While *The Whitecomers* followed a standard documentary format with archival images and voiceover narration, the other episodes included hosted pieces and a set of interviews with historians. Koch and Tovell sought advice for *Images of Canada* from a number of professional historians and hired them not only as advisors but also as writers, episode hosts, and interviewed guests.

The National Dream was Nash's blockbuster. The docudrama series about the building of the Canadian Pacific Railway (CPR) got top billing as proof of the value of the CBC in both the nation-building and public service contexts. Nash, also capitalizing on the lingering sentiments of nationalism brought forth by the centennial, positioned the series competitively to draw a huge audience, and he delivered. Pierre Berton, as the author of the books upon which the series was based and the driving force behind the television production, was central to this success. Like professional historians he was concerned about accuracy, context, and conveying to the audience information about the historical evidence. He was a popular historian too, with an eye for big subjects, galloping plots, and colourful characters. But he was foremost a journalist, and in the 1970s professional journalists were emerging as the new television producers as well as the new content authorities for Canadian history programming on CBC television. Indeed, Berton was a turning point in the transfer of historical authority from professional historians to professional journalists.

Chapter 4 shows the CBC operating within a production model in which independent producers produced or co-produced a much larger portion of its overall programming. In this context appeared *The Valour and the Horror*, a docudrama series on the Second World War and a co-production of the CBC with the NFB and independent producers. The main production team members were journalists, brothers Brian and Terence McKenna, who sought not to support the existing Canadian war narrative but to challenge it. Their work ignited a highly charged and polarized debate that brought forth an avalanche of commentary from all corners of Canada. The nature and extent of this debate masked serious issues in the content and presentation of the series as history. The analysis offered in this book supports an account that differs from those depicting the producers as victims in an episode of Canada's history wars. It also reveals the deterioration of the relationship between professional historians and professional journalists in connection with Canadian history on CBC television.

Chapter 5 covers *Canada: A People's History*, the second attempt of the CBC to represent the entire Canadian past on television. This docudrama series, like *The Valour and the Horror*, received extraordinary financial and resource support from the CBC. The two came to represent what had become the standard for television history series in Canada: works that had high production values and were heavily dramatized yet were billed as documentaries. But *A People's History*, unlike *The Valour and the Horror*, did not upset conventional wisdom. Some of the subjects were new but the themes and interpretations were old, catering to a renewed feeling of nationalist sentiment brought about by the shock of the 1995 Quebec referendum and the coming millennium. The producers hired professional historians to point out errors, omissions, and imbalances, but the relationship between the two had changed significantly since television began in Canada. *A People's History* was nevertheless a popular and mostly critical success, at least in English-speaking Canada, and widely lauded as proof that the CBC was fulfilling its role as a national broadcaster and essential public service.

This story is about Canadian history documentaries and docudramas on CBC television since 1952. The CBC produced and broadcast these works in a variety of circumstances: from a time when it had little competition to a time in which it struggles to maintain relevance among a multitude of channels and platforms. From *Explorations*, the low-cost experimental anthology series beginning in the 1950s, to *Canada: A People's History*, the expensive millennial series that was in many ways conventional fare, CBC television is the only form of electronic media with a continuing tradition of producing and broadcasting Canadian history programs. Their themes and subjects have become familiar to us as the building blocks of Canadian history. Their interpretations have become the widely accepted ones. Why did producers choose these themes, subjects, and interpretations? And why did they present them the way they did?

1 | CBC Television Presents ... Canadian History! *Explorations*

Ernie Bushnell, CBC director general of programmes, was concerned about the future of the new medium soon to come under his direction. Returning in 1949 from a trip to the BBC headquarters in London, where television broadcasting was already under way, he reported back to his CBC bosses what he had learned. He cautioned them that television needed to be a "new form of entertainment and a new form of education that [would] have to stand on its own two legs or go under."[1] Bushnell was already a long-time CBC employee with expertise in radio programming. But he quickly realized that television had to be more than "photographed radio," as a BBC colleague suggested it was.

Bushnell knew that CBC television could build on the strengths of its radio counterpart. And as he and his radio colleagues had shown, the many programs they had produced on Canadian history helped the CBC meet its goals related to public service, nation building, and entertainment. These radio broadcasts, with titles like *They Came to Canada, The Birth of Canadian Freedom, The Heroes of Canada, The Building of Canada, They Build a Nation,* and *Canada as a Nation,* highlighted the achievements of the explorers, politicians, and military men perceived to be Canada's nation builders.[2] They were entertaining and informative, unique to Canada, and invoked a feeling of national connectedness.

When television arrived in 1952 there was not much change in CBC upper management or reporting structure. At the helm were the same Board of Governors and chairman (Davidson Dunton). CBC radio veteran, J. Alphonse Ouimet, became general manager, and under him was Bushnell as assistant general manager. The headquarters remained in Ottawa, and Toronto and Montreal continued to control most of the national program planning and production.[3] In the first few years national television coverage was limited, but, within ten years of the first broadcast, almost all Canadians had access.[4] The CBC was then a powerful entity as not only did it regulate the entire broadcasting industry in Canada, initially it also enjoyed a monopoly in that no private television station could operate in the same area as a CBC station until the national system was fully functional.

Funding for the new television service came from a combination of a small tax (which did not last), an appropriation from the federal government, and advertising. In spite of dire warnings from the Massey Commission and public broadcasting advocates about the Americanization and commercialization of Canadian broadcasting, the first television schedules featured many American, commercialized programs.[5] Although these programs were unsuited to the CBC's nation-building and public service goals, when the CBC first went to air it was obliged to offer this fare in order to fill the television schedule, meet perceived audience demand, and help pay for its existence. The conflicts arising from this contradiction characterized CBC policy making for the rest of the twentieth century and beyond.

In the 1950s, the CBC categorized most adult documentary and docudrama history on television as adult education, which was then under the auspices of the Talks and Public Affairs Department.[6] A set of guidelines for public affairs programs directed production practices. The guidelines stated that the format for any show would depend on the target audience; unless a large audience was anticipated, which would enable the producers to be less serious and to display more variety, producers were to use a "straightforward presentation." They were to solicit commentary from the regions and not just Toronto or Montreal (noted as being easier for radio than for television). They were to work with universities and organizations like the Canadian Labour Congress and the Canadian Association for Adult Education (CAAE), and hire subject matter experts as writers, consultants, or on-screen presenters.[7]

In addition to Talks and Public Affairs, departments like Drama, School Broadcasts, and Children's Programming also produced works based on Canadian history. The series *Folio*, from Drama, served as a vehicle for Canadian and other plays, sometimes on historical figures. School Broadcasts and Children's Programming produced many works on Canadian history for children. An early example was a highly touted series from Children's Programming on the adventures of the seventeenth-century French explorer Pierre-Esprit Radisson. *Radisson* was expensive, filmed on location in Quebec with a large cast of characters, and much-hyped in the press. Although the CBC cancelled it after two years on air, it marked an early attempt by the corporation to create a Canadian television historical hero who, in this instance, could compete with the widely popular American television and film historical hero Davy Crockett.[8]

Four years into the television era, Eugene Hallman, supervising producer of Talks and Public Affairs, proposed a new anthology series. Hallman envisioned *Explorations* as a transfer to television of the kind of programming that the *Wednesday Night* CBC radio series offered: cultural and educational, featuring eclectic content from all facets of life, with specialists and experts as consultants, panelists, writers, and hosts.[9] In keeping with the Irwin-Dunton agreement with the NFB, it would incorporate NFB film.[10] In encouraging submissions from the regions, it would help to satisfy corporate goals of being more inclusive of regional input and providing the regions with an opportunity for national broadcast. And it would include content from smaller CBC units like Farms and Fisheries, which had to fight for air time. For Hallman, these potential benefits also meant a lot of headaches.

Explorations became the primary CBC vehicle for the broadcast of Canadian history documentaries and docudramas, and it introduced long-standing patterns in theme, subject matter, interpretation, and presentation. The first question confronting Hallman was what to feature in terms of content. Ideas came from a number of sources, including professional historians. Historians shared with the producers a desire to educate television audiences on what they felt were the key elements of the Canadian past, and they often worked with them to develop the content. Another question was how to present these histories. The CBC was then the only English-language broadcaster in Canada, and this allowed staff to experiment with various presentation strategies. The programs took the form of documentaries, docudramas,

dramas, interviews, panel discussions, or some mixture thereof, even within the same hour or half-hour. With the documentaries and docudramas, producers often attempted to present history as both a story and as a mode of inquiry.

The germ of the idea for *Explorations* was an earlier series called *Exploring Minds*, produced in cooperation with universities and meant to bring scholarly research to television audiences. Hallman folded it after three years, wanting something similar but with a much more diverse format. His idea was to produce an anthology series similar to the other contemporary series being produced by Talks and Public Affairs at the time, like *Scope*. Although Hallman worried about the lack of available writers with experience in television, he was eager to extend to television the good reputation that CBC radio had already created in programming.[11] "I have the feeling this all sounds very pretentious," he wrote, "and possibly even dull. I do not think it is. Quite frankly I feel that we are on the verge of television rather than very far into it, and in this program I would like to begin to do some of the things which we have done so well in radio and have not even tried in the new medium."[12]

Hallman appointed Eric Koch as program organizer. Koch was a Jewish refugee from Germany who had been deported to Canada, via London, during the Second World War.[13] His first career stop was at CBC radio, where he nurtured his conviction that education was a key responsibility of the corporation. Koch was keen that the new series produce programs on Canadian history, but he admitted that he didn't know much about it. So on his list of program ideas for the first season he suggested a feature about Champlain as a scientist and geographer rather than as a heroic figure. Otherwise, he noted Canadian history as their "main gap."[14]

Nor was Koch confident about how to present Canadian history on television. In that first year of production he approached Hugh Kemp, the script supervisor for *Folio*, for Kemp's insight and advice. *Folio* was preparing a couple of pieces on historical figures, including Joseph Howe, for the upcoming season. Kemp explained to Koch that the idea was to present the figures as if they were "on trial before posterity" and, in explaining their past actions to a television audience, to avoid the "static quality" of a straight play.[15] So this was one idea for presenting Canadian history. But the challenge remained for Koch – how to combine the educational aims of *Explorations* with dramatizations, like those in *Folio*, that would grab the viewers' attention. Or, in his words, how to "devise ingenious ways to make the pursuit of knowledge entertaining."[16]

Explorations went to air in October 1956, appearing every second Tuesday from 10:00 to 11:00 p.m.[17] Most of its producers and writers, like Koch, came from radio. They were inexperienced with regard to television, so some of the early pieces were adaptations from plays and short stories that relied mainly on the original writing.[18] Like the other anthology series in Talks and Public Affairs, *Explorations* included films from the NFB in its lineup. Although relations between the two institutions were sometimes prickly, the CBC benefitted from this arrangement in that the NFB films, as good-quality educational films that expressed ideas about national identity, met the standards the CBC was trying to achieve. One example of NFB offerings on Canadian history to *Explorations*, which aired between 1960 and 1962, was a slate of dramatized biographies on the theme of responsible government and the prelude to Confederation. It included pieces on Joseph Howe, William Lyon Mackenzie, Louis-Joseph Papineau, Lord Durham, John A. Macdonald, and George-Étienne Cartier. The NFB, like the CBC, normally engaged subject matter experts, and, in this instance, the consultants were Maurice Careless from the University of Toronto, along with Guy Frégault and Gustave Lanctôt from the University of Ottawa.[19]

Despite staff inexperience and a less than ideal production situation, in its first year *Explorations* won an award for public affairs programming from the Ohio-based Institute for Education by Radio and Television.[20] Yet Hallman felt that the quality of the series was uneven. He decided that the next season would be improved if the pieces were shorter, thereby forcing staff to treat the topics more succinctly. Reducing the length to half an hour would enable the regions to more readily contribute, and it would also allow Hallman to run *Explorations* weekly instead of every second week.[21] So, for the new season, the regional production breakdown was as follows: Vancouver would produce three programs; Winnipeg, Montreal, and Ottawa would contribute two each; and Halifax would produce one. The remaining sixteen would come from Toronto, for a total of twenty-six.[22]

Koch proposed some changes too. In order to avoid homogeneity he wanted to rotate the producers, editors, and writers on a regular basis. As for the hosts, in addition to having good onscreen personalities, he wanted them to have subject-matter expertise. Koch persisted in his belief that the main goal of the series was to educate, and, while he wanted to avoid a "lecture-hall" approach, he also wanted the content and style to tilt towards the more overtly educational.[23] He stressed that they could still use dramatic techniques to help get their points across, like they did with *Exploring Minds*, but he did not want *Explorations* staff to think of the series as a chance to try out new techniques in drama. "This is adult education," Koch said, "not showbiz. One might even consider a tie-in with CIAE [*sic*] [Canadian Association for Adult Education] with study bulletins and the rest. If it's entertaining, so much the better – but let us worry about this less."[24]

There was some trepidation at the CBC about educational programming because education in Canada comes under provincial rather than federal jurisdiction. Moreover, some CBC staff believed that anything too didactic would result in no audience. Producer Daryl Duke, from the Vancouver office, balked at Koch's ideas on the use of onscreen experts. Duke wrote to Koch that, while he understood *Explorations* as a vehicle primarily for documentary films, he thought that too many experts would result in programs that were above people's heads. "I think we must do everything we can ... to avoid appearing 'educational,'" said Duke, "– to avoid the impression that one sometimes gets from CBC programs that we are being extremely kind in letting the audience have a taste of our bountiful knowledge."[25] Koch replied that the experts would stay and that there was a public demand for material such as he described: "We are convinced that we can put on 'educational' programs – (a term to be used only among ourselves!) – which are *not* condescending."[26]

Koch also had to deal with regional staff discontent regarding the planning of *Explorations*. Complaints about centralization in Toronto and Ottawa had been a long-standing problem at the CBC, so one of the aims of *Explorations* was to involve the regions in a substantial way.[27] Tensions surfaced in 1956, however, when Vancouver's Bob

Patchell wrote that he felt his office was being left out of the planning process and was not being given enough information, lead time, or resources to do a proper job. Koch disagreed, but Patchell railed against what he considered to be the breakdown in communications and the "junior position" of the regional offices: "I don't think anyone in Vancouver would disagree with the fact that there must be some central organization of a program like Explorations," Patchell wrote, "but to be treated as the idiot children of the CBC is not exactly to our taste."[28]

Frank Peers, supervisor of Talks and Public Affairs, intervened and urged Patchell to become more involved in proposing detailed program treatments instead of engaging in "useless recriminations about what Vancouver thinks of Toronto, and what Toronto thinks of Vancouver."[29] But Doug Nixon, from the Winnipeg office, agreed with Patchell. Nixon suggested to Peers that the regional producers should be treated like members of a planning committee and that if the show was to fulfill the national mandate, the regions must be more involved. "There must be a flow of ideas from centres outside Toronto," he declared, and he urged the senior planners for *Explorations* to get out of Toronto from time to time to see what the rest of the country was like.[30]

One problem with the above idea was that too much regional autonomy might have affected the whole CBC nation-building exercise. And in the Canadian history programs, at least in *Explorations*, the central bias in production mirrored a central bias in content. This particular issue came up in the second season (1957–58) in connection with a proposed series on the history of Canadian governors. Koch hired three independent writers to deliver scripts on Champlain, Frontenac, Dorchester, Simcoe, Bond Head, and Elgin, all former governors of the colonies that eventually morphed into present-day Quebec and Ontario.[31] Andrew Cowan, the Ottawa-based director of CBC Northern and Armed Forces Services, protested the choices. Cowan questioned the focus on men from the "east" and the absence of governors from the west, like James Douglas of British Columbia and George Simpson of the Hudson's Bay Company. "I hesitate to think that this geographic limitation sprang from any Eastern provincialism (or even Toronto parochialism)," Cowan said, "since in doing so I would be giving aid and comfort to those detractors of our network programmes who declare this to be CBC's besetting sin."[32]

Koch explained to Cowan that his primary goal was to tell the story of Canada with "a growing sense of North American identity" – an entity that was separate from the United States, Britain, and France. In Koch's view this was the main theme of Canadian history. So a program on a western governor would be "a little peripheral" to the story of Canada's road to nationhood, but they would certainly be producing programs on the west and the Maritimes once they figured out a good way to present history on television. Koch also said that if any region was being neglected in terms of Canadian history, then perhaps the Maritimes would have a better case for complaint.[33] Cowan responded that Canadian history should not be interpreted as a progression from east to west and that the west had developed according to its own logic: "If it can be proved that this phase of our history is 'peripheral' to Canada's growth to national maturity, then I withdraw the charge of eastern provincialism and announce myself to be an unrepentant western provincial and outlander."[34]

Ideas from *Explorations* staff about what was important in Canadian history came from various sources. While personalities like Laura Secord and Tecumseh (two subjects featured the previous year on *Explorations*) had acquired mythical status primarily through monuments, stage and radio plays, and other forms of popular culture, historiographical perspectives also fit with those prevailing at the CBC. Historians of Canada and other Canadian cultural producers were trying to create a distinct national identity for Canada and to construct a common national narrative. Koch's comments show that dominating his understanding was Donald Creighton's Laurentian thesis, the idea that the early economic and political activities along the St Lawrence River system were key to all subsequent development in Canada. He also legitimized Cowan's complaint that the centralization of the CBC was not only embedded in the institutional organization but also extended to program content.

Cowan complained about the exclusion of the west, but Koch's series on the evolution of responsible government in Canada would have been difficult to carry out accurately without including Nova Scotia.

Koch did not consider the colony to be part of the "original 'Canada,'" yet it was the first colony in the entire British Empire to actually achieve responsible government. One of the prime actors in that event was Joseph Howe, who, by 1958, was one of the few historical personalities besides John A. Macdonald to have received star treatment on CBC radio. Historians in the first part of the twentieth century, as historian Ernest Forbes has noted, created a kind of cult about Howe as a hero in the struggle for responsible government and as a key player in the idea of Canada "from colony to nation."[35] Koch seemed unaware of this, but, in any case, his series on the governors did not go ahead as planned. Koch was not altogether happy with the scripts, and, according to producer Vincent Tovell, one of the issues continued to be how to best present Canadian history on television.[36]

The regional disagreement came up again in 1960 when Marcel Ouimet, general manager of the French service, complained about Koch's plans for the Montreal office to produce for *Explorations* three contemporary "'self-portraits'" of Quebec. Ouimet felt that if the programs were to be a study of French Canada, they should include French speakers from areas in Canada other than Quebec. In Ouimet's opinion, instead of helping to improve understanding between French- and English-speaking Canadians, Koch's treatment would only serve to underscore the differences. "Some of our English-speaking compatriots tend to consider Quebec as a region," Ouimet said, "while we prefer to recognize the broader approach that French-speaking Canada ... extends deeply into the Maritimes and is also present in the Prairies and in British Columbia."[37]

There was more to this than semantics for Ouimet, who had been the man in charge at CBC Montreal in the last days of 1958, when producers there went on strike for the right to bargain collectively on their own. The strike triggered a prolonged labour action and caused a serious rift between Montreal staff and CBC employees elsewhere. The occasion saw high-profile personalities like René Lévesque and Pierre Trudeau supporting the cause. By the time it ended in March of 1959, the struggle had politicized Lévesque, who had recently hosted for *Explorations* another two-part program on French Canada.[38] The strike became a symbol for the new kind of French Canadian nationalism with which he became associated, one that focused on Quebec, and was characterized by secularism, urbanism, and dissent from religious and political authority.

The Fall of Quebec: A Battle for Historians

Adding to Ouimet's trepidation about the depiction of French Canada was the mess from which he had just emerged in connection with the attempt to commemorate the two hundredth anniversary of the Battle of the Plains of Abraham. The 1759 victory of the British forces under James Wolfe over the French forces under Marquis de Montcalm is considered a nation-defining event in most English-language histories of Canada. But, as historian H.V. Nelles has shown in his study of the activities surrounding the tercentenary of the founding of Quebec in 1908, such commemoration of the battle had a history of not going over well with all Quebecers.[39]

That winter, with tensions still high from the strike, staff proceeded ambitiously though cautiously with plans to commemorate the bicentennial of the battle. The plans were of grand scale, and, in an indication of the importance and delicacy of the project, senior officials in Ottawa were heavily involved. Similar to the preparations for the tercentenary fifty years earlier, as described by Nelles, the CBC envisioned ceremonies involving government dignitaries and representatives, in this case from the War Museum, the National Battlefields Commission, and the Department of National Defence. Bert Powley, CBC supervisor of Outside Broadcasts, was excited in anticipation of the "television spectacular."[40]

Historical expertise was essential, so he and his colleagues lined up historians Guy Frégault, William Morton, and Charles Stacey as advisors. The three were highly regarded scholars who believed strongly in popularizing Canadian history through various media. Frégault was a professor at the University of Ottawa, a specialist on New France and the "Conquest," and a biographer of legendary figures Pierre Le Moyne d'Iberville, Pierre de Rigaud de Vaudreuil de Cavagnial, and François Bigot. Morton was a professor of history at the University of Manitoba and author of a recent and seminal history of the province (1957). He had written a special report on national museums for the Massey Commission in which he urged historians to strive to reach general audiences and called for the CBC and the NFB to appoint specialist advisors on Canadian history programs or even create their own historical sections.[41] And finally Stacey, who had also contributed a special report to the Massey Commission (on Canadian archives), was Canada's official historian of the Second World War.[42] He was Canada's most esteemed military historian and had actually submitted the idea for the program to the CBC in light of his upcoming book on the subject.[43] Like his colleagues, Stacey was keen on bringing Canadian history to the public, believing it was the duty of historians to be good writers and public communicators.[44]

The production soon ran into trouble. An early warning sign was Powley's scramble in mid-February to withdraw a previous idea of his – that troops re-enact the scaling by the British soldiers of the hill below Quebec. A "theatrical and politically dangerous" re-creation was actually not wise, he said, and had not been part of his original intention. What he had meant in a previous suggestion was merely that troops should demarcate former battle positions and movements.[45] Acting CBC president Ernie Bushnell, in a letter to the minister of defence seeking an opinion about CBC commemoration of the event, included Powley's toned-down idea and stressed that there would be no re-creation but only a few troops to indicate the positions and movements on the battlefield. This would constitute only a small part of the program, Bushnell noted, the rest of the time being taken up with commentary by experts like Stacey. With the use of scale models and paintings, as well as Stacey and a francophone expert, the piece would be an "authoritative pictorial commentary," not "the celebration of a military victory or defeat."[46]

The other possibility Bushnell offered up was a televised ceremony involving the raising of replica flags from both nations as they were in 1759, along with the Canadian ensign. This would be similar to the practice at Fort Niagara, Bushnell wrote, the French-built fort on American soil that had been held consecutively by the French, the British, and the Americans.[47] But Bushnell badly misread the degree of parallel between the symbolism of the Plains of Abraham in Canada and Fort Niagara in the United States. A CBC officer involved with the planning of the program reported that, sometime in late July or early August 1959, the Société Saint-Jean-Baptiste decided not to commemorate the bicentennial in any way and cancelled the tentative plans between its Quebec City branch and the CBC to coordinate activities. The CBC was informed that, furthermore, the Quebec press was growing hostile to the whole idea.[48]

The axe came down on the television spectacular. The producers of *Explorations* had been planning their own program to mark the bicentennial, and they seem to have integrated into it the remnants of Powley's larger-scale project. The problem of how to present it without political fallout remained. Eric Koch and Montreal-based Herbert Steinhouse, the CBC writer/director of the piece, tossed around possibilities. Koch had suggested to Charles Stacey that a "think piece" might be appropriate, while Steinhouse came up with a humorous strategy.[49] What if they based the piece on different versions of the events as found in English and French textbooks? They could have actors dramatizing French- and English-speaking schoolmasters, with each reading the other's textbooks and interviewing the textbook authors as to their motivations. To lighten things up, Steinhouse added, they could use cartoons or even whimsically conclude the piece with a "modern educated Indian" saying that neither version was historically valid.[50]

The final half-hour program, broadcast in English on the English network and in French on the French network in *Premier Plan*, on the same night, comprises bits and pieces of most of the above.[51] "The Fall of Quebec: A Battle for Historians" opens with English- and French-speaking schoolboys reading from English and French textbook versions of the battle, each with a different emphasis. The differences immediately establish the relevance of the program as one of the big questions of the day was whether there should be one version of national history taught in all Canadian schools. Following this is a selection of archival images, among them the famous paintings of the deaths of General Wolfe and Marquis de Montcalm.

Michael Oliver, a professor of economics and political science at McGill University, is narrator and interviewer. He gives a brief introduction before posing the key questions: Has two hundred years been long enough to heal the scars of 1759? Do all Canadians know the same things about the event? And do they feel the same way about it? He begins by asking Stacey, ready with a pointer and a map of the battle area, about the accuracy of the existing accounts of the battle. Stacey responds that most of what has been written in the past has been romanticized rather than having been based on contemporary records. He then summarizes the strategic goals of each side and the subsequent events on the battlefield. He concludes, as he had in his recently published book on the topic, that, although both generals were heroic, neither was "better than mediocre." According to Stacey, the main reason the British won the day was simply that their military efficiency was superior to that of their enemy. The British were the professional soldiers and sailors, and their enemies were the amateur soldiers and sailors.

After Stacey comes a narrative summary of the period following the Seven Years' War, when the French and the British began to live side by side in a "bicultural experience." Illustrated with stills of period paintings, it introduces the next portion of the program, on the bicultural experience in Canada. This portion is made up of very short clips from interviews on this topic with a selection of (mostly male) French- and English-speaking Canadians. Most express the idea that Canadians share a national purpose, with the English and French living together in relative harmony despite their differences. One man says that if the British had not conquered the French, "we would have all been American citizens." Another says that the Conquest could be considered either as a "catastrophe" or as a "providential gift," depending on one's point of view. An exception is a francophone priest, who characterizes the British as a "rather dominating people" and the French under them as divided: the weak who "gave in," while "the strong resisted."

The final and most substantial part of the half-hour special is a parade of clips from separate interviews with historians Guy Frégault, Canon Lionel Groulx, Father Georges-Henri Lévesque, Monsignor Arthur Maheux, Blair Neatby, A.L. Burt, and Hilda Neatby. Oliver's interview questions relate to the immediate aftermath of the fall of Quebec and its legacy, including the present-day relationship between French and English Canada. He poses his first question to Frégault, and it is about the causes of "the war of the Conquest." Frégault, at least in the clip shown onscreen, does not delve into the long prelude to the conflict by discussing the struggle between the British and the

French for dominance in North America; rather, he describes the events as part of a larger "world war" and outlines the circumstances of the French in New France just before the Conquest.

Several clips show the historians responding to the next question, which concerns the implications of the Conquest. One of them is Lionel Groulx, a long-serving historian at the Université de Montréal and an old-school Quebec nationalist who believed that the salient theme in Quebec history was resistance and survival in the face of English Canada. Groulx had written about the history of his province in often romantic and providential terms, helping to create heroes out of men like Jacques Cartier and Adam Dollard des Ormeaux, largely in an attempt to distinguish Quebecers from other Canadians in terms of their history, culture, language, and religion.[52] His response is that the separation of the colony from France, especially in terms of its economic development and intellectual life, is perhaps the most important implication of the Conquest. Frégault has a similar response. In later clips Groulx adds that the loss of political decision making and economic opportunities, such as those connected with the fur trade, are also important consequences.

Hilda Neatby and Blair Neatby also have responses that are similar to each other. Among the scholars interviewed, Hilda Neatby is the only woman. As a female historian on CBC television, as a professor of history (at the University of Saskatchewan), and as a former member of the Massey Commission she was a rarity. In her response to Oliver, Neatby speaks about the psychological aspects of the Conquest, citing Arthur Lower, who had pointed out that it was difficult for people to accept having been conquered: "the resentment, the bitterness, the sense of tragedy." Blair Neatby, a professor at Carleton University and a specialist on the relationship between English and French Canada, also stresses the importance of the emotional consequences of the Conquest. He adds that, for the Canadiens, there was so much more at stake than there was for the British because New France was their home and not yet the home of the British, so it was their fate and not the fate of the British that was tied up in the outcome.

Oliver asks about the historical attitudes of the British and the French towards each other. A.L. Burt, a historian of Canada formerly at the University of Minnesota, gives one response. He says that the awakening of French Canadian nationalism in the early to mid-nineteenth century resulted in the character of Quebec best described by Lord Durham's "two nations warring in the bosom of a single state" and that it was stimulated by a sort of British nationalism. Hilda Neatby offers that it was not an easy co-existence for the British and the French in the first hundred years after the Conquest but that, eventually, the two sides realized that they had to live together. Nevertheless, she agrees with Burt that the Durham Report reinforced feelings of nationalism on the part of the French Canadians.

Oliver puts his next question specifically to Father Georges-Henri Lévesque, founder of the Faculty of Social Sciences at the Université Laval and strong supporter of labour and the arts. Like Hilda Neatby, Lévesque had been a member of the Massey Commission. His position on the commission and his wholehearted support for a united Canada, as well as his later role as one of the architects of the Quiet Revolution, put him in poor stead with traditional Quebec nationalists like Lionel Groulx. Oliver questions Lévesque about the Massey Report and whether he thinks it contributed significantly to English-French relations. Lévesque says yes, it was the first document of its kind to offer such a "fervent plea" to the value of bilingualism and biculturalism. According to Lévesque, evidence of its success was that, after Vincent Massey was appointed the first Canadian-born governor general of Canada upon publication of the report, the next appointment was Georges Vanier, a French-Canadian Catholic.

Oliver: "What about today's attitudes towards co-existence?" Groulx responds that co-existence is inevitable: while the French are too large to be swallowed, they are too small to swallow others. Arthur Maheux, archivist at the Grand Séminaire at Quebec and formerly professor of history at the Université Laval, also answers. He was a professional rival of Groulx who had published a well-known work, *Pourquoi sommes-nous divisés?* (Why are we divided?) on the need for unity between Quebec and Canada during the Second World War (to which Groulx responded with the pamphlet *Pourquoi nous sommes divisés* (Why we are divided).[53] Maheux claims that relations are cordial between French and English Canada, that they are in a moment of "bonne entente." Hilda Neatby's take on the question prompts a discussion with Oliver about the type of history coming out of the Université de Montréal, where Groulx held sway. Like Groulx, historians there generally did not see co-existence as a good thing. Neatby, although admitting that she was taking the perspective of an English-speaking Canadian, says that the interpretations of the Montreal historians are hard to take.

Maheux, asked by Oliver if there should be one history taught in schools, says that if they could "tell the truth on both sides," a book could be written that would be satisfactory to all Canadians. But the question is, would the teachers accept it? Burt, on the other hand, says that such a history book in Canada is not "within the bounds of practical possibility," nor is it necessary. He says that in the United States there is no one prescribed text but, rather, a competition of texts, which tends to eschew stereotyped narratives. To Burt this was a good thing because adherence to just one history tended to lead to nationalism, which he thinks is introspective, "self-pitying, and self-glorifying," and essentially a thing of the past.

Hilda Neatby answers the question in a more subdued fashion than she had in her report to the Massey Commission. In the report she stressed that the divisions between English and French historians in Canada prevented the development of a "common philosophy" that would be needed to form the basis of a common textbook.[54] Here she responds that each community in Canada should choose its own history for its children, though there should be at least some similar facts taught to all. These facts should better explain the events causing resentments between the groups. When Oliver suggests to Neatby that a uniform history might lead to something "deadly and sterile," Neatby agrees that just one version of history would be an "emasculated" one. Also, who would write it?

Oliver ends "The Fall of Quebec" by asking about the conditions for a successful co-existence between the English and the French in Canada. Groulx answers that there are many examples of "the conquerors and the conquered" living together but that French Canadians should never rest assured they will survive. Blair Neatby says that the threat to French Canadian survival will only disappear when English Canada develops an awareness, understanding, and pride in French

Canada and the bicultural nature of the country. Maheux believes that old prejudices needed to be wiped out, that there is no need for divisiveness. The last response comes from Lévesque. While the French and English were once enemies, he says, they are now united in a common cause: "both people having won, in the end, each in his own way, the Battle of the Plains of Abraham."

In the 1950s it was common practice at the CBC to feature on-screen interviews with scholars. In this instance the range of historians with diverse ideas spoke to the CBC's belief in education, to a faith that audiences would be able to grasp the nature of the information they provided, and to a willingness to put the contingency of historical knowledge on full display. Clearly, historical accounts depended at least partly on perspective. The ideas of Burt and Groulx, the intellectual father of Quebec nationalism for at least the first part of the twentieth century, were directly opposed to the CBC nation-building exercise. They were obviously at odds in this respect with fellow interviewees Hilda Neatby and Lévesque, both of whom had been instrumental in the deliberations of the Massey Commission and its quest to help create the foundation of a pan-Canadian national cultural identity.

"The Fall of Quebec" shows that history on television says as much about the present as it does about the past. The end of the Seven Years' War and the Battle of the Plains of Abraham was only a small part of the program. Apart from Stacey's initial synopsis, there is little else in the hour about the original conflict, and even less about its underlying contexts. Rather, the CBC producers attempted to grapple with the present-day resonance of this historical event, arguably an important one with regard to symbolizing the relationship between English and French Canada. In this respect Lévesque's final comments are telling. By suggesting that somehow both the British and the French won the Battle of the Plains of Abraham, he negates the opinions of Burt and Groulx and depoliticizes the battle as an event with no lasting negative consequences. Canadians can be assured that, despite the Conquest and the centuries-long fallout, the country they lived in was a unified one. By concluding with the idea of a "bonne entente," the program says less about "Canada" in 1759 than it does about an idealized Canada in 1959.

Lévesque's conclusion also highlights the fact that the titular battle failed to materialize. Although the often conflicting views of the historians display the contested nature of historical interpretation, the separate interviews allow for no discussion among them. The logistics of bringing all the scholars together would have been difficult as they came from various parts of Canada (Burt was on vacation in Canada at the time of taping), and from a CBC perspective it would have been less controlled. But such a format would have served better had the producers been seeking real debate. As for how it all translated to the viewer, Koch commended Steinhouse on his efforts, but the dizzying array of presentation techniques took its toll. "The Fall of Quebec: A Battle for Historians" did not, as Koch gently hinted to Steinhouse, make for great television.[55]

Winnipeg General Strike 1919

Producers of history on television love anniversaries, and 1959 marked another: the fortieth anniversary of the Winnipeg General Strike. The strike, which took place during May and June of 1919, was brutally put down. But it brought to political prominence some of the strike leaders and indirectly resulted in some improvements for workers across the country. It was not the only labour uprising at the time, but in the forty years between the event and its commemoration on television, the strike had come to symbolize the struggle between labour and capital in Canada in a way that few other events had done. Its interpretation on CBC television only fortified this symbolism.

Staff at CBC Winnipeg believed a program about the strike would make a good contribution to *Explorations*, in part because the strike was already considered to be also of national significance. Leonard Earle, a newspaper columnist at the time of the strike, was host, and the main historical consultants were Harry Walker of the Department of Labour and Kenneth McNaught of the University of Toronto. Walker was writing a history of the strike for his department, and McNaught had just published a biography of strike supporter and first leader of the Co-operative Commonwealth Federation (CCF) J.S. Woodsworth.[56] McNaught appeared on CBC national radio and television programs throughout the 1950s and 1960s, though in 1958 he resigned as a television panelist on CBC Winnipeg's *Roundtable* due to what he considered to be capitulation to interference in the program by private industry.[57]

The producers at CBC Winnipeg placed an ad in the *Winnipeg Tribune* and the *Winnipeg Free Press*, asking for personal photos and artefacts that would help them visually reconstruct the events.[58] In 1919, both the *Tribune* and the predecessor of the *Free Press* had been publicly against the strike. The ad, which indicated that the air date would be Labour Day, the third of September, drew several phone calls and at least three written responses from concerned or angry members of the public.[59] One editorial in the *Tribune* complained that the CBC was doing a "profound disservice" to the people of Winnipeg and should not be treating the strike as ancient history and therefore as something that could now serve as a piece of entertainment. Another person writing to Jim Finlay, CBC Winnipeg's regional director, said that there was still a lot of bitterness about the fact that even the police and firefighters went on strike, so why did the CBC want to bring that up now? People lost jobs and pension rights, and "such a documentary would be re-opening old sores with these people to no good purpose."[60]

Finlay suggested delaying the broadcast in order to more fully investigate the historical issues, but Peers insisted on going ahead as planned.[61] He argued to Charles Jennings, controller of broadcasting, that the BBC had dealt with the British General Strike of 1926, that *Explorations* producers were showcasing other periods of Canadian history like the Battle of the Plains of Abraham and its aftermath, and, finally, that "the issues at stake then have long since retreated into history." On a more practical note, Peers reiterated Jennings's observation that someone had made a mistake with the newspaper ad by saying that Labour Day fell on the third of September that year. Labour Day was actually on Monday the seventh, so since the show would air on the third, which was a Thursday, it had "no connection with it [Labour Day] except that it [was] a program likely to be of more than usual interest to labour organizations."[62] Another CBC manager warned that, even though staff had experience dealing with touchy historical subjects like Louis Riel, caution should prevail and a senior person from Toronto should go to Winnipeg to review the piece before air time.[63]

Given the previous objections from the regional offices about their subordinate position in relation to Toronto, this was a move with the potential to alienate. However, Ouimet reported to the CBC president in late August that Finlay and another staffer from Toronto had carefully reviewed the rough cut and believed the final program would be "adequately balanced."[64] There appears to have been little said about it afterwards in either the *Tribune* or the *Free Press*.

"Winnipeg General Strike 1919" opens with a photograph of the strike, along with the sound of the slow beating of a drum.[65] A hand appears, holding a club. Following the suggestive opening, Earle speaks direct to camera with the context and general description of the event. It is a more complex and detailed introduction than was provided for "The Fall of Quebec." The ensuing story portion shows a series of still and moving images mixed with some on-location filming, while a male narrator delivers the account to the sound of the drum. The drum gives way to a multitude of voices seemingly in a crowd and then to a variety of other sounds, all pairing to dramatic effect with the stills and the film.

The narrator's account: On 6 May 1919, at the Winnipeg Labour Temple, the (Winnipeg Trades and Labour Council) delegates vote to strike on the issues of the right to organize, low wages, and the high cost of living. The background, in terms of the "social cross-currents of the day," are the Russian Revolution, the growing awareness of labour of its own power, unequal standards of living, and the difficult transition from war to peace. Other workers respond in solidarity, and approximately thirty thousand people walk off the job. The disruption virtually shuts down the city as most employees, even those providing essential services like police and firefighters, will not work without the permission of the Central Strike Committee. But there is no violence or demonstrations on behalf of the strikers, the narrator explains, as they are told to merely "stay at home, keep out of trouble." A group of residents opposed to the strike, who wanted to maintain essential services, come together as the Citizens' Committee of One Thousand.

The Borden government sends representatives to Winnipeg under the direction of Minister of Justice Arthur Meighen (future prime minister of Canada), who report back that there is no justification for the strike. Returned soldiers stage silent parades mainly in support of the strikers, but other soldiers parade against the strikers. The mayor of Winnipeg forbids the parades and hires hundreds of special constables (equipping each with a horse and a bat), who eventually replace the city police, whose officers had refused to not support the strike. Sympathy strikes erupt across the west and in Ontario. The federal government, believing that the strike leadership is made up of "immigrant agitators," make amendments to the Immigration Act that allow for the deportation of anyone born outside of Canada who sought to overthrow the government. The strike leaders are arrested with a view to their possible deportation, but they are eventually released.

On 21 June, a group of returned soldiers prepare to stage another silent parade, in support of the strike, and people begin to gather at City Hall. The mayor warns the soldiers, but the crowd grows, and so he calls in the federal mounted police. The police charge in, armed with revolvers and clubs. The mayor reads the Riot Act in an attempt to disperse the crowd but to no avail, and the police charge again, firing three shots. The confrontation, which becomes known as "Bloody Saturday," results in two people dead and many others injured. The police arrest more than one hundred people, and the strike is called off. The trials begin and the leaders are convicted. A number of them eventually get elected to the Manitoba Legislature, one to Parliament, and another becomes mayor of Winnipeg.

A variety of perspectives emerge throughout the program. These come from Leonard Earle's introduction, the narrated documentary, and the first-person testimony that forms the bulk of the remainder of the piece. The testimony consists of a series of separate interviews that a Reverend Douglas Laughlan conducts with four people associated with the strike: R.B. Russell and F.G. Tipping, two former members of the General Strike Committee; F.W. Crawford, a former volunteer firefighter and member of the Citizens' Committee of One Thousand; and Hugh Phillips, a lawyer who had been attached to the Office of the Chief of Police.

Each of the men had been involved in the strike in a manner somewhat more complex than it appears onscreen. Russell was a Scottish immigrant, having arrived from Glasgow in 1911, who became a union leader and then, in 1919, one of the leaders on the Strike Committee. In the end he and seven other leaders on the Strike Committee were arrested and charged with seditious conspiracy; he was convicted and sent to prison. Tipping, for his part, explains in the program that he had not been an officer of the Strike Committee but that, before the strike, he had been an executive of the Trades and Labour Council and so automatically became a member of the Strike Committee when the action was declared. He also represented the Strike Committee in its request to Arthur Meighen that those arrested receive a trial by jury. Crawford, a member of the Citizen's Committee and a volunteer with the Fire Brigade, was one of the returned soldiers who was against the strike. And finally, Phillips stands in for Winnipeg's elite. He was a retired lawyer, describing himself in the program as a Queen's Counsel with fifty-five years experience in the practice of law. At the time of the strike he says he was asked "to associate [him]self" with the chief of police.[66]

The interviewer poses questions concerning the causes of the strike, as laid out in the introduction, and the guests respond with the known causes. When it comes to the subject of the violence, however, their answers differ considerably. Russell, of the Strike Committee, blames the violence on the federal authorities as well as on the Citizens' Committee of One Thousand, which colluded with the authorities in opposing the strikers. The workers did not intend to replace government, he says, they only wanted change. And to keep things as peaceful as possible they met regularly with the Winnipeg City Council to ensure that key service providers like bakers and milk company employees were allowed to work. He later insists that although returning soldiers had paraded through the streets in support of the strike, this was something that the strike organizers were against: their original intent was peaceful and their motto was "do nothing."

Phillips, the lawyer, blames the strikers for the violence, having noted earlier that the authorities acted as they did because they had seen the strike as a rebellion that had spilled over from a similar but aborted plan for a strike in Vancouver. In his opinion the strikers validated this idea by upsetting streetcars and preventing employees of the Hudson's Bay Company from getting to work. Crawford, of the Citizens' Committee of One Thousand, also comes down against the strikers but in a more circumspect manner. He says that when people have nothing to do this can lead to violence, and with the length of the strike and the frustration of the situation, "some people probably did some unwise things."

Like "The Fall of Quebec," "Winnipeg General Strike 1919" reveals something of the historical process at work. The program allows the four participants to contradict one another, and while the interviewer does not probe the responses of his guests, at least onscreen, their answers vary enough one from the other to show that for every narrative there is often an alternate narrative. The interviews are an early example of the use on CBC television of first-person historical testimony, with actual participants in the events acting as informants and authorities. For the producers, with their initial fears about broadcasting the program, it was also a way to deliver a variety of perspectives without taking an obvious stand.

The final summing up of the story adds further complexity. When the host asks Leonard Earle if the arrest and trial of the strike leaders was wise, he replies that it was "not wise" because the strike was on the verge of being settled, and negotiations on some form of collective bargaining looked about ready to begin. Violence could have been avoided if federal authorities had not intervened and arrested the strike leaders, which led to anger and resentment on the part of the strike supporters. Laughlan ends the piece by summarizing the significance of the strike, quoting William Morton and historical sociologist S.D. Clark. Morton had written that, while the trials and sentences were an abuse of justice brought about by class fear and rancour, the strike had challenged public order, "the victors were comparatively lenient," and the sentences "relatively mild." Clark had placed the strike in a more positive light, as opposed to Morton, who thought that it had disturbed the status quo. Clark's view was that it signalled an important phase in the development of a political community in the west and that it was, in part, an expression of "the West's urge to build a better world in which to live."

The idea of the west as exceptional in Canada due to its progressive politics was largely born of the Winnipeg General Strike. The success of colourful leaders like J.S. Woodsworth and R.B. Russell, the program participant who became head of the One Big Union after his prison term, encouraged this idea. The later prominence of these men helped to strengthen the perception of 1919 as a watershed moment not only in the history of western Canada and Canadian labour history but also in the history of Canada overall. The west and the strike as the birthplace of and catalyst for the creation of unions, cooperatives, and progressivism in Canada became the accepted narrative.

The notion developed at the expense of Atlantic Canada in particular. The strike in Winnipeg was not an anomaly in Canada but, rather, was representative of numerous labour protests that were occurring nationwide well before the war.[67] The events in Winnipeg, while perhaps comprising the largest manifestation of labour unrest in Canada to that date, did not occur without precedent elsewhere in the country, nor were they a reaction unique to Winnipeg or the west. Workers had been building tremendous momentum already. Historian Ian McKay has shown that, in the thirteen years before the outbreak of the First World War, workers across the Maritimes went on strike at least 411 times.[68] In the story portion of the CBC program, the narrator recounts a long list of Canadian towns and cities in the western provinces and Ontario in which there occurred sympathy strikes in support of the workers in Winnipeg. But there were other contemporary labour actions across Canada that took place in response to conditions similar to those in Winnipeg, including a general strike in Amherst, Nova Scotia, which was happening at the same time as the strike in Winnipeg.[69] This contextual absence in the program, as well as Clark's final statements suggesting that the west was exceptional in its struggle, upheld and reinforced persistent ideas about Atlantic Canada as a comparatively conservative region.[70]

"Winnipeg General Strike 1919," like "The Fall of the Quebec," has a short running time of only thirty minutes. This partly accounts for the absence of context as well as for the absence of some of the more particular elements of the strike, like the makeup of the strikers and the different motivations for their actions. The narrator does mention the immigrant component of the strikers and the government reaction to it in terms of the amendments to the Immigration Act, for example, but does not mention the experiences of the female strikers – and women played important roles in this and other labour actions across Canada at the time.[71] The relative paucity of historiography on the strike in 1959 may also partly account for the gaps, though the two main consultants were both specialists, and the producers would have had access to other former strike participants in Winnipeg. In sum, the Winnipeg producers chose a story to showcase the national significance of their region to other Canadians, and they highlighted the elements that they believed were most relevant.

The producers also aimed to achieve balance in the program, hence the strikers and the opposition are each represented by two participants. In 1959, the collective memory of the Winnipeg General Strike was still part of individual memory – relatively little time had passed since the event, and many who had lived through it and suffered the consequences were still alive. While those who initially complained about the plans to produce the program had not actually seen any footage, the mere idea of a television interpretation of an event whose central issues were still of some concern was cause enough for protest. Yet, by 1959, unlike the impact of the fall of Quebec, the impact of the strike as a widespread symbol of past wrongs had waned considerably. Thus Clark's summary of what the strike achieved did not require a neutralizing claim, as did Lévesque's final statement about the British-French conflict.

A Long View of Canadian History

In 1959, the Toronto producers of *Explorations* tried a simple format for Canadian history programming: an interview with historian Donald Creighton. Creighton was still at the University of Toronto, a towering figure in Canadian historiography, and one of the best-known historians of Canada. Beginning in the 1930s, he developed an influential body of work based on the economic development of the St Lawrence region. Where Harold Innis had framed his seminal histories on the trade in staples like fish and fur, Creighton extended it to encompass the whole range of economic and political activities occurring in the St Lawrence River system. To Creighton, these were the activities that mattered in Canadian history and this was the region in which they first evolved – the heartland of Canada that, to him, remained vital to any subsequent developments. He first outlined his Laurentian thesis in *The Commercial Empire of the St Lawrence, 1760–1850* (1937) and expanded it with *British North America at Confederation* (1939) and *Dominion of the North* (1944). Creighton believed that

British character and British institutions built the country, and he advocated Canada's maintaining them.

Creighton was famous for his evocative writing, most evidently on display in his books on John A. Macdonald. The two volumes also represented his foundational belief about history, that it all came down to the confluence of character and circumstance: "however much you consider circumstances and forces and contingencies, you've got ultimately to come back to the individual and what he will make of himself and his environment."[72] With these two books, published in 1952 and 1955, respectively, as *John A. Macdonald: The Young Politician* and *John A. Macdonald: The Old Chieftain*, political biography in Canada had arrived. And also with these, oddly enough financed by the American Rockefeller Foundation, came the securing of the idea of Macdonald as mythological nation builder par excellence. The volumes were also a big step towards bridging the gap between scholarly history and mass appeal history, a gap recognized by a number of historians, including those involved with the Massey Commission.

Hilda Neatby was one of them, though she wasn't completely impressed with Creighton's achievement. She wrote to historian Frank Underhill that, although she was happy the books were so "useful and readable," in her opinion they were bad history: "[Creighton] finds it hard to approach the old chieftain except as a faithful clansman and he must have his knife into every enemy of the clan."[73] For a biographer, not being critical enough of his or her subject is a common enough charge, but in Creighton's case, a hail of honours and accolades, including the Governor General's Award for academic nonfiction in both years of publication, overshadowed most complaints. Still arguably the definitive work on Canada's first prime minister, Creighton's biography was the foundation of several contemporary CBC radio and television productions about Macdonald.[74] Political biography was already popular with radio producers, and, in the 1950s, Creighton himself was involved in at least three radio and television features about Macdonald. Tommy Tweed, CBC writer and creator of two of these features, acknowledged that the work of both Creighton and historian Maurice Careless was indispensable.[75]

Paul Fox, a political scientist at the University of Toronto, conducts the interview with Creighton in Creighton's own home. The first half hour includes Creighton's take on the general trend in Canadian history ("a struggle for survival"), a discussion on the staples thesis, some thoughts on John A. Macdonald's national policy, and an explanation of the American "frontier thesis" and whether it applies to Canada (no). Creighton responds to Fox's invitation to identify the "single most important event in our history," with "Confederation." The 1867 union remained to Creighton the sine qua non of British existence in the North. It unified and strengthened the country, and allowed Macdonald to build the CPR and stem the potential tide of Americans into Canada. With it, the provinces connected and reoriented on an east to west axis. For Creighton, unification meant rejection of the American project, and the beginning and continuation of a Canadian nation in the north. Confederation "sums up the past, it collects provinces which wanted to be separate and which were yet not quite united among themselves, brings them together and gives them an unparalleled future."[76]

In the second half hour Fox asks Creighton about the importance of the rebellions in Lower and Upper Canada in 1837 and 1838. The Lower Canada Rebellion and its chief architect, Louis-Joseph Papineau, remain important symbols in Quebec of French Canadian nationalism and resistance to the British. Creighton downplays this legacy, though he agrees that the rebellions were important in that they eventually led to responsible government, which he notes was actually a development of the British tradition. Otherwise, according to Creighton, the importance of the rebellions is exaggerated and their meaning ambiguous. Although the uprisings in both colonies lacked "purpose and direction," Creighton reserves his most negative assessment for the course of events in Lower Canada, where the inhabitants exhibited "a blind kind of resistance" and Papineau behaved "with cowardice and incompetence."

Nineteen fifty-nine was also the year of the CBC Montreal producers' strike and the two hundredth anniversary of the fall of Quebec. It was therefore a good time for Fox to ask Creighton about his views on French Canada and Canadian national unity as Creighton was known not to be enamoured of French Canada. In conversation with Fox he expresses admiration for the distinctive culture of the French in Canada, but this is mainly because they help to distinguish Canada, as a dual nation, from the American "melting pot." He even dismisses the contemporary difficulties between Quebec and Ottawa as nothing special. Canadian history, he says, has long been fraught with provinces (such as Nova Scotia, Manitoba, and Ontario) that have argued with Ottawa: he maintains that nothing consequential had come came of it in those instances and that this would be the case for Quebec as well.

These remarks could have been predicted by any student of Creighton, who tended to minimize the significance of Quebec and its history on its own terms, including with regard to anything, like the rebellions, that had posed a threat to British order and unity. On the other hand, he tended to highlight external threats, chiefly from the United States, which he believed resulted in maintaining the British influence on Canada.[77] Indeed, Fox keeps Creighton mainly to topics concerning the United States and its influence on Canada as Fox knew that his interviewee despaired of this influence. Fox asks him if he agrees with Arthur Lower that the War of 1812 was the most decisive event in the history of Canada. Creighton agrees because he sees the event as a turning point in the struggle against threats from the United States. The Americans went to war because they wanted to make Canada part of the continental system: "For almost a solid century, from the beginning of the American Revolution down to the Washington Conference of 1871, we've been oppressed [by the United States] by threats, wars, rumours of wars, unofficial wars, diplomatic pressure." According to Creighton, the War of 1812 was the worst of the lot. He believes the conflict is important because it was so devastating and because it cemented anti-American feelings on the part of Canadians, which is something that continued to resonate.

Fox to Creighton: "Did it [the War of 1812] have the effect of creating a sense of Canadian national unity?" Creighton cautions that, at the time, British North America was still just a collection of separate colonies, though, despite this, they resisted being amalgamated into the American continental union. He says later that the weight of the United States was so great that Canada would not exist as an entity if it had not been for the British and that, although British support is no longer what it once had been, the association with the Commonwealth is still important. According to Creighton, Canada has had two national objectives in its history: the most important is survival inside North America, and the much less important is autonomy inside the British Commonwealth. He stresses to Fox that the American threat continues, and he warns that the United States is now a global "imperialist power."

Fox asks Creighton about the writing of contemporary Canadian history and whether Canadian historians in the past have been "obsessed ... with rather parochial things." Creighton answers that, if they have, they have had good reason because they are writing about Canada, which is something other historians were not doing. And, in his opinion, Canadian historians seem to be in the public talking about Canadian history and ways of life more than anyone. Creighton, though very different in his personal politics from Frank Underhill, who is the other interviewee in this series, believed, like him, that historians had a duty to convey the meaning of Canada to the larger public. In fact, in his personal papers is an undated proposal for a television history of Canada.[78] Creighton says to Fox that historians must engage with the public about history "and [that] not merely its end products but its whole process [has] got to be made available to the lay reader." "History cannot be too much professionalized," he says, meaning that it had to be made understandable and interesting to the layperson.

Creighton's interview was broadcast in two half-hour segments in June 1959, a week apart, under the title *A Long View of Canadian History: An Interview with Donald Creighton*. The two pieces were rebroadcast in June 1960, just after the airing of *A Long View of Canadian History, with Professor Frank Underhill* (published in script form as *The Radical Tradition: A Second View of Canadian History*,) which comprised two more half-hour interview segments, with historian Frank Underhill. The four together ran under the title *A Long View of Canadian History*, which the CBC billed as the personal interpretations of "Canada's historical development and its impact on the present."[79]

Underhill's views were often controversial, but it was the pairing that was provocative. Underhill and Creighton, two of the most influential historians in Canada, had been colleagues at the University of Toronto and infamous archrivals.[80] Since *Explorations* had a poor time slot and relatively few resources, its producers had to be crafty in order to create interest and maximize viewership. One way to do this was to run back-to-back interviews with two prominent scholars who happened to disagree on most key aspects of Canadian history and politics. Their personalities were equally at odds. Creighton's contemporaries described him as crusty and bad-tempered, generally not well liked but highly respected by colleagues and students. Charles Stacey, for example, noted in his memoir that he got on well with Creighton despite Creighton frequently insulting him, "but then," Stacey wrote, "he insulted practically everybody."[81] Underhill was well liked by his students, but he left his friends and colleagues, at least in his earlier days, exasperated over his continually inflammatory public statements.[82]

Underhill was raised in small-town Ontario and spent the first part of his career at the University of Saskatchewan. Unlike his other prominent historian colleagues, he was not known for any one or two seminal publications but, rather, for a lifetime's work consisting of articles, reviews, speeches, debates, and radio interviews. It was this involvement in public affairs that made him known as more than a historian. Underhill was an anti-imperialist and when in the west immersed himself in progressive politics, mixing with the likes of J.S. Woodsworth and John W. Dafoe, editor of the *Manitoba* (now *Winnipeg*) *Free Press*.

Underhill arrived at the University of Toronto in his early forties. The university in the interwar years was not exactly welcoming to socialists, but Underhill continued his association with the left as a founding member of the League for Social Reconstruction and as a co-founder of the Ontario branch of the CCF. His opinions, expressed in print and speech, laced with wit and barb, were often dissenting and did not sit well with the establishment. This not only brought him under RCMP surveillance for subversive activities but also brought him multiple near-dismissals from the university.[83] In his later years he became known as a liberal, though in the interview for *Explorations*, retired and seventy-one years old, he still described his main beliefs as those of a leftist.[84]

Underhill felt that history was essential for understanding contemporary affairs, and his teaching and many activities outside of the university were a public expression of this belief.[85] He was a regular on radio, and, despite his penchant for stirring things up, or more likely because of it, he was highly sought after as a commentator and participant on panels. From the 1930s to the 1950s alone he contributed to many CBC radio programs, including *The World Today, Of Things to Come, Mid-Week Review, Wednesday Night,* and (frequently) *Critically Speaking.* But *A Long View of Canadian History* was a rare television appearance. He was not as confident in this medium, and Fox had to reassure him of the quality of the results before he saw the final cut for himself.[86]

Underhill's television interviews, like the rest of his output, are a mix of history and politics. Among the topics in the first half-hour are the dual French/English nationalities in Canada, the nature of the political ideological movements in the country, and the disappointing failure of the 1837 rebellions (the Upper Canadian one was "a more ridiculous fiasco"). He thinks it unfortunate that there is no real radical tradition in Canada, despite the various attempts over the years at reform, protest, and rebellion. This he blames on the British connection, which, he argues "helped to immunize us against these American radical influences."

On the relationship between Canada and Britain, Underhill says to Fox that it is primarily a colonial contact. "Culturally, I don't think we've really been very close to England despite all our protestations of our devotion to the British connection." Underhill maintains that Canadians have been a long way from London or Oxford and that, culturally, New England has closer connections to old England than Upper Canada or the rest of British North America ever did. On the relationship between Canada and the United States, Fox asks Underhill which American ideas have the greatest influence on Canadian politics. Where Creighton highlights the positive influence of the British on the development of Canada, Underhill stresses the positive influence of the Americans on Canadian democracy, insisting that much of the democratic push in Canada has come from the United States. He adds that the idea of the public school came not from the English or the Scots but from the Americans. Underhill views the American influence on

Canada as generally a good thing, and another reason for this is because he believes it had encouraged movements of the left.

Fox: "Isn't the fact that we still are a nation the result of our struggle to maintain our separate identity from the Americans?" Yes but we make too much of this, Underhill says. There is "a schizophrenia in the Canadian mind" about this separate identity. We should not be "a continental Ulster, always worrying about the pressure of the people from the south." He feels that the Canadian concern with defining a national identity, as distinct from that of the United States, is a waste of time and "a neurotic worry." When Fox asks him to explain his lack of concern about the American influence on Canada in terms of things like American commercial television and magazine advertising, Underhill responds that Canadians would probably have these things anyway and that they may just be a mark of the twentieth century. He views the Canadian embrace of so much American culture merely as something that was typical of a functioning democracy.[87] Canadians should stop worrying about Americans and Canadian national identity, and start thinking about what kind of a larger community they could identify with instead.

This last idea underscores a big difference between the thinking of Underhill and that of Creighton. In his earlier years, Underhill advocated for Canada to break ties not only with Great Britain but also with the United States. Like most of his colleagues, he regarded the American economic and cultural encroachment on Canada as cause for great concern, illustrating his views in a 1927 speech, in which he noted Laura Secord's "pathetic little monument" in the shadow of a huge plant in the service of making newsprint for the *Chicago Tribune*.[88] Later in life, though he was still an anti-imperialist and stressed the breaking of Canadian ties with Great Britain, Underhill came to believe that Canadians should *encourage* ties with the United States. He came to feel that the influence of American literature and ideas was beneficial for Canada, and this, along with his social democratic ideas, put him at odds with many of his contemporaries. Canadians were criticizing Europeans and Asians for indulging in too much nationalism, he says to Fox, and here we are doing the same thing. And, he argues, if we want to be culturally distinct, then it is up to Canadians "to produce a culture that is worthwhile."

Fox asks Underhill about this change of mind regarding Canada's relationship to the United States. Underhill supposes it might have to do with the fact that he has spent twenty-eight years in Toronto. He suggests that there was an "anti-American virus" in Canada and that this is perhaps resulting in his becoming more pro-American. Fox asks if it is true that Canadian historians in general are anti-American. Underhill says that it is increasingly true and that, although the liberal "whig" historians in the past were not of this ilk, the "newer, conservative Tory" historians are suffering from "an anti-American mania." Underhill is certainly alluding to Creighton, whose views on national identity and Canada's relationship to the United States were at great odds with his own. Creighton held that Canadian national identity was based fundamentally on British characteristics, with American culture posing the ultimate threat.

Fox also asks Underhill, in the first half-hour, about the writing of Canadian history and the role of historians. He actually agrees with Creighton in saying that the historian is not a scientist but "a literary artist." The parochialism in their writing (this prompted by Fox), at least in the past, occurs because Canada is a new nation and they are writing about it as they were literally watching it develop. They are writing as national advocates, and the earliest example of this is in French Canada, with François-Xavier Garneau, who, in the 1840s, published a three-volume history of French Canada. Garneau wrote this work in response to the Durham Report, whose author suggested that the French in Lower Canada had no history or literature that was worthwhile. Garneau set out to prove Durham wrong and produced, in Underhill's words, "a great glorification of French Canada," which "made it live."

In the 1960s, many of the major daily newspapers had a column on television. The *Montreal Star* columnist Pat Pearce was impressed with *A Long View of Canadian History*, calling Underhill's shows "witty" and "provocative," and the series as a whole "rewarding" and "individually challenging."[89] It was a time when historians were regarded as public intellectuals who were expected to bring to the public their expertise on history and its contemporary relevance. Both of these historians had much more experience with radio than with television, but they were eager to expand their reach, and Creighton at least was delighted with the outcome. It had been an experiment for him, he wrote to Fox, but he "could not resist the chance of talking to a possibly wider audience."[90] Both interviews were transcribed, published, and sold by the CBC in booklet form for twenty-five cents each.[91]

Durham's Canada

In 1960, a historian appeared in *Explorations* who would be a recurring figure in the series until its run ended. Jack Saywell, then teaching Canadian political history at the University of Toronto, had done some commentary work for CBC radio and television, and had acted as a consultant for some of the episodes in Koch's proposed series on Canadian governors.[92] In 1963, at age thirty-three, Saywell would leave the University of Toronto to become York University's first dean of arts. He would become a household name as a guest on the CBC public affairs show *701* and then, in the late 1960s, as co-host of *The Way It Is*.

Historian Donald Wright has suggested that, by 1960, Saywell was part of a new cohort of historians who represented an increased professionalization in Canadian history, and that this professionalization closed the field to the layperson.[93] But in the 1960s, through his work for television, Saywell also did more than any other professional historian to popularize Canadian history. Creighton and Underhill were evocative and erudite, but here was Saywell, young, suave, and smart, with the looks and manner made for television. On top of his duties at the university, over the course of the 1960s Saywell wrote, co-wrote, consulted on, or hosted five Canadian history series on CBC television. This body of work included *Durham's Canada*, on Lord Durham and his 1839 report on British North America, and *A War for Survival*, about the War of 1812.[94]

Saywell's main interests at the time were the varying historical crises that, to him, affected national development and gave rise to some of the pressing contemporary problems in Canada. Chief among these were the crises related to English-French relations, so *Durham's Canada* was a fitting topic.[95] For this three-part series, Saywell directed the research, helped with the storyline and writing, and appeared on-screen in the last episode.[96] Eric Koch had originally commissioned someone else to write the scripts on Durham, but, in the end, he and Vincent Tovell rewrote them based on the previous research and with the help of Saywell.[97] The director was Daryl Duke, who had cautioned Koch earlier against involving too many scholars.

The story recounts the activities of Lord Durham, governor general of British North America in 1838. That year the British government tasked Durham to investigate the causes of the recent rebellions in Upper and Lower Canada, and to make recommendations on their future system of government. Control over most matters in the colonies was vested in the British governors and their appointed executive councils and advisors of elites. Protests against the lack of popular representation in this system led to uprisings in Upper and Lower Canada in 1837 and 1838. The rebellions played out differently in the two provinces, but in the end both were quashed, the leaders went into exile, and some of the rebels were put to death.

Durham spent several months mostly in and around Quebec, and upon his return to England he produced a report with a series of recommendations, the chief of which was the union of Upper and Lower Canada. Durham believed that the rebellions and other protests in Lower Canada had resulted not from political or economic issues but, rather, from ethnic tensions between the French- and English-speaking populations. He concluded that the situation – "two nations warring in the bosom of a single state" – could only be resolved by combining the two Canadas into one and assimilating the majority French-speaking population into the minority British population.[98] Durham praised the progressive nature of the British in the Canadas and felt that the French, whom he considered inferior, would only benefit from this. Moreover, the two colonies together would be better off economically.

A second major recommendation in the report was that a form of self-government be granted to all of the colonies in British North America: the United Province of Canada, Nova Scotia, New Brunswick, Prince Edward Island, and Newfoundland. Although Durham had not visited these other colonies during his stay, he acquired information on them from their lieutenant-governors and other informants. Changing the system of government would do away with the ruling cliques that, to varying degrees, existed in all the colonies and would replace them with executive councils created from and responsible to elected legislative assemblies. A division of power with Great Britain would see the British government involved with the colonies in matters of external importance only, leaving the colonies responsible for their own domestic matters. The British Parliament, upon receiving the report, moved quickly to unite Upper and Lower Canada, and with the Act of Union, 1841, created the one province. It was this event, along with its foundation in Durham's idea that the French had no future unless assimilated into the British population and its ways of life, that resulted in long-lasting tensions with Quebec.

Koch and company created *Durham's Canada* in the style of *You Are There*.[99] *You Are There* (1953–57) was a popular American television show, originally broadcast on radio, that dramatized "newsworthy" events in history. *You Are There* featured a young Walter Cronkite and his roving reporters interviewing actors playing historical characters ranging from the philosopher Plato, in ancient Greece, to the survivors of the *Titanic*. The on-air set resembled a contemporary television news show, with Cronkite as anchor and with the reporters conducting interviews with the characters in their historical settings. Cronkite later claimed that the writers had been victims of the McCarthy-era blacklist and that, as a result, a number of episodes centred on witch hunts like those involving Galileo and Joan of Arc.[100]

By 1960, historical dramas and docudramas were more familiar to CBC television audiences than were historical documentaries. This familiarity came from historical dramatizations and plays broadcast by CBC radio since the 1930s and from episodes in other CBC television series (like *Folio*). Koch had been interested in experimenting with a *You Are There*–type of presentation since the aborted series on governors a couple of years earlier. Injecting dramatic elements into a complex story was a way to make history more colourful and entertaining. There were other benefits too. The Durham Report was a sensitive subject in Quebec as many there considered it tantamount to a second Conquest. The dramatic sections would allow the actors to express a range of viewpoints, including those from the rebel leaders, their opponents, and the government representatives. The documentary sections would feature period paintings to help place the action in the 1830s. And Saywell would provide commentary and explanation, and generally authenticate the dramatic parts.

The first half-hour episode of *Durham's Canada* went to air in December 1960. After a short, dramatized teaser, journalist Charles Lynch steps into a period setting, where he begins to interview actor Barry Morse, playing Lord Durham, dressed in full period costume. Durham, prompted by Lynch, provides background and explains his situation, also addressing the perceptions that modern-day Canadians likely have of him. The camera moves to other dramatized scenes, featuring Durham interacting with characters such as British prime minister Lord Melbourne and the young Queen Victoria. A short documentary sequence with Lynch as narrator comes up next, along with further explanations from Durham and Lynch. Both Lynch and Melbourne raise the spectre of the revolutionary Americans as a cautionary tale for the Canadas.

In episode 2, Durham arrives in Quebec to investigate the grievances at the root of the rebellions in the Canadas. Actors portraying four men whom the real Durham actually interviewed show up to argue their respective causes. From Upper Canada is Robert Baldwin, Toronto lawyer and reformer, and John Beverley Robinson, chief justice and influential leader of the elite "Family Compact," who together give Durham conflicting advice regarding how Upper Canada should be governed. In another scene, Denis-Benjamin Viger, Montreal lawyer and spokesperson for the Canadiens, and Adam Thom, anti-French newspaperman and spokesperson for the English-speaking merchants in Montreal, give contrasting versions on the background of the troubles and the future of Lower Canada. All refer to the influence of the Americans and the American experience: Robinson dismissing Americans and their "cult of equality," and Viger praising them as believers in "the equality of men."

The original leaders of the rebellions were Louis-Joseph Papineau, in Lower Canada, and William Lyon Mackenzie, in Upper Canada. The real Durham did not actually interview them as they were in exile in the United States at the time of his stay. So in the television program the two make the case for their actions to reporter Alan Millar and further argue for what should happen in the future. Although not covered in the program, the real Papineau, like many Canadiens, was outraged by Durham's report. He refuted it almost immediately with his own publication, *Histoire de l'insurrection du Canada en réfutation du rapport de Lord Durham* (1839), in which he provided the context of the grievances in Lower Canada that led to rebellion. Papineau was granted amnesty and returned to Canada, and for many in Quebec he became an early symbol of French Canadian nationalism.

Episode 3 takes place after the issue of Durham's Report. In a time-period reversal of *You Are There*, in which modern-day reporters visit historical settings, Durham shows up at a 1960 television press conference to field questions about his report. Before the action begins, Lynch summarizes the report as something that "appeased the Canadian rebels of 1837, recommended responsible government, and somehow laid the groundwork for a relationship between England and Canada that anticipated the Commonwealth." After Lynch, and intermittently throughout the episode, the camera turns to Alan Millar with Jack Saywell, who provides background and context. Durham sits down with a panel of newspaper reporters representing a range of perspectives: a francophone reporter from Quebec city's *Le Soir*, a reporter from the *Winnipeg Gazette*, and a reporter from the *Sunday Herald* in London, England.

The reporter from Winnipeg presents a further twist on the historic and contemporary mix of this approach. Neither the city of Winnipeg nor the province of Manitoba existed in Durham's time, so even though the press conference takes place in 1960, the Winnipeg reporter does not have the same ties to the events of 1839 as the reporters from London and Quebec. The choice to include him expanded the regional representation of the program, but in this case a reporter representing the Atlantic colonies would have been the more appropriate choice. Nova Scotia had strong connections to Durham's report as it was there that responsible government, with an assembly elected by the people and an executive created from the members of the assembly, was first achieved in the British Empire.

A prime mover in this development was Joseph Howe, owner and editor of the *NovaScotian* newspaper and general thorn in the side of the colonial governing elite. For years, Howe had been criticizing the colonial system and pressing for greater popular representation in both levels of government. Thus his delight at Durham's recommendations, but his response and the results in Nova Scotia are not covered in *Durham's Canada*. In fact, the entire Atlantic region, though not the focus of Durham's actual visit, had made its way into his report. While Durham assured his superiors in England that the Atlantic colonies were not in imminent danger of rebellion, he warned that the situation should not be taken for granted. In order to be more representative of the people, the system needed to change there too. Among the Atlantic colonies he singled out a particular "evil" – the long-disputed absentee landlord system in Prince Edward Island – which he warned must end if the colony was to prosper.[101]

During the *Durham's Canada* press conference, the reporters prompt Durham to answer questions, which allows him to provide context and background. They ask questions about the British and British-style government and interests in North America and the influence of the United States on British North America. On the idea of preventing the British colonies from eventually being absorbed by the United States, Durham stresses the importance of giving the people in the colonies a nationality of their own, first through the granting of responsible government. The reporters also ask about Durham's mission, his mandate and process, and wonder, for example, why he had spent such a short amount of time in the Canadas and with whom he had met while there. It becomes clear that Durham did not meet many ordinary people during his five months in the Canadas but, rather, travelled little and listened almost exclusively to the advice of the merchants in Montreal and to other conservative elements. Back in the studio, Saywell confirms that Durham had been easily influenced by this advice because it was consistent with the prevailing ideas of a man of his time and station.

The reporter from *Le Soir* represents the critics of Durham and his actions in Quebec. He pressures Durham to admit that, although Durham considered the reasons for the rebellions to be very similar in both Upper and Lower Canada, without union he could have conceived of responsible government only in Upper Canada, not in Lower Canada. Durham concedes this is true because he "would not allow the British minority [in Lower Canada] to be ruled by the French." The reporter says he finds it strange how Durham could be considered to be the father of democracy in British North America when he would deprive the French of the right to govern themselves. Durham replies that he did not believe the French were qualified to govern themselves: "they were ... primarily a people of peasants, quite untrained for the requirements of a modern society." He thinks it was a deluded dream of the French to think of having a nationality of their own, surrounded as they were by Anglo-Saxons on the North American continent. The reporter later charges Durham with having "misguided" views, saying that, in preparing his report, he was "guided by preconceptions, by anti-French prejudice."

Durham's Canada provides the background events that led to Durham's stay in Quebec, but the idea of responsible government itself is not as contextualized as it is in the actual report. In the report, Durham suggests that French resistance in Lower Canada against the British colonial government found sympathy with "liberal politicians in every quarter of the world."[102] In citing connections with similar revolts in other nations, he references the American Revolution, the French Revolution of 1830, and, in the more distant past, even England's Glorious Revolution of 1688. In the television program Durham does express his admiration of the Americans for standing up to the British in defence of their representative rights, and in reality he was well aware of the impact of American republican ideas on MacKenzie and Papineau.

Saywell, in his final summary of the series, agrees with Millar that the report is the foundation of the British Commonwealth because, several years later, responsible government was achieved in a united Canada under the Baldwin-LaFontaine coalition, and it established a pattern in terms of a relationship with Britain that was followed by Australia, New Zealand, and other nations. Throughout the series, the talk continually returns to Durham as the man who can save the colonies. Lynch describes him in episode 1 as "reformer, fact-finder, and peacemaker"; in episode 2 as a "conciliator and peacemaker" with the future of Canada in his hands; and in episode 3, as having "appeased the Canadian rebels of 1837" with his report. Lynch's final word on Durham is that, whatever his prejudices and mistakes, "it was his greatness to have laid the foundation for a new relationship between nations." He ends by echoing Donald Creighton on the importance of the individual and his circumstances: "once again in history, the right man turned up at the right place and at the right time." Thus, at the end, the reporters and Durham come to no agreement, but Lynch offers the conclusion, contrary to what many Quebecers of 1960 might have thought, that Durham was a farsighted statesman who had led the way to national unity.

Saywell and the others involved in *Durham's Canada* believed that greater awareness of the events of this period was essential to understanding French-English relations in Canada in 1960. They relay the information in a variety of ways. The press conference allows the reporters, who know about the lasting impact of Durham's report, to challenge the governor-general on his motives and to confront him on the outcomes. Although the actor playing Durham does not speak words taken verbatim from the report, Koch and Tovell based the script on the report as well as on other historical records (e.g., Queen Victoria's diaries).[103] The use of straight drama in the other episodes allows the scenes to play out seamlessly. The documentary parts with Lynch and Saywell ground the dramatics and help to make the transfer of history to television more transparent. For example, Lynch reports the first dramatic scene as a conversation that "might have taken place," thus qualifying the evidence on which the dramatics is based. It was important to Saywell at least to convey some idea of what was behind the interpretation onscreen.

Television critics generally liked *Durham's Canada*. Pat Pearce wrote that it was fascinating and imaginative but that perhaps (like some other *Explorations* programs) it had too many different televisual techniques going on. She also wondered, in an indication of how the television schedule affected *Explorations*, if it might have better played out in a consecutive ninety-minute stretch rather than half-hour instalments over three weeks.[104] Columnists for the *Ottawa Journal* and the *Victoria Daily Times* said that *Durham's Canada* was "extremely well done, being both educational and entertaining" and "first-rate."[105] And at least one professional historian wrote a positive review of the series and the accompanying booklet.[106] Bob Blackburn, television critic for the *Ottawa Citizen*, was less impressed. Blackburn wrote that he was intrigued by the first episode, but he felt the second episode was "as flagrantly and crudely biased a dramatization as you're likely to find," so viewers should note that it was only one interpretation.[107]

The CBC published the script, written by Koch, Tovell, and Saywell, as *Success of a Mission: Lord Durham in Canada*, available for purchase at $1.25.

A War for Survival

A theme preoccupying Saywell and other historians at the time, besides the history of English-French relations in Canada, was the historic and continuing impact of the United States on Canada. After *Durham's Canada*, Saywell and Koch collaborated again on *The Fourteenth Colony*, a docudrama about the successful defence of Quebec against the Americans during the American Revolution. The same year, they produced *A War for Survival*, a four-part series on the War of 1812 on the 150th anniversary of its outbreak. *A War for Survival* married these scholarly interests of Saywell's, a particular focus of the series being the impact of war on the inhabitants of Lower Canada and how they reacted to it.

At least one CBC manager saw a series on the War of 1812 as something that, "as a base point for the development of Canada as a nation," could stir up a greater interest in Canadian history and help create for the CBC a tradition of historical programming.[108] It begins with Saywell, onscreen to deliver the introduction to the first episode, "Judgment at Ancaster." Saywell explains that the aim of the series is to look at what had been considered as "the most important single event in the history of Canadian nationalism" because it confirmed the existence of Canada as separate from the United States. Saywell says that the program will not deal with the familiar symbols of the conflict, like Isaac Brock, Laura Secord, and Tecumseh. Their approach, while unorthodox, will be more about the ideas around the conflict: "For the chief result of the war was an idea, or a myth." These ideas, Saywell says, "[were] about ourselves and our neighbours," and "about conservatism, radicalism, and loyalty."

The series featured yet another blend of the documentary and dramatic elements in the *Explorations'* programs. The dramatic components thus far had taken the form of a televised play. Film-like dramatics were not common in CBC documentaries or docudramas at the time, and there was no budget for them anyway. But there was still a lot of room for creativity. After Saywell's introduction in this first episode, the camera follows him as he joins a group of men standing in what looks like a sparse theatrical set. The men are actors, and, as their director, Saywell gives them the background to the upcoming scene: the 1814 Ancaster trials that saw a group of settlers in Upper Canada tried for treason for joining the Americans. Saywell outlines to the actors what is known about the historical characters they will be playing: Chief Justice Thomas Scott, Chief Crown Prosecutor John Beverley Robinson, and the accused, Stephen Hartwell. Saywell steps off-camera and the men act out the scene. Afterwards, Saywell re-enters and explains to the actors how they might play the next scene with a set of new historical counterparts, given what is known about them. He tells the man playing the Canadian-born British general Drummond that Drummond was "irritable, impatient, and contemptuous," while the actor playing Colonel Benton can play him however he wants since there is nothing known about him.

In other instances Saywell stresses that some parts of the dialogue are taken directly from the historical record, while some parts are improvised because little is known about the details. In *A War for Survival*, Saywell occasionally qualifies the historical information to make more evident to viewers how the original source material is being used. At the end of episode 1, the judge announces the sentence for the traitor Adam Crysler: he will be hanged, cut down while still alive, and drawn and quartered. The details about the gruesome punishment heighten suspense for episode 2. But at the beginning of episode 2, Saywell explains that, although the sentence was recorded as such and Crysler was definitely hanged, it is not clear from the historical record whether the rest of the sentence was actually carried out as ordered.

The second episode, "Mr. Madison's War," explores the causes of the war. Saywell and company wanted to bring forth multiple perspectives at once, so the episode departs from the historical record by interpreting a hypothetical trial rather than one that actually took place at Ancaster. Adam Crysler, back from the dead, and Justice Scott, the judge who tried him, join forces to investigate. They begin by putting on trial James Madison, the American president who had declared war. Saywell informs the actor playing Madison that the president was weak, and a contemporary had described him as petty. In the scene, both Crysler and Scott condemn the president for his actions, with Crysler complaining that he was hanged in Canada because of the war the president had started. Madison protests by explaining that people need to understand how contemptuously the British treated the Americans. The British were obstructing American progress and interrupting American trade during their war with Napoleon by seizing American ships and impressing sailors.

The actors then play out a short impressment scene on a part of the stage outside of the courtroom. Afterwards, they return to the court setting and put Henry Clay on the stand. Clay was one of the so-called "War Hawks" in Congress who had pushed Madison to declare war. Clay claims that the British had been urging the "Indians" to rise up against the Americans, and that it was American manifest destiny to possess Canada. Madison returns to the stand. He defends himself against charges that he could have called off the war when the British rescinded their Orders-in-Council (enacted to prevent American trade with France) but that he did not do so because he wanted to be re-elected. Saywell steps in and clarifies that there are elements of truth in all the previous statements.

Episode 3 is entitled "Loyalty," about the involvement in the war of the Canadiens in Lower Canada under the governorship of George Prevost. Université Laval historian Fernand Ouellet was special consultant for this episode. Saywell explains that Prevost had replaced Governor James Craig, who had enacted a "reign of terror" over the Canadiens by trying to wipe out French culture. The story initially unfolds in scenes between Prevost and Bishop Mountain, the Anglican bishop in Montreal. Mountain represents the English-speaking minority in Lower Canada, and he seeks the assimilation of the French. Bishop Plessis, the head of the Roman Catholic Church, also features prominently in these scenes. He is loyal to the British and assures them the Canadiens will be too. Napoleonic ideas are not supported, he later says; American republicanism is "the forerunner of atheism," and the American idea of the sovereignty of the people is "a diabolical doctrine."

Prevost seeks to help win over the Canadiens in part by recruiting Charles de Salaberry to lead a regiment of Canadiens against the Americans. De Salaberry mentions the young Louis-Joseph Papineau to

Prevost, who then appoints Papineau as a captain in the militia. When the actor playing Papineau receives his commission, he stops himself in mid-sentence, protesting to Saywell that this is out of character since Papineau will later become a leader of the rebellion in Lower Canada and, thereafter, an icon in Quebec. Saywell responds that Papineau's aim was to outwit the members of the British Executive, who had been claiming that the Canadiens were disloyal to the British cause. By showing his loyalty, he was trying to gain more rights for the Legislative Assembly, which was made up mostly of Canadiens.

At the end of each episode, Saywell highlights its main theme. Episode 1 shows that the war strengthened Canadian nationalism as well as "the conservative forces" in British North America. Reminiscent of Frank Underhill's discussion about the radical tradition, Saywell explains that, at the time, anything questioning the British way of doing things, or that smacked of radicalism or Americanism, was regarded as disloyal. So with the War of 1812 the radical tradition in Canada suffered a setback. Episode 2 explains the complex events that led to war and the fact that neither side was wholly innocent with regard to its outbreak. Episode 3 is about the loyalty of French Canada. According to Saywell, the loyalty of the Canadiens was due just as much to the conflict within Lower Canada between the French and the English, and between the Catholics and the Protestants, as it was to the fear of the Americans or an American invasion.

At the end of episode 3, Saywell announces that the fourth and last instalment of the series, ("Fact and Myth"), will be a discussion with three other historians about the war and its lasting implications. In the draft script for his sign-off (which did not air), Saywell had written that historians themselves had been perpetuating myths that get in the way of real knowledge about the past: "as time passes history becomes what the historians say it was," Saywell was to say. "Around the War of 1812 the historians have built a formidable wall of myths. We have discovered that it was not the conquest of Canada; not a war which found a united Upper Canada; not a war in which French-Canadians breathed nothing but the most altruistic sentiments of loyalty." And, with the discussion in the upcoming and last episode, he hopes that he and the other historians can "rewrite Canadian history."[109]

The episode is a panel debate. Unlike the series of individual interviews in "The Fall of Quebec," this format allows the participants to interact with each other and debate the issues in person. Its aim, as Saywell indicated, was to explore the facts of the war as well as the myths that swirled around it. Paul Fox is facilitator and the participants are Saywell, Charles Stacey, Jean-Pierre Wallot (then a young doctoral candidate in history at the Université de Montréal), and Arthur Lower. Lower is the senior authority of the group. Along with Donald Creighton and other scholars he had helped to develop a Canadian nationalist historiography. But he differed from Creighton in that in works like *Colony to Nation* (1946) he explored Canada as a nation apart from the British, as a nation on its own terms within North America.

The debate begins with the question of who won the War of 1812. The panel members agree that the British, Americans, and Canadians all had some degree of victory. Wallot adds that it was most beneficial for Canada because out of it came a vision and "the principal elements of today's Canada." Fox to panel: "Was the War of 1812 the beginning of Canadian anti-Americanism?" Wallot says yes, particularly for Upper Canadians, but the war also made the French Canadians wary of the great risk posed to them by the Americans. Lower says that this sentiment had actually started earlier under the guise of anti-republicanism (after the American Revolution), which led to anti-Americanism after the War of 1812 broke out. Stacey says that anti-Americanism existed before the war and agrees with Lower, adding that the 1812 conflict merely revived those earlier hostile sentiments: "we always have to have our anti-Americanism revived by successive crises." Lower adds that this was typical as every nation needed to have an enemy. The Americans, in turn, found theirs in the British.

Much of the debate takes up the topic of episode 3, which is about the role of French Canada in the war and the place of French Canadians in British North America afterwards. "Was the war the birth of nationalism in Canada?" Fox asks Wallot. Wallot replies, "Yes," for English Canada. The Canadiens stayed on the British side mainly because they thought they had a better chance of becoming a nation under the protection of the British Crown, thus being fortified against not only the Americans but also the British settlers in Lower Canada. On the Canadien militia fighting with the British, Wallot says, "French Canada was fighting for its life." Later, he adds that those actions helped the British realize the Canadiens could be trusted, and while they still needed to politically subordinate them, they realized that they didn't need to assimilate them. Thus, argues Wallot, the threat of the United States was the most important link between the British and the French in Canada.

Fox reads a contemporary text speaking to the iconic status of the Battle of Châteauguay and asks Wallot if it illustrates a nascent national mentality on the part of the Canadiens. Wallot says that the point of the battle and the subsequent celebration of victory was not to show off the loyalty or nationalism of French Canadians. Lower interjects that this idea of Châteauguay was the beginning of a myth that "has been affirmed and reaffirmed," and that it served to augment French Canada's sense of identity. When Wallot adds that de Salaberry was the first hero for both the French and the English, Stacey agrees, claiming that here is another part of the myth, in connection with the idea that the militia was crucial in defending the country, as de Salaberry was in fact an officer of the British Army. The importance of the militia at Châteauguay and elsewhere to the outcome of the war was something Stacey had been refuting as mythology. Indeed, Saywell adds that now they were hitting on one of the key results of the war – its "hordes of myths." He maintains that the myths created an artificial foundation for Canadian nationalism but that, on the other hand, if they chipped away at them too much, this nationalism might collapse.

The sparring among the panel members reveals as much about the nature of myth, and historical interpretation, as it does about the events and outcomes of the war itself. Like the historians in "The Fall of Quebec," the historians of the War of 1812 express great differences in their interpretation of the same events. Lower, perpetuating the idea that the militia in Upper Canada won the war for the British (an idea now rejected by most scholars), had already made it clear that he rarely agreed with Stacey on anything. The following exchange occurs after Fox quotes a statement from Bishop Strachan of York (Toronto), made late in 1812, that the Canadian militia had "twice saved this country," thus contradicting Stacey's point of view:

> STACEY: I've always rather regretted that Sir Isaac Brock was killed before that was said because it would have amused him very much.
> LOWER: [reads a quote from Brock himself, expressing his appreciation of the Canadian militia].
> STACEY: I was quite astonished at the Canadians doing so well!
> LOWER: Well ... I have another quotation ...
> STACEY: Yes, quite, quite. Have you ever looked at the casualty lists?
> LOWER: Yes, I've got them right here ...

Saywell was right that historians themselves were fortifying myths about the war, but this hit closer to home than he may have thought. Mythmaking requires some things to be emphasized or exaggerated, and some to be diminished or ignored. *A War for Survival* focuses on the people and events in and around the Great Lakes and along the Upper St Lawrence. There is no discussion of people in the Atlantic colonies or the events there and along the eastern seaboard of the United States. Yet Halifax was then the principal British naval station in North America, and substantial human resources from the entire Atlantic region augmented the British forces in Upper and Lower Canada, in the American theatres of war, and along the eastern seaboard. The panel, with members from Toronto, Kingston, and Montreal, reflect this absence. The scholars stuck to the people and events in present-day Ontario and Quebec, and on English-French relations in Canada. This meant there would be no room for discussion of other aspects of the war effort in British North America, including those connected to the Atlantic colonies.

Nor was there an indication of the role of Indigenous people in the war. Indigenous people were key players in all the major wars involving the British in North America, including the Seven Years' War, the American Revolution, and the War of 1812. Saywell notes in his introduction that one of the legendary heroes of the conflict, who will not be discussed in the upcoming episodes, is Tecumseh, a Shawnee chief who led a confederacy of First Nations in alliance with the British. Not only the Shawnee but also thousands of Indigenous warriors, like those from the Six Nations, Abenaki, and Mohawk, fought with the British against the Americans. And along with the virtual unanimity of the panel on the idea that the war concluded with multiple victors, there is virtual silence about the losers. In the negotiations at the end of the war, the British did not push for their Indigenous allies to regain land lost to them. The British and the Americans returned to their antebellum borders. But the Indigenous people in the United States were left to the mercy of the unstoppable American push westward.

This pattern of absences or silences alone can be the basis of myth creation. Yet the historians in *A War for Survival* at least seem aware of their own role in mythmaking and the part that myth played in building and maintaining nationalist sentiment. As William Morton had put it regarding the connection between historians and writers of poetry: "each is a maker of myths, only the historian has neglected his job of making myths in this decadent, analytical age."[110] The panel members in *A War for Survival* address myth outright. Lower and Saywell discuss the nature of myth in general and agree that it can be useful, that it is not necessarily a bad thing. As Saywell says, if we examine our myths too much, our nationalism might collapse. Lower adds that myths are necessary to every community: "The Battle of Bannockburn and all that sort of thing – Falkirk!"

The debate ends simply with Fox cutting off Jean-Pierre Wallot in mid-sentence and signing off. The CBC paired and broadcast *A War for Survival* with an NFB series of biographical teleplays entitled *The Road to Confederation*, which features John A. Macdonald and his colleagues in their quest for union. The CBC ran the two series on *Explorations* under the umbrella title *The Formative Years*. This was the title under which all Canadian history programs for *Explorations* would thereafter run, a label indicative of the importance of nationalist history leading up to the centennial in 1967.[111]

Eric Koch championed *Explorations* as an educational vehicle. While the educational elements were evident in the documentaries "The Fall of Quebec," "Winnipeg General Strike 1919," and *A Long View of Canadian History*, Koch also stressed them in the more creative docudramas, like *Durham's Canada* and *A War for Survival*. They were evident in the professors and panels, the interviews and narrative commentary, and the concluding lessons to be learned. This was an attempt to show history not just as an account of past events but also as a process of critical inquiry dependent on original sources and incomplete or conflicting evidence, often resulting in differing interpretations.

Explorations also sought to put the past in contemporary focus and to highlight its continuing relevance, to promote knowledge of a shared past in order to help build national unity and a sense of national identity. Almost all of the historians involved with *Explorations* were working in Ontario and Quebec, which reflected the CBC's focus on the histories of those provinces. Other themes and subjects in Canadian history could have been explored, but the producers believed that those brought forth by Creighton, Stacey, Saywell, and others were the ones essential to learning about Canada. Koch, Tovell, and other staff worked collaboratively alongside these historians; in fact, it was policy and practice in Talks and Public Affairs to work with experts in all fields as consultants, writers, commentators, and narrators.

Although Koch positioned *Explorations* as an educational series, he also sought wider audience appeal than did the more specialist-oriented pieces of the earlier *Exploring Minds*. There was little in the way of established practice in presenting history on television, so producers retained some of the didactic aspects of *Exploring Minds*, along with some of the dramatic aspects of the three-act plays common on CBC radio, which was the former home of Koch and Tovell. This combination of educational and entertainment values reflected a wider middlebrow approach to programming at the CBC.[112] One of the interesting things about *Explorations* was the sheer variety of different techniques even within the same program. While it may not always have worked well with viewers, people tuning in each week never knew quite what to expect. This changed as the 1970s approached. Increasing commercialism and competition in the industry overall led to greater homogeneity within the programs themselves and within the entire schedule. Technological developments and a new Broadcasting Act were additional features of the changing times.

2 | A New History of Canada?
Images of Canada

As *Explorations* wrapped up in 1964, plans for the 1967 centennial programming were already under way. The federal government had begun preparations as early as 1960 by supporting a multitude of commemorative projects across the country.[1] The celebrations fed a growing English Canadian nationalism, reoriented from British tradition and represented most tellingly by the usurping of the Red Ensign by the new Canadian flag. Writer Robert Fulford wrote about the early 1970s that this new nationalism was one of the most surprising and "striking aspects of life" in English Canada. "Certainly no one predicted," declared Fulford, in *Saturday Night* magazine, "that it would appear so suddenly and in so many fields at once, reaching into everything from legitimate theatre to popular music."[2]

For the centennial, the CBC needed to stake its position as an essential national service. Officials created a special committee for history programming and appointed Bert Powley, who had been involved with the precursor to "The Fall of Quebec," as special programmes officer.[3] Powley put forward a list of ideas, stressing that he did not envision a "dogged, school-masterish attempt to teach history, but rather a search for highlights that will make good story-telling or re-creation or dramatization or whatever."[4] Yet Powley still believed he needed the help of professional historians. He asked Eric Koch for some names and wanted the centennial committee to consult with the universities too, to see "what new historical research was being carried out in Canadian universities, and by whom."[5] He praised the work that *Explorations* had done on historical documentaries but lamented to Doug

Nixon the lack of sustained Canadian history television programming at the CBC. "In the United States and Great Britain," he wrote, "the history learned in school is reinforced by thousands of children's stories, adult novels, plays, movies and television productions ... This is the gap which Canadians have to fill."[6] The centennial programming featured a wide variety of mostly one-off historical dramas and documentaries, though in the end it did not address Powley's desire for a lasting vehicle for Canadian history.

In 1968 the federal government passed a new Broadcasting Act. The act only made official the nation-building role the CBC had long assumed and practised, but the confirmation renewed continued questions about that role given the continued preponderance on the English network of American programs.[7] This relative lack of distinctive Canadian programming on CBC television did not square with the nationalist sentiment still running high from the centennial. The new act also included requirements for regional programming and stated for the first time that the CBC had an obligation to serve "the special needs of geographic regions." CBC officials generally interpreted this to mean attention to regional production for local, regional, and national consumption, including production in the regions by outside personnel.[8]

Images of Canada, the first attempt at a television series on the entire history of Canada, was conceived largely as a response to these challenges. It was pure Canadian content supporting the nation-building mandate. In keeping with public service values, it was an educational documentary series of high quality. And supporting the increased emphasis on regions, it included a subseries called *The Whitecomers* on the history of Canada's regions. Overall the series interpreted the history of Canada as the development of Canada as a nation, but this regional framework paralleled contemporary developments in the writing of Canadian history. Following the pattern established by *Explorations*, Koch and Tovell consulted widely with some of Canada's top historians and also hired them as consultants, writers, onscreen presenters, and interview guests.

With the passing of the Broadcasting Act, the CBC conducted a major corporate reorganization. The headquarters of the English Services Division, along with the headquarters of the French Services

Division in Montreal, moved to Toronto, and the two became semi-autonomous units encompassing both radio and television production. In each of the cities, a vice-president and general manager ran all operations. This rendered obsolete the position of vice-president and general manager, regional broadcasting, as all regional offices in the English network now reported to Toronto.[9] Eugene Hallman filled the new position in Toronto. His responsibilities included the two new television departments of Information Programming and Entertainment Programming under Knowlton Nash and Thom Benson, respectively. Nash, reporting to Hallman through Managing Director of Television Norn Garriock, managed five production teams: Agriculture and Resources; Religious; Schools and Youth; Current Affairs, which now included the news; and Arts and Sciences, which included most of the history programming. Eric Koch continued in a role similar to that he had held previously, as area head of Arts and Sciences.

Nash had just returned from a high-profile position as the CBC's correspondent in Washington, a posting that provided him opportunities to interview newsmakers as diverse as Robert Kennedy and Che Guevara.[10] He later recounted lots of battles in his quest to make "hard news" a priority, but "current affairs programs and historical documentaries were almost as critical."[11] His appointment signalled an important change not only in the amount of history programming but also in the type of history programming. Nash allowed the incorporation of dramatic elements into the history programs mainly because he felt it could help attract larger audiences. Yet he was at heart a newsman, more comfortable with the type of factual programming associated with the news and journalism. Although there had always been program policies and standards in Talks and Public Affairs, Nash's tenure coincided with a tightening of controls in information programming, including a series of policy guidelines to ensure journalistic standards pertaining to areas like ethics, objectivity, accuracy, integrity, and balance.[12] As communications scholar David Hogarth put it, in these years "documentary programming was largely colonized by journalism."[13] But some of the key staff under Nash who had previously been associated with Canadian history documentaries and docudramas, like Eric Koch and Vincent Tovell, had not built their careers as journalists. They identified themselves as television program organizers, producers, and directors.[14]

The CBC was also operating in a different industrial landscape than it had during the run of *Explorations*. In addition to the new Broadcasting Act, a national private broadcaster, CTV, was now on the scene. CTV started up in 1961 as an amalgamation of eight affiliates from Halifax to Vancouver. It was not an immediate concern to CBC staff as it initially struggled with finances and an unwieldy ownership and management scheme, and its schedule amounted to game shows, music shows, and *The Littlest Hobo*.[15] In the late 1960s, however, a reorganized and profitable entity emerged under John Bassett and his CFTO station in Toronto. It featured lots of American shows that Canadians wanted to watch and that were lucrative to the broadcaster.[16] The CBC now had to compete for advertising dollars that, in the past, had underwritten a good part of its own Canadian content.

Nor was the CBC any longer the only public service broadcaster in Canada. Another change, written into the new Broadcasting Act, allowed for the creation of independent educational broadcasters. In developing its original mandate, the CBC had followed the BBC in its promise to "inform, educate, and entertain." But with education in Canada a provincial responsibility, the CBC mandate became "inform, enlighten, and entertain." Yet officials had always interpreted educational programming as part of CBC's responsibilities. These were the programs for schoolchildren, like *Canadian School Telecasts*, and its provincial counterpart, which was produced in association with provincial educational authorities and used by teachers in the classroom.[17] It was also the formal educational programming for adults, like *Live and Learn*, produced in association with universities and organizations like the CAAE.[18] And then there were the informal educational programs of a public affairs nature, which included shows like *Explorations*, *Man at the Centre*, and *The Nature of Things*. Staff were careful not to label them "education," as noted by one employee, "although their effect [was] educative."[19]

CBC officials therefore argued that the infrastructure and expertise already existed for educational programming at the CBC and that the creation of other educational broadcasters would have a negative effect on its informational programming overall.[20] Nevertheless, in 1970 the Canadian Radio-television (and later Telecommunications) Commission (CRTC), now the regulatory body for Canadian broadcasting, began to extend licences to the provinces. By 1973, the Quebec Broadcasting Bureau, the Ontario Educational Communications Authority (now TVO) and broadcasting on Channel 19, and the Alberta Educational Communications Corporation (ACCESS) were in operation.[21] The Council of Ministers of Education and provincial educational authorities soon took over the *School Telecasts*, with the CBC providing airtime.[22] Moreover, because the Broadcasting Act was imprecise in its definition of educational broadcasting, Channel 19, for one, began to compete with the CBC in public affairs and informational programming as well.[23] This marked the end of educational programming as the exclusive purview of the CBC.

This was the new environment in which Nash waged his Canadian history campaign. The programs in this campaign were nation building; high-quality educational works, and they counted as 100 percent Canadian content. Canadian content regulations had been put in place following the previous Broadcasting Act (1958) to ensure that broadcasting in Canada remained "Canadian in content and in character."[24] The criteria depended more on Canadian production control and Canadian personnel than on the actual content of the program, but until the early 1970s, educational works could receive a 100 percent Cancon rating. Similarly, any program produced in a Commonwealth or French-language country qualified as full and 50 percent Canadian content, respectively.[25] This was the case even if the subject matter had nothing to do with Canada. CBC Canadian history programs, whether drama, docudrama, or documentary, for children or adults, always qualified as full Canadian content.

The first of these programs produced under Nash was *The Tenth Decade*, on federal politics from 1957 to 1967 – the tenth decade after Confederation. Cameron Graham and staff from the Ottawa regional office produced the series, which went to air in 1971 in eight one-hour parts. It consists of archival stills and film, news footage, and interviews, most significantly with the two prime ministers of that decade: Lester Pearson and John Diefenbaker. *The Tenth Decade* highlights both the personal and political lives of the prime ministers, following them throughout their careers as they deal with the events of their time and with each other.[26]

The Tenth Decade was a critical success and provided the impetus to produce more content on political history and Canadian history in general. The Ottawa unit immediately developed a proposal for another series following a similar model of archival stills, film, and interviews, with some basic dramatization. *The Days before Yesterday: Struggle for Nationhood*, covers the years between 1897 and 1957 and the leadership of prime ministers from Laurier to St Laurent. It was televised in 1973 as a kind of prequel to *The Tenth Decade*.[27] Critics liked this one too, as well as two more series based on the interviews with Pearson and Diefenbaker made for *The Tenth Decade*, only portions of which were televised in the original series. These were *First Person Singular: Pearson – The Memoirs of a Prime Minister* (1973) and *One Canadian: The Political Memoirs of the Rt. Hon. John G. Diefenbaker* (1976–77).[28]

A big influence on the content and presentation of CBC Canadian history programs was the foreign (mostly British) content that staff purchased to help fill the schedule, provide educational and quality programs, meet Canadian content quotas, and entertain audiences.[29] Some examples, on air from the late 1960s to the mid-1970s, are *Civilisation*, featuring British art historian Kenneth Clark; *America* (1972–73), British-American journalist and broadcaster Alistair Cooke's take on the history of the United States; and *The World at War* (1973–74), the series on the Second World War by Thames Television, with which the CBC had some production affiliation. CBC producers referred to these works in their proposals for new shows, and television columnists referred to them too, for comparison purposes in assessing CBC offerings. They were often presenter-led with archival images and film, and no dramatic elements.

The international success of the BBC's *Civilisation* provided the inspiration for *Images of Canada*, created by Eric Koch with Vincent Tovell as executive producer. Where *Civilisation* traced the history of Western culture using art and architecture as touchstones, *Canadian Civilization* (one of *Images of Canada*'s early working titles) would do the same for Canada. The plan for *Images* was to continue the emphasis on Canadian history featured in the centennial programs and

The Tenth Decade. Where *The Tenth Decade* had focused on politics and political personalities, the new series would focus on Canada's cultural and social history, including the historical development of the regions. Although Nash said later that the centre/region dichotomy was not a factor in *Images of Canada*, following the recent Broadcasting Act, the CBC renewed its emphasis on more regional production for national programming.[30]

There was also a political reason for the series. The CBC had vocal critics in the House of Commons who questioned its taxpayer support given the similarities between CBC programming, with all its commercials, and the American and American-style programs. The history programs counted as 100 percent Canadian content, which the CBC was trying hard to augment. They were educational and were considered to be high quality compared to the superficiality of many of the American shows. Nash had been looking for a program like this, and early in 1971 he pressed Koch and Tovell to get the first two episodes ready for the following season. Nash was not sure how much time they had to make an impact on the CBC critics. "The only really effective way we can demonstrate that the CBC is performing the job set out in the Broadcasting Act, and is performing the job that is vital to Canada," he said, "is by the presentation of programming of a character we foresee in 'Canadian Civilization.'"[31]

The original proposal outlined twelve one-hour episodes organized around the themes of the nature, law and order, and communications.[32] Over the course of the next several years, Koch and Tovell pared it down and transformed it into a series of five one-hour thematic shows on different topics about Canada, and another subseries of five. The topics of the themed episodes are: the work of historians of Canada, the Parliament Buildings in Ottawa, colonial settlements across Canada, popular ideas about Canada, and, finally, northern Canada and the Inuit. The subseries is *The Whitecomers*, a title announcing the work as a history of the colonial settlement of Canada's regions. With all the other episodes, it would form "a mosaic of Canada's development."[33] Unusually for a major documentary series at the time, Tovell hired for the *Whitecomers*' episodes a female producer/director, Carol Myers, and, as part of the writing and narration teams, Barbara Moon and Mia Anderson.

From early on, the production team envisioned *Images of Canada* as an educational film series. Koch in particular, parlaying his experience with *Explorations*, was keen on presenting something thought-provoking that reflected new ideas and approaches to the study of Canada and its past. Vincent Tovell, the main driving force of *Images*, alone helped to fill that bill. Tovell was a member of the influential Massey family and had taught English literature at the University of Toronto before abandoning a PhD at Columbia University in order to work at the United Nations (UN). Eventually he became the CBC representative for the UN and worked there first in radio and then television. So by the time Tovell arrived back in Toronto in 1957, he had experience in both media.[34]

For *Images*, Koch and Tovell felt there was a need to go beyond the political and economic-based historical narratives and create a more challenging presentation of cultural history.[35] Tovell wanted to establish connections with museums, universities, and archives to ensure that *Images* would be highly esteemed among experts as well as among the general public.[36] To that end he and Koch consulted a range of individuals and scholars, mostly professors in Ontario universities, for "guidance from leading thinkers."[37] They wanted well-known scholars to appear onscreen. But not everyone agreed. One staffer felt that, with this idea, Tovell was in danger of "over-intellectualism" and "bloodlessness," and so was happy to see in one of the proposals the possibility of including people like Pierre Berton or Lorne Greene.[38] In the end, neither was approached as the fear about Berton, at least, was not only his probable demands for editorial control but also his certain negotiations for residual rights.[39] If the intellectuals were bloodless, at least they were cheap.

The format and the choice of participants also reflect the educational intent. Each episode would be broken up into three eighteen-minute acts, seamless to the television viewer but divisible for school broadcasts and in-classroom use.[40] The producers retained part of this original plan, but they eventually dropped or parcelled off into individual episodes the specialist advisors and committee of scholars initially deemed necessary for the whole series. The exception was Ramsay Cook, who served as the overall consultant. Donald Creighton hosts the first thematic episode in the series, and Northrop Frye hosts the last. The first episode, "The Craft of History," features Cook's interviews with three senior historians: Creighton, Arthur Lower, and Michel Brunet.

Images of Canada was the last substantive Canadian history series on CBC television to engage professional historians other than as consultants. The 1960s and early 1970s was a pivotal time in the historical profession. While in popular culture there was a surge of English Canadian nationalism, in Canadian historiography the nation as a theme was losing its dominance. Canadian universities had begun to multiply, and, as history departments grew, so did the number of historians of Canada and the diversity of their subject areas. Earlier historians, from various perspectives, had sought to explain how Canada developed into a unified and self-governing nation, first as part of the British Commonwealth and later as a nation in its own right, apart from the British and distinct from the United States. Most of these accounts told the story of Canada as one of unrelenting progress, of unity and conformity within which internal conflicts were either resolved, diluted, or ignored altogether.[41] But they served a purpose by providing a scholarly foundation for a Canadian historical narrative where none had previously existed.

The newer scholars, even those who still used the nation-state as a framework, began to probe and unravel these nationalist narratives. They saw them as exclusive and dismissive, and no longer necessary. Many of these younger historians were Americans who had been exposed to new social movements south of the border, especially the civil rights movement. They began to create a historiography that filled the gaps in the existing narratives, which focused on "great white men," with histories of women, workers, Indigenous peoples, and others. Oral history was used as a way to capture these experiences. Scholars turned their interest to regional and local histories as well, and a much fuller picture of the Canadian past began to emerge. Maurice Careless has explained this shift through the concept of "limited identities," an idea first introduced by Ramsay Cook. Careless suggested that these identities – region, culture, class – were units other than the nation with which people could identify themselves and that might provide an answer to the quest for a Canadian identity.[42] Most of the Canadian history programs developed under Nash, however, with the exception (in some respects) of *Images of Canada*, did not respond to this shift.

The first episode is "The Craft of History," televised in March 1972 in the *Tuesday Night* time slot of 10:00 to 11:00 p.m. Ideas varied as to the goals of this first episode. Its producer/director George Robertson saw the piece as the prologue to the series. He explained to Nash that the goal was to explore the character and ideas of each scholar and to convey a sense of history as a living entity that was constantly open to re-evaluation as new sources and ideas came forth: "There is no 'one' history of Canada, and would not be even if we were formed of only one language and culture."[43] Robertson deflected potential concern about the piece as "talking heads," or a radio show on television, by insisting on the visual potential of each historian being situated in an environment that had some relation to his work. Tovell wanted "The Craft of History" to reveal the major themes running throughout each historian's written works, including their ideas about "survival north of the St Lawrence." Cook, for his part, wrote in the introduction to the published version of the interviews that the episode brought out a key preoccupation of the three historians, which he thought was shared by all historians writing about Canada: "[the] search for the characteristics of our national identity, for the convincing image of Canada." And finally, a press release put out in advance of airtime announced that one aim of the episode was to reveal insights into the past that would shed light on present-day situations.[44]

"The Craft of History" lived up to most of these expectations. Common threads in the interviews are the state of the Canadian federation and English-French relations. This was particularly apt given the growing popularity in Quebec of the idea of sovereignty. Cook begins with Lower, still sharp at eighty-three, on location in Lower's home, on Lower's boat in Lake Ontario, and at the table during lunch with Lower's wife. The conversation centres on two topics: Canadian relations with Britain and the United States, and English-French relations in Canada.

On Cook's question about when the problems began between the English and the French in Canada, Lower responds that it began with the Conquest and that it continued long afterwards in the form of its traumatic repercussions. Lower's interest in the history of Quebec, which itself was unusual among his anglophone contemporaries, extended beyond Quebec's relationship with English-speaking Canada and included the social impact of the fall of New France.[45] He says to Cook that historians had not done enough work on the psychological aspects of being conquered, "the most devastating experience that a people can have." He asks Cook to imagine how he would feel if he were walking down the street one day as a Canadien of New France and met up with the sharp end of a British bayonet. According to Lower, this accounts for the French cry of "la survivance" ever since.

When Cook raises the possibility of a colonial mentality on the part of French-speakers in Canada, Lower says that all Canadians have a colonial mentality and even an inferiority complex, which makes them act like "dumb, driven cattle." "They'll take any decisions that are made for them," he says. On the work of the historian, he maintains that historians are doing more than just writing history: "they're making the nation." Lower believed that this was their primary task and that, like Donald Creighton, Frank Underhill, Charles Stacey, Lionel Groulx, and others, they should undertake it by engaging the public in their work. For example, according to Lower at an earlier time, CBC radio could have done a better job of producing talk programs that would have interested more people at different levels, as opposed to some "high-falutin" CBC dramas.[46]

Michel Brunet, Cook's next guest, was also interested in history as the essential component in the development of national identity. But for him, the nation of concern was Quebec. Brunet was among the top scholars of the history of Quebec and a recent recipient of the Governor General's Award for non-fiction (French) for his book *Les Canadiens après la conquete, 1759–1775: De la révolution canadienne à la révolution américaine* (1969). The interview highlights Brunet's views on historic and contemporary English-French relations, and on the history of Quebec overall. He says that Canada and Quebec should exist as two nations and that dual leadership, similar to the Baldwin-LaFontaine coalition in the 1840s, will be the key to effective cooperation. Like Lower, he assigns the Conquest the central position in Canadian history and holds that many contemporary problems of Quebecers are a direct result of it. Brunet further believes that these problems are not just the fault of the British but also of the Canadiens, who afterwards collaborated with the British. On a provocative note he describes French Canadians as having a "servant's mentality" in that, since the Conquest, they believed that Canada did not belong to them and therefore wanted to work for the English: "the richest master."

Brunet's debunking of what he considered to be traditional French Canadian mythology, promoted by his predecessors (e.g., Lionel Groulx), was part of the changing brand of Quebec nationalism that had begun to gain traction in the late 1950s.[47] He challenged traditionalist views of the province's history by promoting the idea that its basis was not in agriculture and religion – as scholars like Groulx and Lower believed – but in commerce. In his interview, Brunet talks about the early negative opinion some in Quebec had formed about him as a result of these ideas. To Cook's question of whether the history of French Canada was being badly served by English writers, Brunet replies that francophones themselves were doing a poor job of it. And if *they* were defining themselves and their ancestors as agrarian and religious, how could English-speaking Canadians be blamed for not understanding them?

Cook's interview with his last guest, Donald Creighton, occurred at an interesting time in the senior historian's career. Creighton's approach to Canadian history had served him well in the past, but it was beginning to fall out of favour with his colleagues. In 1970 he published *Canada's First Century*, a work that continued his criticism of what he considered to be the disintegration of Canada. It was panned by many of his colleagues for its cranky diatribes, most notably regarding Canada's position vis-à-vis the United States, Quebec, and English-French relations, and the weakening of the federation caused by the provinces. Creighton saw that the new nationalism emerging in English-speaking Canada, expressed so vigorously in 1967, was not the type of nationalism that he advocated. Gone or going were the attachments to the British institutions and symbols that he held so dear and that underscored much of his illustrious writing. His anxiety over the future of Canada led him to produce the book that his biographer described as Creighton's "lament for a nation."[48] In a CBC television interview that year about *Canada's First Century*, Creighton appears bewildered by the response to it, noting that only small, controversial parts of his work were condemned, while the rest of it was ignored. He simply wants to work as a historian, he says, instead of having to make television appearances as a "propagandist."[49]

The interview with Cook, one year later, finds Creighton less defensive. He does not deny that *Canada's First Century* is "despairing" (in Cook's words); he merely wanted to show how Canadian federalism was declining due to the forces chipping away at it. The two men talk in Charlottetown, at the lieutenant-governor's house, and at Province House, where the Charlottetown Conference, leading to Confederation, took place. They also travel to Ottawa and the Parliament Buildings, where they talk in the former office of John A. Macdonald. Here Creighton conducts himself much as he did in his 1959 *Long View of Canadian History* interview with Paul Fox: he is serious and articulate, passionate and expressive. Much of the interview is about the nature of Canadian national unity, but Creighton also discusses his biography of Macdonald, and his thoughts on Louis Riel. Cook is particularly curious about Riel, but Creighton is cagey. His callous treatment of Riel in the biography, as well as his more recent take on Quebec nationalism and French Canada, had drawn widespread criticism.[50] He tells Cook that he can never quite satisfy himself on the contradictions surrounding the Métis leader.

Due to the growing negativity in television circles towards scholarly "talking heads," some saw "The Craft of History" as risky television. The CBC Research Department found that, in terms of audience numbers, the episode was the lowest for *Images of Canada*. Still, the department considered the 6 percent rating as average for a documentary in that approximate time slot and on par with other *Tuesday Night* offerings. CBC Research also conducted qualitative research on its programs, and the "index of enjoyment" level for the episode was a "moderate" seventy-three.[51]

The critical response to "The Craft of History," however, got *Images of Canada* off to a positive start. Though the *Montreal Gazette*'s TV columnist deemed it essentially a radio dialogue (contrary to George Robertson's earlier statement that it would *not* be like a radio dialogue), at least three of his colleagues at the major dailies were impressed. The television columnists from the *Globe and Mail* and the *Ottawa Citizen* wrote that the three professors were "fascinating, delightful and provocative," that they "almost upstaged history."[52] And Ted Ferguson at the *Vancouver Sun* registered surprise at having his preconceptions about historians destabilized: "Nothing, I reasoned, could be duller than a tweedy scholar serving a life sentence in an archive's Canadiana section. It was the CBC's excellent documentary, 'The Craft of History,' that changed my mind."[53]

During the planning and consultation for the series, Koch said that the time had come to go beyond the political and economic approaches to Canadian history. Although "The Craft of History" does not stray too far from these approaches, the topics under discussion may not have been familiar to the average television viewer. And basing the episode solely on the interviews with the historians did mark a change from the recent slate of political documentaries. As George Robertson had hoped, the discussions provide a unique insight into the historians' work and their diverse perspectives on the Canadian past. It also reveals the dynamic nature of historical knowledge, for example, where it connects to current realities such as the relationship between English and French Canada.

Still, the piece highlights some of the limitations of the history profession at the time. One of these was that all four scholars (except for Cook) are older men. In the early 1970s there were relatively few women in the field of Canadian history, let alone senior scholars working on the subjects that Cook covered in this episode. Another limitation was that all four were living and working in either Ontario or Quebec. When the working title for the series was still *Canadian Civilization*, one CBC manager complained to Nash about too many potential consultants from Toronto ("not even Vincent thinks Toronto warrants a place in a series on civilization").[54] At least the importance of Quebec and its history are well recognized – Cook says about Canada, in his voiceover narration, that "a country of two nations is a country of two histories." But the focus remains on national history, which is important because "The Craft of History" was supposed to be a framework within which the next episodes would fit.

The nationalist emphasis continues in the second and third instalments, beginning with "The Folly on the Hill," about the Parliament Buildings in Ottawa ("a national self-portrait").[55] Tovell himself directed this piece about the construction, architecture, and role of the buildings, called "absolute folly" by George Brown of the *Globe* newspaper, because of its cost overruns. "The Folly on the Hill" opens with a short filmed segment of a female stone carver working on a sculpture inside the centre block of the Parliament Buildings. The narrative voiceover begins with the story of the design proposal competition. This competition takes place, the narrator explains, within the context of the Industrial Revolution, "Manifest Destiny" in the United States, nation building and wars in mainland Europe, and "the cult of progress" in Britain.

"The Folly on the Hill" moves back and forth, from the various Blocks and architectural elements of the buildings, and some of the political personalities who work inside, to the national events occurring outside their walls. The events included all seem to represent some type of milestone in national development. The fragmented visual and narrative style proves to be a defining feature of *Images of Canada*, though it is employed somewhat less successfully here than in some of the other episodes. Towards the end of the hour, the narrator indicates that, along with the buildings as a symbol of national identity, national identity itself required symbols of the past: "The white newcomers have real estate but no sacred places, traditions but no myths, history books but no heroes. Perhaps they are too impatient – 'a nation,' Disraeli said, 'is both a work of art and a work of time.'"

George Robertson directed "Heroic Beginnings," the next and last episode in the first season. Donald Creighton was writer and host. Creighton uses a selection of national historic sites, designated as such by the Historic Sites and Monuments Board of Canada (HSMBC), as an entry to talk about important beginnings in Canada's past. The beginnings are "heroic," Creighton explains, because they represent the skills, fortitude, and perseverance of the early settlers. The sites are located across Canada in the various regions, but the board had designated them as national historic sites only because of their national significance, not because of their local or regional significance. Creighton was then finishing up a fourteen-year stint as a member of the Historic Sites and Monuments Board of Canada.

"Heroic Beginnings" also reflects Creighton's philosophy of history as "the encounter of character and circumstance." He begins his journey not with Indigenous peoples but with the story of the Norse at

L'Anse aux Meadows in Newfoundland, though the Norse did not establish a lasting settlement there. He continues to places like the Fortress of Louisbourg in Cape Breton and Dawson City in Yukon, ending at the Vancouver Maritime Museum with the *St Roch*. For Canadian history on television, it was a novel approach. Tovell made the cinematography and background music key elements of *Images of Canada*, with original musical pieces by Ricky Hyslop, Louis Applebaum, and Harry Somers. Played by the CBC's own orchestra, this music creates an engaging and impressive backdrop to "Heroic Beginnings." Tovell noted to a reporter that Creighton had never done anything like this before "but [that] he took to it quite well."[56] According to CBC Research, the episode elicited the highest ratings overall for *Images of Canada*: 10 percent of the viewing audience and an enjoyment index of eighty-three.[57] Creighton enjoyed the production process and thought that such television projects were important "to help Canadians visualize the glorious moments of our past."[58] In 1974, Macmillan of Canada published the expanded story in book form with the addition of a prologue on the "Earliest Canadians," who were omitted from the televised version.[59]

Creighton as host and his focus on built heritage mirrored Kenneth Clark and his approach in *Civilisation*. It also supported the activities of the Historic Sites and Monuments Board. In the build-up to the centennial, the National Parks Branch had undertaken extensive restorative and reconstructive projects. Three of the sites Creighton visited for the program – L'Anse aux Meadows, the Fortress of Louisbourg, and Dawson City – had benefitted from this largesse. Historian C.J. Taylor, in his book on the subject, described this time period as the "era of the big project." In an indication that the prevalent interpretation of Canada's past was still one of national consensus-building, Taylor noted that, at Louisbourg, one official suggested reconstructing the fortress as it had been at different time periods with an explanation of how it developed and was then destroyed by the British. But the project went the way of another, who preferred to interpret "the story of the progress of Canada's two major races from armed hostility to their national partnership and unity in the Canada of today."[60]

The next five episodes of *Images of Canada* formed a subseries called *The Whitecomers*. In Tovell's words, they were "original visual essays on white men in Canada, from 1600 to the 20th century, in a format that melds poetry, music and narration."[61] It was an interpretation of the history of Canada's regions, coinciding with the growing scholarly interest in regional history and an attempt to feature more regional content in national programming. Popular regional and local histories were not new, and certainly the heritage movement was strong at those levels. But scholarly regional and local histories, in English Canada at least, were still relatively scarce. Professional historians were only beginning to consider the region in its own right, apart from the nation and for the regular person, as a unit of identity possibly as important as the nation. In Atlantic Canada, for example, historian W. Stewart MacNutt published histories of New Brunswick (1963) and the Atlantic provinces (1965).[62] And, in 1971, a group of scholars in Atlantic Canada founded the journal *Acadiensis*. *Acadiensis* provided a forum for studies on the Atlantic region for historians like T.W. Acheson and Ernest Forbes, who were instrumental in challenging myths and stereotypes about the region and its past, especially those depicting it as complacent and conservative.[63] These were the myths and stereotypes that also served as a contrast to popular ideas about western Canada as progressive and dynamic.

Region can refer to a common geographical space or one created by imposed geopolitical boundaries. In the 1970s, there were CBC regional offices for the Atlantic, Newfoundland, Quebec, Ontario, the Prairies, Alberta, British Columbia, and the North.[64] *The Whitecomers* depicts the primarily European settlement and development of five "regions": the Maritimes, Quebec, Ontario, the Prairies, and British Columbia. The overall pattern is traditional documentary: roughly chronological sequences, archival stills, filmed segments, and voiceover narration. Unlike most of the previous Canadian history programs that depicts individuals or single events, each episode of *The White-comers* covers a vast period of time. This forced the producers to be more selective about what to include. The reliance only on documentary conventions made the visual demands of television more evident. For the earlier periods, in the absence of archival stills and with no dramatic elements, the screens are filled with short filmed pieces showing dramatic features of the landscape. There is little overt dramatization aside from the cinematography, music, and the narrators occasionally reading from historical records. The two primary narrators are actors Mia Anderson and Douglas Rain (whose voice was famous as HAL in the Stanley Kubrick film *2001: A Space Odyssey* [1968]). Additional narrators joined them.

The first instalment of *The Whitecomers* is "The Magic Circle," about the early history of what is now Quebec, beginning in the New France era. This episode hinges on the individual, starting with Champlain, "the father of Canada," and the founding of Quebec, though in reality Champlain's time in the country began in present-day Nova Scotia. A theme repeated through the subseries is that these newcomers will "'explore, expropriate, and exploit' this raw landscape." Following Champlain, the narrator recounts the experiences in New France of Marie de l'Incarnation, Jean de Brebeuf, Bishop François de Laval, and various others, including Wolfe and Montcalm, and later, Louis-Joseph Papineau. Many of these figures had already appeared on CBC television in some form or representation. After a telling of the fall of Quebec and life in the now-British colony, the narrative ends just before Confederation.

"The Ties That Bind" is about the maritime colonies. This second episode in *The Whitecomers* begins with the founding of Port Royal by Champlain and the Sieur de Mons, and life in Acadia. Then follows the fighting between the French and the British, the Acadian Deportation, life at Louisbourg and the final siege of the fortress, the American Revolution (including the experiences of Simeon Perkins during this time), and the massive influx of the Loyalists. The last part is the establishment and early development of Halifax. Joseph Howe is featured in connection with responsible government and freedom of the press. While this episode is ostensibly about the entire maritime region, Halifax and Nova Scotia are clearly the focus and stand in, respectively, for the urban and rural experiences of the entire region. New Brunswick and Prince Edward Island only warrant specific mention in the sequences on the Loyalists and the creation of New Brunswick, and the Charlottetown Conference, after which the episode ends.

"Peace, Order, and Prosperity," about Upper Canada and early Ontario, is the last episode in the second season. It opens with visuals of pictographs created by Indigenous artists before the arrival of "the whitecomers." It is here, narrator Anderson explains, where the British would "explore, expropriate, exploit" in "Canada's power centre." She recounts the circumstances of the arrival of the Loyalists and moves to the War of 1812, the Upper Canada Rebellion, the gaining of responsible government, the influx of Irish and Scottish immigrants and newcomers from elsewhere, and the building of infrastructure of all kinds. This episode highlights events, though politicians like John Graves Simcoe, George Brown, and John A. Macdonald are prominent. While the first two instalments of *The Whitecomers* end just before Confederation, this one ends in the early part of the twentieth century.

The second season of *The Whitecomers* (1974) covers western Canada. It relies less on traditional approaches and the elite male figure, and displays more consideration and empathy towards Indigenous peoples. The first episode is "The Promised Land," about the Prairies. This story begins early in the history of Europeans in Canada, with the fur trade and the Hudson's Bay Company, and the European explorers and their relationship with Indigenous peoples. Later, with white settlement on Indigenous lands, this relationship becomes one of antagonism, leading in part to the Red River Resistance and the later 1885 uprising. An unusually detailed sequence on Louis Riel's trial describes the jury of all English speakers and the trial in Regina, adding that had the trial been held in Winnipeg, Riel might have gone free. The latter half of the piece covers the mass European settlement of the west, including a bit on the Ukrainians ("much of the rough work of nation building in Western Canada is being done by them") and the building of towns and cities. Winnipeg, like Halifax for the Maritimes, represents the urban experience. The account covers the Winnipeg General Strike, women and the vote, and the Depression, with background music and talk from radio bible programs. This episode ends after the Depression.

The last entry of *The Whitecomers* is "Splendour Undiminished," about British Columbia. It begins with an outline of the early exploration of the Northwest Coast by men like George Vancouver and James Cook, and it includes perspectives from First Nations people through voiceovers and visuals of their totem poles and other artefacts. The men of the fur trade and the forts they build continue the story into the eighteenth and nineteenth centuries, followed by the founding of Victoria and the governorship of the colony by James Douglas. It also covers the Cariboo gold rush, the arrival of the North-West Mounted Police, the completion of the CPR, and the arrival of non-European immigrants, many of whom were unwelcome at first. This episode also ends in the twentieth century, with artist Emily Carr and her work, and shows the totem poles of the Indigenous peoples of British Columbia: "an old culture, engulfed."

Since the first episodes on Quebec and the Maritimes end just before Confederation, it initially seems that the focus of the *Whitecomers* is the colonial past of the regions. But the episodes on Ontario and the west continue beyond the Confederation era. So the termination of the first ones in 1867 imply that Confederation is not only the major turning point in the history of Quebec and the Maritimes but also that their important years are over after that. The pre-Confederation period was the focus of most history-writing about the Maritimes as well. As Forbes has noted, even by the early 1960s most of the serious work on the Maritimes and Newfoundland ended before Confederation, and the extant post-Confederation studies on Prince Edward Island (1951), Nova Scotia (1957), and New Brunswick (1961) were political works published by political scientists.[65] But by the time *The Whitecomers* went to air, more historians were exploring the post-Confederation era in the region, and certainly there existed a body of work on the post-Confederation history of Quebec.

With the importance of English-French relations in "The Craft of History," there was some balance in favour of Quebec. But Nova Scotia and New Brunswick, in 1867, comprised two-thirds of the colonies that federated. The union could not have happened without them, yet their stories end there. The portrayal recalls Frank Underhill's 1964 reference to the maritime region as a place where nothing much happens. The depiction of Ontario's history, from 1776 and truncated around 1900, may indicate that the episode on the Maritimes was cut short due to the time constraints of television. But it remains that much of the European-based span of history in the Maritimes was not covered, while the episodes on the Prairies and British Columbia continue well into the twentieth century.

Another difficulty in the one-hour presentations is the portrayal of the regions as having one history. One reviewer in the *Calgary Herald* complained that the presentation of the "three 'Prairie' provinces as if they were one geographical, economic social unit ... [gave] a misleading impression of homogeneity."[66] The piece on the Maritimes displays some distinctions between the provinces but, conversely, important events that affected them all, and in different ways, are associated with just one. The Acadian Deportation, for example, is represented by Grand-Pré in Nova Scotia, a site first made famous by the publication of Longfellow's epic poem *Evangeline: A Tale of Acadie* (1847). But substantial numbers of Acadians and French were also deported from the Chignecto Isthmus (the present-day border area between Nova Scotia and New Brunswick), Cape Breton (Île Royale – politically separate from mainland Nova Scotia at the time of the Deportation), and Prince Edward Island (Île Saint-Jean). The only event in the series associated with the island province is the Charlottetown Conference that led to Confederation. Islanders actually resisted the union, only joining six years later under financial duress and desperate to get their railway completed. Yet in *Images of Canada* it fares better than Newfoundland. Despite its long history of European occupation, Newfoundland does not appear in *The Whitecomers*. In fact, in *Images of Canada*, apart from Creighton's visit to L'Anse aux Meadows, it does not register at all.

Still, in addition to the region as an organizing principle, *The Whitecomers* introduces some new elements to Canadian history on CBC television. While the usual (white, male) political figures are certainly conspicuous, at least considered are little-known personalities, including women and people of colour, like Marie de l'Incarnation, a nun serving in New France, and Sarah Tilley and Boston King, Black Loyalist arrivals to Nova Scotia after the American Revolution. These latter underscore the irony of the title, as blacks and other people of colour also lived in the regions during the time periods depicted in *The Whitecomers*. The title further emphasizes the marginalization of Indigenous peoples in national histories. Yet *The Whitecomers* at least makes apparent the continual presence of Indigenous people from the earliest periods of exploration and reveals some of their challenges in dealing with the effects of white settlement on their lands.

In other CBC histories, producers used dramatic techniques in an attempt to establish visual connections to the present and to better animate the past. The producers of *The Whitecomers* used still images and short moving images showing cultural and natural vestiges. This was the main premise of Creighton's "Heroic Beginnings," but it is also on display in *The Whitecomers*, particularly in the episodes on Quebec, the Maritimes, and British Columbia. These are the astrolabe attributed to Champlain, parts of eighteenth-century French shipwrecks in the harbour at Louisbourg, and broken totem poles lying in an overgrown forest. This display of artefacts, in their more deteriorated state, highlight the time gap and the reconstructive aspect of history on television. While the overall program content does not strongly deviate from past Canadian histories on CBC television, the presentation is not completely linear or predictable. It hints at a distant past perhaps not so easily understood through a present lens, or neatly told in an hour of television. The Upper Canada episode, for example, spends as much time on the actual events of the War of 1812 as it does on Brockville and the later erection of the Brock monument and its symbolism to Upper Canadians of the time.

These aspects of *The Whitecomers* help to convey a sense of complexity about the past. But, unlike some earlier CBC Canadian history programs, there is little overt reference to historical sources or other means to help viewers understand the nature of what is onscreen. When the narrators read from letters, diaries, or other original written testimony, the change in voice and tone is usually enough to indicate a break from the narration. Yet the sources and context of the original documents are not always clear. In the sequence on the Acadian Deportation, for example, the narrator reads words, presumably from an external text, that the Acadians "are notoriously litigious, always involved in boundary disputes," but the source is not identified. Is it written testimony from someone who might have had first-hand experience or a later interpretation? These kinds of statements are difficult to assess without knowing who uttered them, when, and in what context.

Until the end of *The Whitecomers*, the press reaction to *Images of Canada* was positive overall but mixed, depending on the episode. Most columnists agreed that the documentaries together presented a stunning visual portrait of Canada but that the content was uneven, with generally positive reviews of the episodes in the first two seasons and rather lacklustre reviews over the last two seasons.[67] The last two episodes went to air in the shadow of *The National Dream*, however, which was the most hyped television series of the 1970s and, due to the bestselling books, came with a pre-sold audience.[68] Still, CBC audience measurement statistics showed that the episodes of *Images* captured average or above average audience percentages. Its enjoyment index ranged from sixty-five for the *The Whitecomers'* episode on New France to eighty-three for Creighton's piece.[69]

After the end of *The Whitecomers*, a full year passed before the last two episodes of *Images of Canada* went to air. The first is "Journey without Arrival: A Personal Point of View from Northrop Frye." Frye was a famous literary critic, a University of Toronto professor, and a board member of the CRTC. "Journey without Arrival" is his take on the "Canadian consciousness," and it mirrors the personal approach to the past taken by Kenneth Clark and Alistair Cooke in *Civilisation* and *America*, respectively.[70]

Frye frames his essay with ideas that originated in his influential "Conclusion to a Literary History of Canada" (1965).[71] It begins with the question "Where is here?" rather than with the more common question about Canadian identity: "Who are we?" He explores the various perceptions that existed in the past about "where here is" and the "habits of mind" that produced these perceptions. One example is the mindset of the early Europeans in Canada and their attitude towards Indigenous peoples ("We never lost the sense of the absolute cultural rightness of what we came to do"). Frye explains his ideas against a visual backdrop of frequently changing landscapes and archival images, with Champlain and Macdonald serving as two points of departure. Intermixed are his observations on the differences between Americans and Canadians with regard to their attitudes towards their own history and national experiences, for example with the War of 1812 as "Canada's war of independence." Echoing Creighton, he talks about the St Lawrence River as the spine of the country and the national railway as an extension of it, and Macdonald's conception of the railway as a link to the empire, given his colonial mentality that was bound up in the idea of a "head office somewhere else."

Another mindset Frye addresses is his notion of the Canadian "garrison mentality," meaning the impact on a community resulting from its awareness of being in a hostile environment. After the early settlers came to terms with their surroundings, they developed a mistrust of outsiders – the Americans, the French, the radicals – and became defensive and separatist. Frye points out that, in the larger world, Canada as a whole acts as a garrison, and rather than Canadians thinking of their cohesion in terms of an east-to-west axis, this garrison mentality might be the answer to Canadian unity. He cautions that people must not confuse this with Canadian identity, which, in a country like Canada, is restricted and localized. To his original question, "Where is here?," he responds that, in Canada, "there are as many answers as there are places of identity across the land." Like "The Folly on the Hill," "Journey without Arrival" is a complex presentation. And Frye, though world renowned and respected, does not display the flair of a Donald Creighton or a Jack Saywell in making his ideas, expressed so eloquently in written form, understandable to a general television audience.

The last episode of *Images of Canada* is "Spirit in a Landscape: The People Beyond," a poignant piece meant as a cultural essay on the Inuit and the North, the one region (besides the province of Newfoundland) left out of *The Whitecomers*. In previous years, the CBC had produced and broadcast a few programs on Indigenous peoples in Canada, but stories about the Inuit were relatively unfamiliar to television viewers. "Spirit in a Landscape" is the first CBC television program ever broadcast in English, French, and Inuktitut.[72] It opens with various scenes of the North juxtaposed with a mix of sounds, including an Inuit radio announcer asking that a pair of boots taken from the nursing station be returned. A number of Inuit narrators join three main narrators, one of whom, Minnie Freeman (an Inuit woman), recounts traditions, myths, and historical events related to the people in the North. It includes the arrival of the whites, and the missionaries and the adverse effects the adoption of Christianity had on the Inuit.

"Spirit in a Landscape" also highlights the contemporary way of life of the Inuit, including their relationship with the land, hunting and fishing practices, and beliefs and traditions. Yet their artwork defines the piece; the still images are almost entirely composed of Inuit sculptures and prints. The latter part of the hour ends with an explanation of the larger Canadian interest in this artwork and the development of a market, beginning in 1949, which eventually leads to worldwide demand. Despite this success, the narrator suggests that, aside from the money, the artwork serves no purpose to the Inuit. And with the changes in Inuit lifestyle brought about by white culture, in the future there would be no basis for the unique nature of this artistic imagery. Like Northrop Frye's "Journey without Arrival," "Spirit in a Landscape" tackles issues of identity, in this case the changing identity of the Inuit. Yet this narrative, even with its episodic style and multiple narrators, is more effective than was Frye's in connecting past and present.

Images of Canada wrapped up in 1976.[73] The series overall met most of the intellectual and artistic goals that Koch and Tovell had set for it. It agrees with traditional historiography in that it covers who and what were considered to be the important individuals and milestone events as they fit into the national story. But it also hints at some of the new history that was emerging. The Whitecomers is not a radical departure from the content in previous CBC history programming, but it is nonetheless a departure. The region is its framework, and it includes and emphasizes some marginalized and forgotten groups of people. The other episodes also present some challenges to traditional Canadian history-writing in English Canada. "The Craft of History" showcases the perspective of a French Canadian nationalist. Northrop Frye openly questions the existence of a Canadian national identity. And "Spirit in a Landscape" explores the history and contemporary culture of the Inuit, who until then had been only rarely included in any type of historical account.

Images of Canada, compared to the basic sets and improvisation of Explorations, is a more artistic creation for television. With increased competition in the television industry, the CBC had to pay more attention to the entertainment aspects of television in order to prevent people from changing the channel. The relative sophistication of Images is due also to the production team members and, in particular, to the vision of Vincent Tovell, who ensured that art and music were important components. The Images team used standard documentary conventions and techniques, but the CBC was still in an experimental phase with regard to the presentation of Canadian history, and Nash and Koch allowed Tovell the autonomy and flexibility to fashion the series as he saw fit. This included collaboration with historians; indeed, it was the last CBC series on Canadian history to involve professional historians in a substantive way.

Images of Canada also met the political goals that Nash had set for it. With around $120,000 in total costs per episode, during its first season *Images of Canada* was one of Information Programming's highest priority programs.[74] That changed as the production of *The National Dream* progressed. But the two together, along with the previous success of *The Tenth Decade* and plans beginning in 1973 for *The Days before Yesterday*, gave Nash a critical mass of high-profile Canadian history programming that showcased the public service values of what his team was doing. Nash clearly saw *Images of Canada* in this light; Tovell also hoped the series would provide evidence that people had "faith in public television."[75]

Images was only one piece of a grand design, not only of a larger Canadian history program but also, according to Nash, of "a growing nationalism that's now reflected in CBC programming."[76] Newspaper columnist Bob Blackburn agreed. He wrote that the CBC's Canadian history programming at the time was one of the few things he could turn to when he was "wondering whether there's any bloody justification for having a CBC at all."[77] Nash summed it up in *Canada in Perspective*, a glossy promotional booklet from 1972 with Champlain's 1632 map of New France on its cover. Praising the various series as a translation of history "from dusty pages to the lusty, thrilling drama" that it was, Nash identified two main problems as the most relevant from Canada's past: how to unify the country and how to protect Canadian identity from American dominance.[78] His history campaign – "the most exciting and the most popular Canadian history course ever known" – would provide the answers.[79]

The National Dream was the most compelling part of Nash's Canadian
history course. The series was based on *The National Dream* (1970)
and *The Last Spike* (1971), Pierre Berton's bestselling books on the
building of the Canadian Pacific Railway. It was high-quality, audi-
ence-pleasing, and distinct from American fare. According even to
Berton, the main reason for its success was that it followed on the heels
of 1967 and Expo.[1] Where *Images of Canada* featured regional content
along with some of the more ordinary people from the Canadian past,
The National Dream was unadulterated national celebration. As a
docudrama it differed from Nash's documentaries, and in the evocation
of national pride, it was without equal. While CBC officials seemed to
accept that the more cerebral *Images of Canada* would draw a relatively small number of viewers, for *The National Dream* they expected
mass viewership. "Nowhere in Canadian history," according to Nash,
"is there more meaning for Canadians today than the story of the
building of the CPR."[2]

Fuelling these expectations were the popularity of the books and
the author himself. Berton was not a professional historian, but he
had much in common with the professional historians of his day, including a shared passion for public service broadcasting. He was a
founding member, for example, along with Arthur Lower and Frank
Underhill, of the Canadian Radio and Television League (later the
Canadian Broadcasting League), once the main advocacy group for
public service broadcasting in Canada. He also shared with the historians a commitment to historical accuracy, process, and transparency,
his roles as content expert and onscreen host for *The National Dream*

being similar to Jack Saywell's in *A War for Survival* and Donald Creighton's in "Heroic Beginnings." But Berton was different from them in that he dominated the entire rest of the production as well. In addition to his career as a writer and popularizer of Canadian history, he had a long history as a journalist behind him. Indeed, his involvement with *The National Dream* marked an important development taking place in Canadian history programming on CBC television: the transfer of content authority from professional historian to the professional journalist.

As for Nash, he needed success with *The National Dream*. Throughout the late 1960s and 1970s, licence renewal hearings, external and internal inquiries, and incessant press and audience criticism continually put CBC officials on the defensive. Commercialism, and the American programs with which it was associated, was one of the key complaints, but no one could agree on what to do about it. Despite statements in the new Broadcasting Act touting the CBC as a proponent of cultural sovereignty, much of its prime-time schedule still consisted of American programs. This left the Canadian content – now supposed to be 60 percent of the primetime (7:00 p.m. to 11:00 p.m.) schedule – for the worst time slots within that window. Along with the Americanized CBC schedule came the beginning of a shift in audience measurement. The balance was tilting from an attempt to reach a range of viewers through diverse kinds of programming, as per public service broadcasting practices, towards targeting audience size per program, as per commercial broadcasting practices.

At least three CBC staff members were concerned about the commercialism and the increased emphasis on audience size. In 1970, Eric Koch wrote to Nash that he did not have much of a problem with some one-off programming being sponsored, but a weekly series carrying advertising was not acceptable and would make the CBC seem no different from the CTV.[3] In 1972, Vincent Tovell objected to filling out a section of a proposal form asking for potential "audience ratings and response." Tovell said that it indicated a move from quality to quantity and was "an abdication of our editorial responsibilities and opportunities."[4] And, in 1973, Arthur Laird, the head of audience research, also complained to Nash about the overt commercialism. Laird said that it was leading to the ratings being used to justify changes in the schedule, and he worried that the CBC was becoming a slave to advertising.[5]

But at the CRTC 1974 licence renewal hearings, CBC president Laurent Picard argued that commercials kept the CBC competitive. Programming to the masses was essential, in his opinion, in order to avoid an "ivory broadcasting tower," especially with the loss of viewers and competition from provincial educational broadcasters, cable television, and the new private broadcaster, Global Television Network. The CRTC agreed about avoiding an "ivory broadcasting tower" but disagreed with the premise underlying it, saying that broadcasting for mass audiences was the antithesis of public service broadcasting.[6] Many intervenors disagreed as well, including the Committee on Television and supporter Donald Creighton, who had once been among the strongest of CBC's supporters but was now among its most ardent critics.[7] In the end the CRTC renewed the CBC's licence with conditions that called for the gradual end of commercials.[8]

Just before the next CBC licence renewal hearings in 1978, both the CBC and the CRTC issued reports on CBC programming. In the CBC report, the new president, Al Johnson, tried to pre-empt the criticisms about commercials that he knew would be in the CRTC document. Among his proposals was a second CBC television channel. This second channel (never realized) would be commercial-free and feature high-quality programming like "book reviews, news for the deaf, specialized analysis in the areas of social issues, economics, arts, politics, and a host of other programming areas serving specialized constituencies."[9] In short, it would feature much of what other public service broadcasters around the world were already doing. The CRTC report again criticized the CBC for its quest for mass audiences and its over-reliance on commercials. It cited the greater commitment to quality over audience as shown by the BBC, referring to its highly regarded documentary series *Civilisation*, which was the model for *Images of Canada*. *Civilisation* had garnered only 10 percent of the national audience.[10]

For the actual hearings, the CBC submitted a massive formal report to the CRTC entitled "The CBC – A Perspective." The authors wrote that, with audience fragmentation, the criticism about programming for mass audiences was moot. They argued that, although current practice was to measure and evaluate audiences for various purposes, there was also an obligation to try to reach large numbers through popular programming. They too worried about Canadian audiences and their taste for American popular programs. But they insisted that the CBC would feature more in-house productions of this kind in order to meet its responsibilities "to contribute to the development of national unity and provide for a continuing expression of Canadian identity."[11] In an attempt to underscore the importance of the CBC in these terms, Johnson referred to the Canadian history programs: "most of our kids know more about the Alamo than they know about Batoche or Crysler's Farm," he said. "They know more about Davy Crockett than Louis Riel."[12] It was not uncommon for CBC staff to refer to the negative impact of American icons on Canadian culture, even though it belied the continued dominance of American programs on their own television network.

These opposing arguments about commercialism mirrored clashes within the CBC itself. The prime contestants were Nash at Information Programming (the fare more associated with the public service and nation-building roles of the corporation) and Thom Benson at Entertainment Programming (the fare more tied to revenue from commercials). In 1971, Nash pointed out to Hallman that the prime-time schedule aired only five hours per week of information programming, as compared to twenty-one and a half hours for entertainment. This was not balanced, in his opinion, in terms of "information, enlightenment, and entertainment," as was outlined in the CBC mandate.[13] Continuing to rail against this inequity over the next few years, he detailed in one long epistle a litany of complaints: the "ghettoizing" of information time slots; the amount of pre-emption by sports programs (including hockey, football, and baseball, which fell under entertainment and frequently disrupted the schedule); the move in local units from informational to (American) commercial programming; and the scheduling of works as entertainment programming that were logically categorized as informational programming. In short, he was tired, said Nash, of Information Programming getting "screwed, blewed and tattooed for so goddam long now that it is time to begin to rectify the damage."[14]

As Al Johnson realized, a strong counter to the criticisms about the CBC not fulfilling its public service or nation-building roles was the

Canadian history projects associated with Nash. CBC staff, for the 1974 licence renewal submission, stressed that these documentaries "on the Canadian historic heritage" – *First Person Singular*, *The Tenth Decade*, and *The National Dream* – were important as unifying vehicles.[15] Nations must define and continually redefine themselves, so the history programs were also useful when the CBC attempted to show how its programming complied with the new national policy on multiculturalism, passed in 1971. In that instance, Bob Patchell, who had replaced Koch as head of Arts and Sciences, offered up *Images of Canada* and *The National Dream* as the prominent examples. "And what a conglomeration of nationalities participated in this venture," said Patchell, about *The National Dream*: "from city-slicker Americans to totally dislocated Chinese laborers!"[16]

The appeal of *The National Dream* to the CBC was undoubtedly related to similar aims of nation building that underwrote CBC broadcasting overall. It was technological nationalism, an idea advanced by communications scholar Maurice Charland, that space-binding transportation and communications technologies were instrumental in creating the Canadian nation.[17] In many ways the story of the building of the CPR was the story of the creation of the CBC as well. Berton's take on the railway added some distinctive elements: a linear account of heroes and villains, conflict and conciliation, and obstacles and upsets overcome by ultimate victory.

In February 1971, with the *The National Dream* at the top of the bestseller lists and *The Last Spike* soon to follow, Berton and Lister Sinclair discussed adapting the books for television. Sinclair was executive producer of *Man at the Centre*, the CBC Arts and Sciences series that had produced, among many other programs, biographies on Susanna Moodie, Grey Owl, and William Lyon Mackenzie. This last was "Mackenzie the Firebrand," based on the book of a similar name by historian William Kilbourn, in which Berton played a *You Are There*–style journalist.[18] Sinclair was distinguished as a playwright and television producer, and as a lifelong and trusted friend of Berton's, the perfect liaison between the author and the corporation. Berton told his friend that the CTV had approached him to develop the books as a television series but that he preferred to work with Sinclair and the CBC. Sinclair apprised Koch of the idea, and Koch suggested to Nash that it be taken under serious consideration, perhaps as a co-production with the Drama department. Nash agreed and asked Koch for a more specific program proposal.[19] Nash was hoping that a production of *The National Dream* would help improve public perception of the broadcaster and "play a major role in perhaps turning around public opinion about the CBC."[20]

Berton and Sinclair's proposal followed. The first outline indicated that the series would target a mass audience and consist of six one-hour "dramatized documentaries." Berton would be onscreen host. The team would work under the auspices of Arts and Sciences, and would consist mostly of freelancers, with some CBC staff members seconded on special assignment.[21] Berton later expanded the outline to eight episodes, and in its preamble were his overall objectives: each episode would stand alone though still build up expectation for the next; the series overall would avoid superficiality while remaining simple enough to follow; balance would be maintained between the action in the interior and exterior scenes; and each part of the story would incorporate dramatic conflict and tension, with appropriate character development throughout. The prescription was much like the layout of the chapters and the cast of characters in his bestselling books. Berton also outlined how the series would be shot, with himself front and centre:

(a) On camera commentary by myself on location;
(b) On camera commentary by myself in studio;
(c) General location work;
(d) Graphics;
(e) "Interviews" of historical characters by myself either in studio or on location;
(f) Straight dramatic scenes using actors.[22]

Berton was no stranger to television. Having begun his career as a newspaper journalist, he first appeared on the small screen in 1952 in one of the CBC's inaugural public affairs shows, *Court of Opinion*. In 1957, he began both co-hosting duties on *Close-Up*, and what turned out to be a thirty-eight-year stint as a panelist on *Front Page Challenge*. And, from 1963 to 1973, he hosted the independently produced *The*

Pierre Berton Show, a vehicle for one-on-one interviews carried primarily by CTV.

Berton, in addition to television, had a knack for writing books on Canadian history that people liked to read. He put to work his skill at writing lively prose not only in his many books, beginning in earnest with *The Golden Trail* in 1954 and *Klondike* in 1958 but also in their presentation for film and television. It started in the late 1950s with two documentaries: his narration of the NFB's award-winning *City of Gold* and the CBC's *Trail of '98*, both based on his books about the Klondike. In 1960, although his involvement was limited, *Klondike* was also the basis for a short-lived television dramatic series by American broadcaster NBC.[23] In 1974, the same year the CBC broadcast *The National Dream*, he created *My Country*, which dramatized episodes from the Canadian past and ran on Global Television until 1977. As with *The National Dream*, with *My Country*, and with his later creation of historically themed plays called *Heritage Theatre* (1986–87), Berton was intimately involved in most aspects of production and governed his residuals with a sharp eye.

With *The National Dream* it was clear from the start that Berton, extraordinarily for a non-CBC employee, was in charge. With regard to negotiating the original contract, Berton told his lawyer that he was selling four things: the rights to his books, and his services as consultant, program host, and writer of his own commentary.[24] It remains unclear why the CBC assigned this last task to William Whitehead, but Berton, though very involved in it, long held on to the idea that he should have been doing it himself. From the beginning he implicated himself in almost every other aspect of the production, including the dramatic portions of the script, the filming, and the balance of his time onscreen relative to the rest of the work. After Sinclair left early in the production to assume the mantle of CBC vice-president of English Language Services, Berton once hinted to him to see what he could do, in his new position, about what he felt was the poor handling of the bidding for the French dubbing of the series. He did not want it done in a shoddy manner.[25]

One staffer concerned about *The National Dream* proposals was Ken Black, the assistant director of Information Programming. Black's main problems were with the dramatization and high costs overall.

He also worried that the discussions with historical characters in a *You Are There*–style, as outlined in Berton's earlier proposal, was "an old-hat gimmick."[26] The CBC had used this technique fairly frequently up to that point, and Berton himself had recent experience with it in "Mackenzie the Firebrand." Black also cautioned that, since it looked like some of the episodes were almost full dramatizations, they must call upon the expertise of staff in the Drama department. Despite earlier complaints from Nash about Information Programming getting relatively less resources and airtime, CBC management could have categorized *The National Dream* as a docudrama coming under the auspices of Entertainment Programming. The fact that they did not prompted a heated debate between the two departments.

The mixing of drama and documentary at the CBC involved some politicking. Series that had routinely run documentaries, like *Explorations* and *Man at the Centre*, had often incorporated drama without much friction. But the stakes were higher with an expensive and high-profile project like *The National Dream*. In November 1971, Black, Garriock, and two representatives from Drama held a meeting to discuss the series as a dramatic production. Nash's counterpart in Entertainment Programming, Thom Benson, therefore understood the series as a production for his department and endorsed as producer Harry Rasky, a well-regarded independent filmmaker with international experience.[27]

Nash and Bob Patchell, upon learning of the meeting, took great umbrage at what Nash saw as Entertainment's "larcenous instincts": "it seems to me that we are in the position of a robber baron having entered our house and been caught trying to make off with the furniture, with the robber now protesting his innocence and demanding to know what we are doing in our house in the first place." Nash had envisioned the working arrangements as similar to what had been done with "Mackenzie the Firebrand," in which Drama had collaborated with them with little problem.[28] Further, since the project until then had been discussed and developed within Arts and Sciences, and, according to Patchell, the episodes were documentaries that would incorporate some dramatization on a level yet to be determined, it most definitely belonged in Arts and Sciences. Patchell also argued that not only was he himself competent to handle any dramatic portions but that Lister Sinclair had been showered with awards for his dramatic productions. He pointed out that Berton had been very specific about working with only one person, and that person was Sinclair. As a final claim, Patchell drew comparisons between the departments: "I recognize also that this department has had its failures as well as its successes," he said, "but then, the same might truthfully be said of the Drama department."[29]

On the failures of Drama, Patchell could not know that the CBC signature dramatic series, about to be broadcast, would be a disaster. *The Whiteoaks of Jalna* was a costume drama of thirteen episodes, based on the books written in the 1920s and 1930s by Mazo de la Roche. The CBC saw the series as Canada's answer to the popular British television series *The Forsyte Saga*. *Jalna*, produced by John Trent and written for television primarily by Timothy Findley, who was then relatively unknown as a novelist, was cancelled even before all the episodes were broadcast. Although this was partly due to complications caused by a CBC technicians' strike, as a television program it was a failure. No expense had been spared in production or promotion, but critics complained about its constant flashbacks and disjointed storytelling, even with the Whiteoak "family tree" that the CBC distributed to help viewers identify the characters and understand the complex storyline.[30] The occasion sent a chill throughout the institution that took years to live down, and, as one journalist noted, it also left the CBC with a gap that season in terms of a major series.[31] This put under the spotlight that other blockbuster serial in period costume, *The National Dream*, especially as half of its writing team was in the person of Findley.

Findley had made a name for himself as an actor at Stratford, and in the years before *Jalna* he had also begun to write novels, and for radio and television. While *Jalna* was still on air, Sinclair secured his services for *The National Dream* as well as those of Findley's life companion and writing partner, William Whitehead. Findley, with his background as a dramatist, was to craft the dramatic scenes. Whitehead, who had more experience with documentaries and was actually beginning to write an episode of *Images of Canada*, was to write the documentary sections as well as Berton's commentary. Findley wrote in his diary that he was nervous upon first meeting Berton but impressed with Berton's efficiency, energy, and ability to immediately address whatever was said.[32]

It was from Berton's now eight-episode outline that Findley and Whitehead, part of a team that now included Sinclair as executive producer, and Doris Gauntlett as associate producer and script editor, went to work. Whitehead created the initial content breakdown according to what Berton had supplied and, in Findley's words, provided the discipline to himself and Gauntlett, both of whom had more experience in drama. The dramatic sections included "any scene, sequence or shot which includes an actor – even though he might be no more than a figure placed on location." Despite the trouble with Drama, Findley noted that two of his first draft episodes were "almost straight drama." These particular scripts would require twelve actors each: two lead roles, three second leads, and seven support roles. For the final scripts they would then decide who was expendable according to a rule set by Berton, which was that each character must in some way tell the story.[33]

Augmenting the amount of drama helped to meet a recent directive from Hallman on the subject of the Association of Canadian Television and Radio Artists (ACTRA). ACTRA was pressuring the CBC to guarantee a fixed annual expenditure on its members, so in order to avoid that scenario and still show good faith, Hallman directed the television units to create more opportunities for ACTRA writers and performers as well as for members of the American Federation of Musicians (of the United States and Canada). He warned there would be no increased production in any information or features programs not in line with this position.[34] Like the Canadian content rules, such directives illustrated the industrial motives of the corporation, whereby the CBC was supposed to help create work in the television industry.

ACTRA was a fairly formidable body protecting the interests of its members. In a letter to ACTRA, the CBC supervisor of talent relations carefully referred to "Pierre Berton's – 'The National Dream'" as a documentary: "we want all programmes in the series to be considered to be documentaries beyond any doubt in the minds of any participants." In his original proposal, Berton himself referred to it as a series of dramatized documentaries (and still in 1985, for the rebroadcast of the series, as a "drama-documentary.") The CBC staffer stressed that no episodes would have more than 50 percent re-creation, even though it might look that way to the performers as the intent was to "block-shoot" the dramatic scenes. For both the writers' agreement and the film agreement, he wanted the series and episodes to come under one package of rights for documentary.[35]

There were several reasons for this position. An important one was the potential friction with Entertainment Programming if there was too much drama in a series in which the Drama department was not involved. Another was that Nash wanted the series to be on par with the authenticity and authority of documentaries like *The Tenth Decade* and *Images of Canada*. While docudrama had been the accepted format for many of the earlier Canadian history programs, documentary represented authenticity more than did either drama or docudrama. Just as significant was the financial aspect of it. Documentary meant a different and less expensive package in terms of the writers' and actors' contracts. ACTRA, in response to the CBC memo, allowed that, if the dramatic portions did not constitute a major part of any episode whereby it would render the episode or series into a drama, the production could come under the rates for documentaries. But they refused to negotiate such a package for the series as a whole.[36]

This created considerable stress at the other end, with CBC staff in Talent Relations even talking about getting Berton (a member of ACTRA) involved to help with the negotiations.[37] In the end it was not necessary as ACTRA clarified that, as a documentary, the 50 percent dramatization limit was acceptable and that if the CBC paid the actors the appropriate buy-out rates, it could intermingle and block-shoot the dramatizations as it saw fit.[38] It all went according to plan except in one scene, when the director of drama decided that a group of actors in non-speaking roles would sing a song in support of John A. Macdonald. As this inadvertently rendered their parts into speaking roles, an extra forty thousand dollars was technically due them. But ACTRA, according to Nash's memoir, let it go.[39]

So the dramatic parts of *The National Dream* raised a sticky issue. Over 50 percent re-creation would constitute a drama in terms of ACTRA, and that would not do for Information Programming. But if it was to have the dramatic intensity of shows like "Mackenzie the Firebrand," then the balance of documentary and drama would have to be carefully considered. Just where the docu/drama line was drawn previously had not been of much consequence, but it was a growing concern. This was not just because of internal conflicts between Information and Entertainment Programming but also because it was not typical of the practices in news and current affairs, with which Nash was more familiar. In the past, it had been less of a concern because the *You Are There*–style programs had strongly distinguished between the two elements.

Findley, as an actor and novelist, understandably gravitated towards heavy drama, and in his and Whitehead's own notes on the outlines they wondered how they were going to cut down the onscreen time of the actors. With his background Findley felt that the documentary parts were a "problem," but since *The National Dream* was supposedly a documentary series, he had to figure out ways to make the dramatic parts as authentic as possible. To that end, he and Whitehead devised a plan to create still photographs of the principal actors in sepia-tone, as if the actors were actually the historical characters they were playing. These "custom stills," as they called them, could mark the end of a dramatic sequence, followed by a documentary sequence using authentic period photos.[40] Thus, in the television series there were lots of archival images of settlers, towns, and trains, but none of John A. Macdonald, William Van Horne, or any of the other characters for whom actual photographs existed.

Berton, as the script consultant, spent much of his time ensuring that the content was historically accurate. But he also controlled the balance of drama and documentary as well as most other aspects of the writing. His long and detailed, blunt, and often cutting comments on Findley's and Whitehead's first outlines must have made this immediately and abundantly clear to the writers. One of Berton's biggest problems was with Findley as a dramatist and how this fact, as Berton saw it, got in the way of the history. Findley's work was full of scenes, Berton said, that not only had no basis in historical fact but that also, in some instances, were highly improbable. In the quest to create conflict, tension, and drama, Findley had the historical personalities speaking in overly flowery speech, saying and doing things out of character, and over-sensationalizing already sensational events. According to Berton, this would not only damage the authenticity and the documentary nature of the series but also lessen the impact of scenes in which overt confrontation and outrageous behaviour actually *did* happen. "It makes for good theatre," he said, "but bad history."[41]

He was speaking from experience – a few years earlier he paid historian Michael Bliss to provide him with critiques of the drafts of the two books on which *The National Dream* was based. On the first one, Bliss was generally positive, but commented on Berton's black-and-white characters, contrived scenes, and his "'gee-whiz and gosh-and-golly' approach to history."[42] Later reviewers of the published books drew the inevitable comparisons with the work of Donald Creighton.[43] With all that in mind, Berton produced pages and pages of notes on the scripts for the television series, correcting both general aspects of the writers' texts as well as the minute details of the history that he himself had mastered. He told the writers again and again that any speeches, public addresses, or anything said in the House of Commons had to follow some kind of contemporary reportage or verbatim public record, like *Hansard*. He told them how the characters would have addressed each other; what expressions or specific words they would have used; the nuances of characters' behaviour, likes and dislikes, and the probable nature of their interactions with others; what the railway crew would have eaten; what instruments the surveyors used; and what the landscape would have been like at different points along the way.

Berton also made clear his opinions about the filming of the series. This included the balance of scenes in eastern Canada (meaning Ontario and Quebec) versus western Canada, the locations where certain scenes should be shot, at what points his commentary should come in, what kinds of visual effects should be used, the episode titles, and the need for superimposing some dates and place names.[44] Some of his concerns about content and filming can be displayed effectively in merely two pages of comments to Findley and Whitehead, which are worth quoting at length. It gives some idea of his overall concerns about the project, his command of the historical details, the importance he placed on some details and not others, and the visual effects:

Page 52: Note the custom still of Stephen on the phone. He didn't use the phone.

Page 57: This poses a problem. There is no evidence that Van Horne and Haney went out on a handcar together ... I see no reason to use a handcar. (Nor can a handcar go anywhere near 60 miles an hour) ... It's stretching things a bit but it might be possible to indicate in the opening commentary that Van Horne might have gone off on a brief inspection trip with Haney ...

Page 78: It may be that the navvies started forest fires to celebrate some holiday but we have no evidence of it. We do know from Tyler's correspondence that they set a fire especially for him ... I would stick to what we know.

Page 82: I think we should much more graphically describe the Indians' plight. They were forced to eat their dogs and their horses and when those were gone, to scrabble for gophers and mice and eat those, often raw and after that, even to consume the carcasses of animals found rotting on the prairies.

Page 85: Van Horne's decision was daring alright but it was also callous and we shouldn't overlook that. And the commentary here needs to be much stronger...

Page 91: We're making a point here which I have no evidence for in my books that people were fired for frivolous reasons. I doubt that anyone was fired for complaining about the food ... If you fired a man for complaining about the food, you wouldn't have anyone left in your camp ... Again, let's stick to the facts. I am not crazy about the sequence that follows. Why not follow the historical record that we have ... – we are a year out but I don't think that matters much ...

Page 103: Have you considered the value of shooting this against the actual rock of Craigellachie? I am not sure it's as expensive as it sounds ...

Page 106: Any evidence for Macdonald hating to wear white gloves? It doesn't really sound in character.[45]

The producers of *The National Dream* did not engage professional historians and, except for the producers of *Images of Canada*, neither had their immediate predecessors. This included the producers of *The Tenth Decade*, the series perceived as the launch of Nash's new "Canadian history course," and its prequel, *The Days before Yesterday*. In both, most of those who appeared onscreen were politicians and journalists.[46] In *The Days before Yesterday*, the only person identified as a historical consultant was not a professional historian but television producer Jean Bruce, who wrote and directed some of the episodes along with journalist Brian Nolan. The host of *The Days before Yesterday*, Bruce Hutchison, was also described in the credits as a journalist and historian (he was a writer of popular history books). At least one television columnist, L. Ian MacDonald of the *Montreal Gazette*, noticed this absence of professional historians. He was pleased about it, as, unlike Donald Creighton and the other scholars of *Images of Canada*, he wrote, Hutchison did not "seek to impose a theory of Canadian history" on the audience. For support MacDonald quoted Brian Nolan: "That's because Bruce is a journalist," Nolan said, "not a historian."[47]

Here was an early inkling of the idea, on the part of some journalists, that their work was objective, dialogic, and relevant, while the work of historians was subjective, one-sided, and irrelevant to the regular person. Yet interrogation of the status quo by contemporary journalists was not unlike what the new historians were doing with former historical narratives. Even Creighton was a curious subject for criticism because he excelled at narrative, and "Heroic Beginnings" had received a good rating according to the audience enjoyment index. True, he was an old-school scholar, but in *Images of Canada* he did not impose his views on the audience any more than did Bruce Hutchison in *The Days before Yesterday*. Both interpreted a set of historical facts for the audience, with neither host more detached nor more objective than the other. Both Creighton and Hutchison based their narratives on their understandings of the historical record, and both accounts were mediated by television.

Rather, the primary difference between the two works was that in *Images of Canada* the interpretation came from a professional historian, while in *The Days before Yesterday* it came from professional journalists. By the 1970s, a major difference in the two professions was that most Canadian historians had abandoned the idea that complete objectivity was possible and understood that value judgments were a necessary part of their work. But in the Western world, at least, a professed commitment to objectivity continued to be the mantra of the journalism profession. Media scholars have argued that this claim to objectivity is part of the occupational ideology and that journalists believe that it forms the basis of their credibility.[48] It was a sentiment that newspaper journalists seemed to offer in support of their CBC television counterparts as the better authorities for Canadian history.

By the 1970s, journalism was becoming more professionalized, with an increasing number of journalism schools and associations, and a changing perception of professional codes and norms. These arose largely from the reporting in the United States on the civil rights movement and the Vietnam War, and the presidency of Richard Nixon, brought to public attention most vividly through television journalism and most spectacularly through the investigative reporting connected to Nixon and Watergate.[49] The scandal that brought down a president made stars of Bob Woodward and Carl Bernstein, the two young *Washington Post* journalists who helped uncover the story. Media studies scholar Mark Deuze has explained that journalistic ideology also involves the journalist as a public servant, an idea that legitimizes aggressive investigating and reporting because it is done on behalf of the people, with the reporter serving as a "watchdog."[50] Now the job of the journalist, at least the idea of the journalist in popular culture, was to question established authorities, whoever they were, and to reject official narratives wherever they were found.

Canadian historiography was undergoing a similar shift. It too was part of a larger movement in the fight for social and civil rights, mainly originating in the United States, where scholars of all stripes became eager to expose the fault lines in traditional narratives upholding the establishment. Historian Jack Granatstein, in his 1998 book *Who Killed Canadian History?*, claimed that this turn in the writing of Canadian history occurred at the expense of national history – political and military history in particular – and that it led to the easy takeover of popular history by journalist-historians.[51] But there have always been professional historians writing on political and military history. The displacement, at CBC television at least, was more a result of the growing belief of professional journalists that they were best equipped, better than professional historians, to bring Canadian history to mass audiences. It was another outcome of events south of the border, where the investigative reporting on the civil rights movement and the Vietnam War exposed widespread government corruption and created a distrust of authority and official accounts of all kinds, including historical ones. The sensational accounts of uncovering secrets and cover-ups cemented, in popular culture, the idea of the journalist as a flouter of the powerful and a champion of the people.

None of this applied to Berton, who, even by that time, had done more than anyone to cement dominant versions of the national narrative into the minds of Canadians. His participation in *The National Dream* was more like Jack Saywell's in *Explorations* than anything his contemporaries in journalism were doing at the time. He was fastidious about the use of historical evidence and adherence to original texts (he made allowances in order to solve structural issues, like presenting events slightly out of sequence if he thought it would have little negative impact and would enhance dramatic effect). During production of *The National Dream*, for example, Italian film producers approached Berton and pitched him a movie version of the books. Berton insisted on controlling the future script to ensure there would be no distortion of history. In that project, however, distortion was looking pretty likely since the Italians wanted Sophia Loren to star. As the books and television series clearly demonstrated, and as Berton himself told the Italian producers, in *The National Dream* there was no starring role for any woman.[52]

Berton's role as historical consultant for *The National Dream* came about not just because of his content expertise but also because of his need to control projects having anything to do with his material. Until then, most CBC productions based on works by professional historians had involved the authors in some capacity, but none of them had anywhere near the power that Berton had with *The National Dream*. Judging from his records and CBC documentation, he had an unprecedented amount of influence in the CBC television programming connected to his work – in *The National Dream* but also in one-off programs like *The Dionne Quintuplets* (1978) and *Spirit of Batoche* (1985).

Appearances to the contrary, Berton had no monopoly on the story of the CPR. The mythology of the railway as the sine qua non of Canadian unity had been long established in popular culture, mainly by the CPR itself through its massive promotional machine, which was in place even before the completion of the railway.[53] Harold Innis and James Bonar had published substantial works on the subject well before Berton came along. And even the CBC, as early as 1962, had considered a thirteen-plus episode series on the CPR. Bert Powley, then special programs officer for history in the lead-up to the centennial, supported it. Powley did not like the idea in the original proposal of also covering Canadian Pacific steamships and airlines, as in his opinion doing so would render the work "a glorified commercial." But he reasoned that, if Canadian Pacific would agree to fund the series, it would go a long way to helping the CBC create "our own Davy Crockett style of serial."[54] The project never came to fruition, but CP Rail did become involved in the Berton series. Upon the CBC's request for cooperation, the company provided travel, access, and resources like rolling stock as well as the services of its resident archivist and historian Omer Lavallée. Berton often directed Findley and Whitehead to his own railway books and the sources he used to write them, and Lavallée is one of very few others to whom Berton referred them. When he did, it was usually for details on the railway's institutional or construction matters.

Findley, on his own, consulted the person who had previously been the acknowledged expert on the era of Macdonald and his National Policy. Donald Creighton agreed to help with Findley's questions but asked to remain anonymous since he guessed that he and Berton might not have similar views on events.[55] Some professional historians actually had regarded the railway books favourably, but many had not.[56] Berton was well aware, from the reception of his books, that with the television series it was necessary to be conscious of the potential reaction of professional historians. He cautioned Findley and Whitehead many times how essential it was that they stick to presenting the facts "without embellishment." Scenes had to be based on actuality, he said, or "we will be subject to the severest criticism for mythologizing history."[57]

Yet Berton had a taste for myth in history and he understood the public's taste for it as well. In his address to the CRTC just two years earlier, he bemoaned the American influence on Canadian broadcasting, and he stressed that broadcasting in Canada had to reflect Canada as a nation "'with its own mythology, its own heroes, its own songs, its own character, and its own idiom.'"[58] The CBC, too, in its submission to the CRTC only a few years later, stressed that history programs in the service of building myth and folk heroes was a vital part of the CBC's legacy in terms of building Canadian unity.[59] The importance of myth to the national psyche was an idea that was also shared by a line of professional historians like William Morton, Hilda Neatby, Jack Saywell, and Arthur Lower. In *A War for Survival* Lower proclaimed that myths were essential to the building of national identity. And, as Jack Granatstein wrote, Berton and other journalists filled this very gap – "creators and keepers of the national mythos" – that the new historians had abandoned.[60]

Knowlton Nash did not get overly involved in the scripts for *The National Dream*. But, from the start, one of his main concerns was also one of Berton's: the author's onscreen time. Ken Black, commenting on the early proposals for the series, pointed out that Berton's on-air time seemed excessive.[61] Just before the writers' first draft outlines were delivered, Nash alerted Patchell that he wanted to be kept informed on how the author's scenes were evolving and that he wanted reports on them before the final cut.[62] Later, as Berton's scripted screen presence was then clocking in at around nine minutes per episode, Nash worried that the program might be viewed as a lecture forum for the author rather than as "one of the greatest adventure stories in Canadian history." Nash was also concerned about what appeared in the outlines to be the author's *You Are There*–style involvement in dramatic scenes. He had firmly quashed the idea of Berton's "interviews" with historical characters early on in the process, but in one of the draft outlines it looked like it was still there. Nash told Sinclair of one instance in particular where Berton seemed to be involved in a discussion between historical characters. This was not compatible with Nash's journalistic sensibilities: not only would it be confusing to the audience but it would also "[bring] to mind memories of the *Jalna* future-past shifts in story line."[63]

A few weeks later Nash was adamant that Berton's scenes be reduced and revised for fear that *The National Dream* would become Information Programming's version of *Jalna*. While acknowledging Berton as the centrepiece of the series, Nash wanted Patchell to put a stop to any more script development until after a major discussion concerning how to cut down the now approximately ten minutes per episode of Berton's onscreen time. Furthermore, any scenes with Berton interacting with historical characters or entering dramatic scenes had to be deleted. Nash warned Patchell that Patchell's reputation, as well as Berton's and Sinclair's, was at stake, that everyone had to realize the huge significance of the project, and that with *The National Dream* they "must have a smashing success."[64]

Patchell replied immediately. He assured Nash that the new outlines, directly forthcoming, would show Berton's pared-down screen time to be between six minutes and six minutes and forty-five seconds. Responding to Nash's fears about the similarities with *Jalna*, Patchell promised to deliver much tighter scripts in terms of chronology and to eliminate any shared scenes between Berton and the actors.[65] When the revised scripts made the rounds that autumn (1972), Berton wasted no time making his feelings known about his diminished onscreen presence. In a memo to Jim Murray, who had replaced Sinclair as executive producer, he argued vehemently that his time in front of the camera was essential to the strength of the series. He seemed to have "practically disappeared": "And I notice in script number four there are entire acts where I appear on camera only once ... I do not want to be divorced from the action to this extent and I think the series will suffer if I am."[66]

Berton was also unhappy about the drafts of his onscreen commentary. Early in 1973 he was not only pushing for longer commentary but was also returning to the idea that he should be writing most of it himself. He wanted to lose the feeling of brevity, he said, and add more depth and humour.[67] Later, he suggested to Murray and Gauntlett that he rewrite all of it. While acknowledging that Whitehead had done a good job of condensing the material, Berton complained that this had subsumed his personality and erased all colour from the story. In a passage of withering comments he compared Whitehead's work to articles from *Reader's Digest* "after they've been reduced by the *Reader's Digest* editors from real articles." For Berton, they just weren't good enough.[68]

In reality, for *The National Dream*, the CBC had assembled a winning team. The production talent was among Canada's best: director of drama Eric Till, cinematographer Harry Makin, and composer of the original score Louis Applebaum. Actors William Hutt and John Colicos, playing John A. Macdonald and William Van Horne, respectively, were headline stars at Stratford as well as regulars on film and television.[69] And Whitehead, remaining on the job and completing the commentary according to Berton's wishes, eventually won an ACTRA award, along with Findley, for best television documentary writing. Berton actually became good friends with Whitehead and Findley, and occasionally sought their help in his future attempts at bringing Canadian history to television.

Unlike the other history programs produced under Nash, *The National Dream* had a sponsor in Royal Trust. But even with criticism coming from all sides regarding the CBC's commercialism, it seemed not to be an issue. Sponsorship was a sensitive business at Information Programming. With *The Tenth Decade*, Nash went back and forth on the matter, finally deciding that such subject matter should be "'totally pure'" and paid for by the CBC itself. This was also certainly due to the fact that the two prime ministers in question were still alive, thus *The Tenth Decade* had the potential to be controversial, and controversial programming was off-limits for commercials or sponsors.[70] For *The National Dream*, the agreement with Royal Trust was part of the company's celebration of seventy-five years in business. Its promotions for the series, tacked on to CBC publicity, trumpeted the fact that Lord Strathcona, the man who hammered in "the last spike," was the first president of Royal Trust. It also announced that, for *The National Dream*, it would only use half of its purchased advertising time.[71]

Something that got less attention was the fact that Royal Trust was also the executor of the estate of William Van Horne. Van Horne, the general manager and then president of the CPR, was one of the principal and most dynamic characters in the television series. Royal Trust, as executor, handled the sale of Van Horne's mansion to a developer who bought it on the condition of getting a permit from the city of Montreal to knock it down. During production of *The National Dream*, a group under the leadership of Jim McLellan, a CPR employee, opposed the demolition and took it to the courts – to no avail. When presented with this information after the mansion had been destroyed to make way for an office building, Berton said that, had he known, he "would have made a statement."[72]

Amid a plethora of promotional activities, "The Great Lone Land," the first episode of *The National Dream: Building the Impossible Railway*, went to air on 3 March 1974. The synopsis on the video jacket touts the overall theme for the series: the railway is something that will see "the rise and fall of political and financial fortunes" and will "determine the destiny of the nation." The episode opens with a long panorama of the first antagonist to appear in the series: a mountainous landscape somewhere in western Canada. It is one of the "impossible" things to be conquered by the railway builders. It also sets the stage for the remarkable cinematography and on-location dramatic filming, a first for a historical documentary or docudrama on CBC television.

The first scene with actors introduces CPR surveyor Walter Moberly, a central character in the episode. Moberly appears in the mountains in search of a pass for the railway line, which he finds. Berton comes onscreen to give context and, over the early part of the episode, introduces the themes of the series: that the railway was built to keep the Americans out of the Northwest (twice alluded to) and that its construction was equal to the task of building Canada itself. Thus, echoing Donald Creighton, Berton at once equates the CPR with the birth of Canada and raises the spectre of the Americans, who are the second antagonist in the series.

The first episode also introduces many of the main characters, all men except for Lady Macdonald and Lady Dufferin, a gender imbalance perpetuated throughout the series. The dramatic parts take turns with the documentary parts, which Berton presents onscreen or with his voiceover commentary. The black-and-white photos illustrate the documentary sections, with either Berton's voiceover narration or actors in voiceover reading excerpts from diaries and letters. Some of these photos are the custom stills referred to by the writers during the writing phase. They could be misleading in that, like the authentic photos, they are black and white, while the dramatic sections and Berton's scenes are all in colour. This technique deliberately blurs the line between the original and the created photos. But what makes them recognizable as fake is that the actors they feature have already appeared in the dramatic sequences.

Berton occasionally conveys that the information onscreen is based on some kind of actual documentation. Commenting on an upcoming scene with a survey crew, for example, he states that one of the featured crew members, Robert Rylatt, kept a diary. Throughout the series he makes similar comments, giving context to the actions of characters based on textual accounts. Along with Berton's extensive notes on *The National Dream* draft scripts, and the commentary about primary source evidence, it indicates his desire to create the proper balance of fact and fiction, and his awareness of the potential to mislead viewers. "In the theatre," he wrote to Murray, "when the audience knows it is seeing a play (Coulter's *Riel*, for instance) theatre wins out over history with the audience's tacit agreement. But in this documentary series history must win out over theatre."[73]

Introducing the next episode, "The Pacific Scandal," Berton again describes the purpose of the railway: "to create a dominion from sea to sea and to keep the Americans out of the Canadian West." Macdonald appears and claims that the Americans will not get the west but that, until the railway is built, Canada will be "a mere geographical expression." The intrigue that follows has Macdonald stressing that the railway must be Canadian-owned and operated, but, in reality, the silent backers behind wealthy Montrealer Hugh Allan turn out to be Americans. When Allan dumps them, the news breaks that their funds helped the Conservatives win the election in exchange for railway contracts and a position for Allan as president of the railway. Macdonald and his government resign, go into opposition, and the next year the Liberals win the election. At the end of the hour, Berton gives his take on whether Macdonald knew about the American backers and the promise made to Allan (that he suspected, but likely did not want to know, the details). While Berton exposes the political ambitions of Macdonald and his quest for power, he also indulges in the idea that, although the hero is down, he will rise again.

The third episode of *The National Dream* covers the complications surrounding the deal made with British Columbia – that it will get the railway line in exchange for joining Confederation. Alexander Mackenzie is now prime minister, and he carries on with the project, suffering the many headaches of contracting and surveying, an economic depression, and political negotiations. The episode shows Mackenzie as not up to the task and, depicting him as dour and uptight, juxtaposes him with the popular Macdonald. One scene features

Mackenzie posing for a portrait photographer who begs him to smile a little, to whom the grim-faced Mackenzie responds that he actually *is* smiling. Macdonald, on the other hand, is affable and personable, and even when drunk, as he often is, proves to be a master orator and political strategist. The allusion to Macdonald's exceptionalism is reminiscent of Donald Creighton's description of him in "The Craft of History": convivial and friendly, and, as such, "a strange, strange politician in sober, solemn, sanctimonious Victorian times."

In the fourth instalment is the defeat of Mackenzie's Liberals, with Macdonald returning as prime minister. Macdonald picks up where his predecessor left off, going back to his wheeling and dealing and fending off the attacks of his political opponents – the third group of antagonists in the series. In this episode, construction of the railway actually begins in earnest. The many battles with the muskeg and rocky terrain in northwestern Ontario play out in detail, though the camera is never long absent from the halls of Parliament in Ottawa. Berton continues to conflate the building of the railway with the development of the nation – indeed, the railway takes on a character of its own as Berton talks about how greatly it has affected the lives of all the major players met to date.

The National Dream clearly connected with the Canadian public. According to the CBC the first episode attracted the largest ever audience for a CBC program, and the series immediately became ensconced in popular culture. Even before it went to air, the previews and heavy fanfare led to its being parodied on a Wayne and Shuster comedy special, a sure sign of its cultural importance. One political cartoon in a newspaper depicted two boys and a train set with a caption saying "No! You be Sir John A. and I'll be Pierre Berton!"[74] After the fiasco of *Jalna*, the press was anticipating either the redemption or the demise of the corporation, and its initial reaction to *The National Dream* was overwhelmingly positive.

With the previews, many columnists wrote reviews before the first broadcast. The heightened expectation helped to create a national audience, and it became something that all Canadians, from Newfoundland to British Columbia, were expected to watch. It was nation-binding in the way the CBC had envisioned, as a shared media experience in which every Canadian watching knew that other Canadians were watching at the same time. Blaik Kirby of the *Globe and Mail* called the first episode "stunning," and he deemed it, overall, "the greatest series of programs it [CBC] has ever made, a series which will be talked about for years and will stimulate many Canadians to feel a chest-swelling pride in their nation."[75] In the *Calgary Herald*: "To watch *The National Dream* is to be surrounded and immersed in the forces which created this country."[76]

Basil Deakin, in the Halifax *Mail-Star*, wrote a review with a comment similar to those concerning *The Days before Yesterday*. One positive aspect of the series, in his opinion, was that Berton was a journalist rather than a historian, "since Canadians have long suffered from the inability of native historians as a profession to instill a knowledge of and an interest in Canadian history in the minds of most of their countrymen."[77] An article in the *Ottawa Journal* echoed this sentiment by partly blaming history teachers, as opposed to what the series would do, for why no one knew anything about Canadian history.[78] The verdict seemed to be in: historians were no longer competent as popular interpreters of the Canadian past.

One of the few negative reviewers of *The National Dream* was Dennis Braithwaite of the *Toronto Daily Star*. He complained that the series was overly nationalistic, that he "half-expected an officer of the ministry of culture to knock on the door" to see if he was watching. Like some others, he compared Berton and *The National Dream* to Alistair Cooke and *America*, but he further observed that Berton covered only fourteen years in the same amount of time it took Cooke to recount the entire history of the United States. He also dismissed Berton in a manner reminiscent of how some journalists were then dismissing professional historians: "He over-researches, over-writes, over-verbalizes and is manifestly unable to see the forest for the trees."[79] In a similar vein, towards the end of the series, Urjo Kareda in the *Toronto Star* stated his dislike for the series. He also commented on Findley's involvement and on how strange it was that, after *Jalna*, the writer had been given another such high-profile opportunity.[80]

After the halfway point of *The National Dream* run, the CBC released its audience numbers and evaluations. According to these figures, altogether the average audience tally for the series was approximately 3 million viewers. This was the biggest of any recent program except for the Wayne and Shuster special and the coverage of Princess Anne's wedding.[81] The average audience ratings (25 percent) were three times that of *Images of Canada*, though *Images* was not sponsored and sponsored programs had garnered more resources and more publicity. The evaluations indicated that the series was most popular in western Canada and, in accordance with other CBC works of televised history, that the typical viewer was educated and at least fifty years old. The average "index of enjoyment" was eighty-three, which was the same figure given to Donald Creighton's "Heroic Beginnings." This number was considered to be high and, in recent history productions, was only surpassed by the program *Was Tom Thomson Murdered?*[82]

At the same time, the BBM Bureau of Measurement, the most prominent supplier of data on the viewing habits of Canadians, issued its ratings for the program. The BBM information, supplied on a quarterly basis, showed that, just after the mid-point of the series, the approximate 3.6 million viewers that were initially captured for the first episode had diminished by around 800,000. The CBC explained to the *Globe and Mail* that, as a heavily promoted program, more people watched the first episode just to see what the talk was about. And even with the lost viewers, *The National Dream* was still just behind the holy grail of the NHL hockey playoffs.[83]

As for Berton himself, the "appreciation index" was eighty-four.[84] Hosts of similar productions, like Lorne Greene for *Last Year in Jerusalem* and Bruce Hutchison for *The Days before Yesterday*, had garnered an eighty-eight and a seventy-four, respectively. Had Creighton's appeal been measured for "Heroic Beginnings," he likely would have compared favourably since "Heroic Beginnings" compared favourably with the appreciation indices for *The National Dream*. The *Globe*'s Kirby, though, noted grumblings from "people who didn't like seeing or hearing so much of Pierre Berton, or his constant costume changes," among other things.[85] On this particular point, CBC audience evaluators strayed from their usual stance of impartiality and noted in their report that the audience did not seem to agree with these kinds of criticisms about Berton.[86] Mel Hurtig, Berton's fellow cultural nationalist, wrote to him: "don't pay any attention to the jealous bastards."[87]

"The Railway General," the fifth episode in *The National Dream*, begins with the newly formed Canadian Pacific Railway and introduces the dominant character of the second half of the series: William Van Horne. The American Van Horne, the CPR's general manager, took to overseeing, with equal vigour, the continuing construction of the railway and the development of western Canada in preparation for immigration. Berton had cautioned in his notes to Findley not to forget that Van Horne could be callous as well as daring. But, onscreen, Van Horne quickly emerges as a hero of the story. He is the personification of the line's now-relentless progress, surmounting all obstacles in the way, including the "problem" of Indigenous peoples.

Indigenous peoples appear throughout *The National Dream*, but they are not an integral part of it. As Berton indicated in the draft script notes, despite his belief in the necessity of the railway and what it represented in terms of national unity, he was sympathetic to the plight of the Indigenous peoples who lived in its path. But the depth of this concern does not translate to the television screen. In the opening segment of each episode appears the face of an Indigenous man, turning to the sound of a train whistle, with a cut to a train careening through a mountain pass. Episodes 1 to 4 occasionally show Indigenous men working with the small survey parties or watching silently on horseback as the workers construct the line. Their first substantial scene is not until episode 5, when they are hunting buffalo, whose numbers, according to Berton, are rapidly dwindling. In episode 6, surveyor Major Albert Rogers expresses the racist attitudes of the day by complaining about the large appetites of the Indigenous men on his crew and their dislike of hard work. Berton describes them as fearless, however, as they had one of the most dangerous jobs a construction crew member could have: setting the explosive charges to get through the rock.

In *The National Dream*, Indigenous people lack both substantial speaking parts and agency. This includes even Crowfoot, who, in fact, played a key role in the events of the time with the negotiation of Treaty 7 and his later decision to not involve the Blackfoot in the 1885 resistance. In episode 5, Crowfoot and his men, on horseback, approach the railway crew as it works on the line near the reserve of the Blackfoot Nation close to Calgary, but they leave without speaking. Father Albert Lacombe, an Oblate missionary and friend of the Plains Indigenous peoples, is a featured character here, and it is only he who relays contemporaneous comments about the distress the building of the railway causes them. Episode 5 does depict Indigenous people and does not depict the falsehood of terra nullius – the colonial and, until relatively recently, pervasive concept that the lands colonized by Europeans had previously belonged to no one. Rather, it glosses over a situation that Berton understood well but that he also knew could not be seamlessly integrated into the story he wanted to tell. A realistic account of the dislocation, starvation, and exploitation of Indigenous peoples, chiefly as a result of Macdonald's policies, could not be reconciled with the tidy resolution that Berton's nation-building television narrative required.[88]

Episode 6, "The Sea of Mountains," introduces Major Rogers and his search for mountain passes for the line into British Columbia. It also depicts the Chinese workers, recruited for the BC sections of the CPR by American engineer Andrew Onderdonk. Like the Indigenous men, the Chinese are subject to discrimination, but, in contrast, they are known to the whites apparently as self-sufficient and hard-working. Berton says that this difficult section of the track could not have been laid without them. The Chinese, like the Indigenous workers, are also required to do some of the most dangerous tasks, including the blasting of rock using nitroglycerine, a substance that is highly unstable but cheaper than dynamite. Like the Indigenous men, the Chinese endure greater construction hazards and lower wages than the white workers (and they also suffer from scurvy as, according to the narration, most of them will only eat fish and rice). However, the Chinese, unlike the Indigenous men, do have a couple of small speaking parts, including one man who lies dying of scurvy while Onderdonk looks in on him.

In episodes 7 and 8, the story returns to the politics of railway construction and the re-emergence of Macdonald, now well ensconced in the position of prime minister. The entire railway project is running out of money. George Stephen, president of the company, continually hounds Macdonald to secure more funds in order to prevent the bankruptcy and collapse of the project. Van Horne attempts to prove the necessity of the railway by offering to transport troops to the northwest, by rail, in order to quell the recently erupted "rebellion" of the Métis and First Nations people in the Plains. This will help support Macdonald's bid to the House of Commons for more funding. It works. Little appears onscreen of the grievances of the Indigenous peoples or the desperate situation in which they find themselves. The troop transport is later described on the video jacket as "the cruelest journey in Canadian military history," yet one that is necessary to avert "the national crisis." There is nothing said of the other crisis, which is the crisis of the Indigenous peoples, which existed precisely because of this nation-building project.

The interpretation of the resistance begins at Duck Lake, in the series a snapshot, in reality a battle between a force of Métis and First Nations, and a force of North-West Mounted Police and Canadian military volunteers. The incident is the prompt that results in troops being sent to Saskatchewan, even though sections of the line north of Lake Superior are still not finished. Much is made of the pomp and preparation of the young men going off to war – noted by Berton as the nation's first war and the first test of the debt-ridden CPR. Their struggles on the snow and ice as they march between sections of the line are well documented onscreen, but the sequence ends before they reach their destination. Berton appears and says of the conflict only that Riel has surrendered and that the CPR has "helped to save the country." Unlike how the producers of *Images of Canada* had treated this event, the producers of *The National Dream* ignored the outcomes from the perspectives of the Métis and First Nations people. There is nothing said of the trial, the sentencing, the petitioning in support of Riel, or of his hanging and the hanging of eight other Indigenous men. In *The National Dream* they are the obstacles whose sacrifice is necessary for the national unity mythologically achieved by the railway, symbolized by the final scene of Donald Smith (Lord Strathcona) driving home the last spike.

The building of the Canadian Pacific Railway did affect Canada in profound and long-lasting ways. It led to the creation of towns and telegraph lines along the track; it facilitated both the transportation of multitudes of settlers to the west and the development of industry and trade. And it also facilitated the displacement and marginalization of Indigenous peoples. Little of this emerges in *The National Dream*. As Berton says in the opening scene, the primary reasons for building the railway were to unify the country and to keep out the Americans.

Themes of national unity and the American threat run throughout many of his other books and television projects as well. In Berton's proposal for a television adaptation of *Klondike*, reissued two years before *The National Dream* went to air, he measured the significance of the gold rush by its facilitation of "the prairie boom" of immigration and the construction of two more transcontinental railways. He also thought the gold rush distinguished Canadians from Americans according to their different reactions to it, which he stressed in terms of contrasting national stereotypes: "The Canadians' love of order imposed from above; the Americans' passion for freedom."[89]

Berton was partial to big symbols of national unity: he laboured to get his books on the War of 1812 and the Battle of Vimy Ridge on television. Along with the building of the CPR, Berton regarded Vimy as the other epic of Canadian history, the battle heralded every anniversary since as the event that marked "Canada's coming of age." He wrote in a proposal that, along with the building of the CPR, Vimy was a subject that was pretty much pre-sold to Canadian audiences. It could be successful in the United States as well, especially if the latter half of what he proposed as a dramatic series was reworked for American and other foreign markets.[90] Thus, he seemed to have no qualms about the possibility of reconfiguring Canadian epics to suit American audiences, though he continually returned to the theme of American culture as the ultimate threat to Canadian identity. Nash joined Berton in promoting this notion. About *The National Dream*, Nash wrote that, in addition to regionalism, the other big obstacle confronting Canadian unity was "the seductive magnetism of the Americans."[91]

Berton's formula worked well. Canadians took to *The National Dream* not only because of all the intrigue and adventure but also because it included thwarting the Americans. The CPR overcomes a multitude of other formidable obstacles as well: the mountains, the political opponents, and the Indigenous peoples. It keeps to the well-worn formula of a latter day romance, featuring heroes Macdonald and Van Horne, along with the other essential elements: villains, conflict, setback, and ultimate triumph. The railway represents not the progress of the Canadian people but the progress of Canada as a nation, similar to Berton's interpretations in his book treatments of the

Klondike, Vimy, and the War of 1812. Before Berton there were few popular history books (let alone television series) on these topics, and Canadians responded by eating them up.

The National Dream was a big financial success for Berton. To capitalize on the series his two books were condensed into one paperback, peppered with photos taken during the filming. This book ended up on the bestseller list, where his first two had been. In addition to selling to the CBC the rights to the written works for an undisclosed amount, Berton received payments for his services for each episode as well as a generous per diem over the approximate two years of production. The CBC acknowledged this was unusually high, but Berton was considered to be worth it.[92] The author/host collected residuals from non-broadcast sales as well as when the series was rebroadcast, as it was on the CBC at least four times in the ensuing years.[93]

Berton also benefited from foreign sales, as the CBC sold *The National Dream* to the BBC as well as to entities in Ireland, Spain, Denmark, Australia, Jordan, and Italy.[94] The corporation was supposed to submit regular statements to Berton regarding his share of all this, and its seeming inattention to this over the years was the subject of fiery letters from him, demanding statements and payments. Before the series had first gone to air, Norn Garriock wrote to Nash relaying his one-word reaction to someone at the CBC who suggested that Berton didn't care much about the money – "Balderdash!"[95]

The National Dream, as Information Programming's highest priority vehicle with its approximate $2 million price tag, raised the profile of the CBC with audiences and politicians alike. But it was a short-lived success as, in the following years, major cuts to the corporation would prevent similar instances of spectacular all-out history programming. Before this became clear, Berton worked hard to push television adaptations of his other books. Even before the first episode of *The National Dream* went to air he proposed the series based on *Klondike*, later envisioned in *You Are There*–style, possibly with Whitehead and Findley as writers.[96] Nash, although enthusiastic about it as a great vehicle for public broadcasting, was not able to commit to it as proposed. He did discuss with Berton a possible "pseudo-documentary" that would be less expensive than the initial proposal, but in the end he dropped it.

According to Nash, this was partly because of potential complaints from the Drama department about another incursion into its territory. But it was also because, in 1978, the CBC was forced to make a $71 million budget cut.[97]

In 1981, the CBC optioned Berton's two books about the War of 1812 – *The Invasion of Canada* (1980) and *Flames across the Border* (1981) – with a view to giving them the same treatment as the CPR volumes. Again the project was eventually rejected on the grounds that it was too expensive.[98] Berton tried to interest journalist and independent documentary filmmaker Michael Maclear in making it and selling it to the corporation, reasoning as follows: "The CBC will get the program much more cheaply than they could have if they produced it themselves; the private stations on a second-run basis could get a large number of points for Canadian content; and we get the thing produced." Maclear was intrigued but replied that, from what he understood, the stumbling block at the CBC was that it had already committed to too many period dramas.[99] The same thing happened to Berton's efforts with his book on Vimy – the CBC optioned it in 1990 but never produced it.[100]

After *The Tenth Decade, Images of Canada, The National Dream,* and *The Days before Yesterday,* the era of the high-profile historical documentary and docudrama series seemed to be over. In 1978, its champion – Nash – left to become the anchor of the national evening news. In the following years, the English network did produce some history-based programming, but these were mostly one-offs or one- or two-part documentaries or docudramas, which had been the more common format for history programs before the big productions of the 1970s.

Nash supported the Canadian history programs because they distinguished the CBC as a nation-building force and as a producer of quality informational television programs. But, in the 1970s, competition from Canadian private and public broadcasters, and cable and satellite distribution, made audience share the most important part of the CBC conversation. Public service obligations to educate and inform viewers got squeezed out among the commercial demands for big audiences. The CBC had to court sponsors like Royal Trust to help pay for programs like *The National Dream*, while at the same time deflect charges of commercialism and superficiality by showing it was fulfilling its mandate as a national public service broadcaster.

The history programs of the early 1970s also stoked the fires of English-Canadian nationalism, at its apex at the centennial, now under threat with the growing popularity in Quebec of the separatist movement. *The National Dream* did nothing if not contribute to that sentiment: it was a clear celebration of what was considered to be a momentous event in the building of Canada. And, more than the other history programs, it met the challenge of competing with American programs on the other stations. Berton's story diminishes the grievances and suffering of Indigenous peoples and has no roles for women, but, for Berton, Nash, and other CBC officials, the series was a testament to national unity and a formidable response to the American cultural invasion. To that end, "entertainment," said Nash, not "lecturing," was key to the success of *The National Dream* – "the greatest adventure story in Canadian history."[101]

This comment hints at the turn away from public education as CBC staffers had previously practised it as well as the changing attitude towards the participation of professional historians in the Canadian history programs. Around 1970, a schism appeared between producers of Canadian history on CBC television and professional historians – a schism that had not existed in the 1950s and 1960s. It is often said that, at the CBC, the stars are the journalists. In the 1970s, the journalists assumed the role of historical authorities as well. In *Images of Canada*'s "The Craft of History," Michel Brunet and Ramsay Cook contend that the public role of the historian as played by Lower, Creighton, Underhill, and others of a more recent generation was moving to "newspapermen and commentators." While Pierre Berton was the most prominent example of this trend, he also attempted to maintain a balance between the narrative account and transmitting to viewers an idea of history as a mode of inquiry. This was not necessarily the case for the next generation of journalists who produced Canadian history programs for CBC television.

4 | Behind the History Wars at the CBC: *The Valour and the Horror*

By the late 1970s, commercial broadcasters, public broadcasters other than the CBC, and cable and satellite distribution had pushed CBC television to the periphery of television broadcasting in Canada. In 1982, the Federal Cultural Policy Review Committee signalled a major shift in policy by recommending to government that the private sector produce all CBC programs except for the news. Until then, CBC staff had produced most of the Canadian programs broadcast, with some from the National Film Board, and purchased most of the rest from international broadcasters. The minister of communications, Francis Fox, rejected the committee's recommendation as it was written, but the idea prompted the move towards private production and development of the Canadian media industry.

The shift included a directive from Fox to the CBC to "re-orient" itself. This meant the CBC would regularly schedule NFB productions, pay more attention to regional production, and raise its Canadian content levels to 80 percent. Most important, it was to begin purchasing half of its television programming, besides news, sports, and information, from independent producers.[1] The CBC began to change priorities. The new focus was drama, and much of the funding for documentaries now went to current affairs and its newly created flagship program *The Journal*. The documentaries and docudramas on Canadian history that did get made were mostly co-productions with the NFB or with the NFB and private producers. These included the documentary series *The Champions* (1978, 1986) and *The Defence of Canada* (1986), and the docudrama series: *Canada's Sweetheart: The*

Saga of Hal C. Banks (1985), *The King Chronicle* (1988), and *The Valour and the Horror* (1992).

The production house behind *The Valour and the Horror* was Galafilm, a Montreal-based company that was well positioned to take advantage of the CBC's turn to independent production. Filmmaker and company founder Arnie Gelbart produced the series along with Galafilm producer André Lamy, past NFB film commissioner and former executive director of Telefilm. But the real forces behind *The Valour and the Horror* were Galafilm associates Brian McKenna, a documentary filmmaker and former CBC producer, and his brother Terence McKenna, a CBC journalist. The two co-wrote the series, with Brian as director and Terence as narrator.[2] The CBC and the NFB signed on as co-producers. The NFB participated through the new NFB Independent Co-Production Program. Galafilm received some funds from Telefilm through the Canadian Broadcast Program Development Fund, a program created to bolster the Canadian media industry. So although *The Valour and the Horror* was a child of independent producers, it was underwritten principally by public funds.

The timing of *The Valour and the Horror* capitalized on the period marking the fiftieth anniversary of the Second World War. The three two-hour episodes covered the experiences of Canadians in the Allied defence of Hong Kong and in the Japanese forced labour camps, the Allied air bombing campaign over Germany, and the Allied invasion of German-occupied Normandy, including the attacks on Verrières Ridge. The producers used a mix of documentary techniques (including eyewitness interviews, archival film, and photographs) and dramatic techniques (including actors speaking direct to camera, and an arresting soundtrack).

Brian McKenna made clear that their aim was to correct what they considered to be the accepted version of these events, to expose the wrongdoing of the Canadian government and military officials, and, finally, "to set the historical record straight."[3] The approach was very much like that of the new historians who confronted the old nationalist narratives, but without the historical methodology. Where Pierre Berton worried about professional historians accusing him of mythologizing history with his account of the railway, the makers of *The Valour and the Horror* accused professional historians of a similar offence with regard to these wartime events. Berton and the McKennas were all journalists, but this was a different era. Berton spent his formative working years in the company of professional historians and cultural nationalists. Their aim was not to debunk the standard narratives but, rather, to create or support them.

Earlier CBC productions had suggested that collective memory about nation-defining events was perhaps not so easily challenged, however, especially when the vehicle was taxpayer-funded television. Not everyone accepted this new television narrative about what was supposed to have been the "Good War." The public backlash after the broadcast resulted in the Senate, the CRTC, and the CBC ombudsman conducting investigations into the content and presentation of the series. All came to different conclusions. The controversy endured for the rest of that year and beyond, casting a heavy pall over the corporation and calling into question the nature of the relationship between the CBC and the NFB, as well as the new CBC reliance on independent producers. More damning was the criticism of CBC journalistic practices, its credibility in interpreting Canadian history, and its fitness overall as a public service broadcaster. Veterans' groups, politicians, media professionals, historians, and everyday citizens took part in the dispute. It was the most public battle to date of the history wars in Canada.

By the 1990s, the term "history wars" had come to refer to clashes over attempts to expose or change widely accepted interpretations of important events in national histories. In 1970s Australia, historians and others faced formidable opposition when they began to advocate for a national history that was more inclusive of Indigenous peoples and more transparent about their near annihilation due to colonization. By the 1990s the debate had moved into the public and political realm, expanding to the Australian museum system and national school curricula. Another prescient example arose in 1994 at the National Air and Space Museum in the United States. That year, curators faced an angry public over plans to display part of the *Enola Gay* (the airplane that dropped the atomic bomb on Hiroshima) in an effort to mark the end of the Second World War. Their attempt to explore the atomic bombing of Japan from multiple perspectives, including those of the Japanese, set off a firestorm of condemnation from veterans' groups, politicians, and others, which eventually led to the departure of the museum's director. It was part of a general rupture happening everywhere in the Western world, where history began to function as a critique of nationalism rather than as its foundation. These challenges affected not only the accepted versions of national history but also, by extension, the very idea of Australian and American national identities. Many were unhappy to think of themselves as inheritors of such uncomfortable legacies.

Most writing and commentary about *The Valour and the Horror* has focused largely on the aftermath of its broadcast as an episode in these history wars; some has focused on its content and presentation.[4] Given the many players fighting to be heard after the series went to air, understanding issues of power and voice is vital to understanding why the debate took the form it did. The following interpretation is an assessment of the presentation and framing of the series within the contexts of its production and the tradition of CBC Canadian history television programming. The broad storylines of the three episodes had many defenders, including some professional historians. It was the presentation, specifically the dramatization techniques and the use of written and oral testimony, which were not new practices at the CBC but which were applied here in new ways and with greater emphasis, that most distorted the historical integrity of the final product. The producers also framed the series as non-fiction and themselves as truth-tellers. They positioned themselves in opposition to historians, claiming that theirs was a journalistic approach to history. But how did their practices differ from those of historians and what were the results? These questions are at the crux of the claims about fact and fiction made by both the producers and their detractors, yet they are not fully explored in the existing literature.

The CBC had produced or televised works about Canada and the Second World War before. In 1962, it broadcast a thirteen-part NFB documentary series called *Canada at War*. That same year it also produced, for its *Close-Up* series a documentary on Dieppe, the site of the invasion considered to be the cause of Canada's greatest wartime tragedy. In 1979, the CBC co-produced with the NFB a two-part documentary series, also on Dieppe. All were standard documentaries, so, unlike with the *The Valour and the Horror*, none mixed documentary and dramatic elements. These versions of Dieppe also conformed to the accepted narrative of Dieppe as a debacle. There was no fallout from the Canadian public.

Yet there was precedent for controversial documentaries on the war as it played out elsewhere. In France, an early version of the history wars erupted with the showing of *Le Chagrin et la Pitié (The Sorrow and the Pity)* (1969). This film by Marcel Ophüls, made for but initially banned from French television, caused outrage in France by poking holes in widely held notions about the upstanding conduct of French citizens under the Vichy regime. Another example, also from France, is Claude Lanzmann's *Shoah* (1985), a cinematic documentary film about the Holocaust and how regular citizens, especially Polish citizens, were complicit in it. Many Poles were scandalized by Lanzmann's depiction of them in wartime as too wilfully ignorant, afraid, or anti-Semitic to help the Jews and others being murdered in their midst. Both works have been praised as two of the best documentaries about the war ever produced, yet in their day they were extremely contentious for French and Polish nationals.

In 1988, the CBC broadcast the first of the docudramas created by the McKenna brothers based on the participation of Canadians in the two world wars. *The Killing Ground* is about Canadians in the First World War. This two-hour piece depicts Canadian soldiers as poorly trained and badly led, and the war overall as a great waste of life and resources. Because there were few remaining veterans of that war and because this interpretation of the war as a tragic futility was already widely accepted, this docudrama did not result in any substantial backlash. Two years later, the producers proposed a similar treatment for a series on the Second World War. Based on the success of *The Killing Ground*, they received approval to proceed from Darce Fardy, CBC head of network television, and Trina McQueen, vice-president of television news and current affairs.[5]

Included in the production agreement for *The Valour and the Horror* was a clause stating that the CBC reserved the right to edit the programs if they were not up to CBC standards. The CBC would also have the final decision regarding the acceptability of the "content, treatment and technical quality" of the series.[6] The NFB signed a separate agreement with the producers, but, unlike the CBC, the film board left the right of final cut to Galafilm. Later, according to Film Commissioner

Joan Pennefather, throughout the production the producers were responsive to requests for changes from Adam Symansky, the NFB lead on the project.[7]

The relationship between the CBC and the NFB had changed dramatically over the years. In the past, the relationship was often one of unworkable agreements and difficult collaboration – their production processes and technical requirements were too different from each other, and some CBC staff had bones of contention with the film board. These included a lack of CBC involvement on NFB projects meant for CBC broadcast, NFB programs meant for CBC broadcast that were not attractive to sponsors (or that even allowed for commercials), and the NFB's submitting to the CBC current affairs programming that was too controversial. In the early 1980s, however, federal policy directed the NFB to reduce production, decentralize, and put more emphasis on its role as a training institute for new filmmakers. The CBC, in turn, was to televise more works from the NFB.

The producers complied with requests for changes from the CBC as well, and during the various stages of the work little seemed out of the ordinary. According to CBC internal documents, however, the CBC legal department flagged (then cleared) the portrayal of some of the characters as possibly defamatory. The main concerns here were Air Chief Marshal Arthur Harris, Wing Commander Mervin Fleming, and CBC wartime correspondent Matthew Halton.[8] Since CBC staff knew the material was controversial, in advance of the broadcasts they established a process in order to deal with any negative responses. Extra staff members were appointed to audience relations. Should anyone press beyond the audience relations staff by telephone, the producers and appointed CBC and NFB staff were to be available to answer any questions. All written inquiries would be sent to the producers for a draft response, then to Fardy and McQueen for review.[9]

The main model for the new series overall was *The Killing Ground*. Early plans for the series included dramatic scenes with techniques borrowed from *Canada's Sweetheart* and *The King Chronicle* as well as from *Culloden* (1964).[10] *Culloden* is the television interpretation by Peter Watkins of the disastrous stand, in 1746, of the Jacobite forces under "Bonnie Prince Charlie" against the British army.

Watkins, who created *Culloden* for BBC broadcast, used an approach similar to that used in *You Are There*, whereby modern reporters interviewed actors in historical settings. But in *Culloden*, the reporter is only heard, not seen, and the actors give their answers direct to camera.

As media scholar John Cook has observed, this type of presentation overturned what was then the dramatic convention that actors not look direct to camera. This transforms the viewer into the object of the actor's gaze. It also contravenes the traditional authority of the television reporter as the only one to speak direct to camera, thus allowing the actors' recounting of events to appear unmediated.[11] But *Culloden*'s stark depiction of brutality, the hand-held camera, and the unprofessional and dishevelled actors are the greater breaks from the television standards of the mid-1960s. By pretending to prepare a newscast in the midst of the slaughter, Watkins turns the spotlight on television itself by capturing the often exploitative nature of television news coverage. *Culloden* also reveals the limited ability of television to present the whole reality of a situation, along with its tendency to not fully provide explanatory context.

In *The Valour and the Horror*, the *Culloden*-style re-enactment was not intended as a critique of television or of mediated history but, initially at least, as a traditional re-dramatization of the events at Verrières Ridge with members of the Black Watch. The rest of the key dramatics in the series consist of multiple costumed actors in period settings and non-verbal roles or, as in *Culloden*, individual actors speaking direct to camera. Most of the actors in speaking roles play people who survived and whose words the filmmakers had taken from their written works or from interviews they had later conducted with them. The filmmakers also used standard documentary tools such as archival photos, war art, film footage, and onscreen eyewitnesses. These eyewitnesses include two veterans per episode who travel back to the scene of the action, describe what it was like to be involved in the various campaigns, and give their opinion as to why things transpired as they did. Altogether, *The Valour and the Horror* was meant to be a combination of "investigative journalism, drama and documentary" as described in the promotions.[12] While some have described this combination of methods as unconventional or "non-traditional," there was nothing very new in the historical approach.[13]

The CBC created a national audience for the series with ample advertising and a primetime Sunday night time slot. It begins with "Savage Christmas: Hong Kong 1941," a story about what happened to the Canadian contingent of approximately two thousand men and women who joined the British troops in Hong Kong in 1941. The episode opens with white letters on a black screen and voiceover narration: "This is a true story. In some cases actors speak the documented words of soldiers and nurses. There is no fiction." The soundtrack plays to the opening credits. Almost immediately, two unnamed Canadian veterans appear, on location in Japan. The narrator announces that they are back for a reunion, which turns out to be a visit to the Japanese graveyard of their fallen comrades.

A costumed actor (playing soldier Roger Cyr), the third to appear approximately four minutes into the program, speaks direct to camera and outlines the main theme: "The thought that my government would knowingly offer a couple of thousand of its young men as lambs to the slaughter, in order to meet some sort of political expediency?" McKenna as narrator then introduces the two veterans: Bob Manchester and Bob Clayton. The details of what happened to them and the other Canadians in Hong Kong "were for a long time suppressed by the Canadian government," McKenna says, and "the terrible story is known to very few Canadians." The account turns to another reunion, of the members of the Japanese contingent that fought against the Canadians. These reunions used to be held in secret, but now there is "an open celebration of the spirit that brought them [the Japanese veterans] together for war."

Then follows a narrated historical sequence of events showing archival photographs and film footage, costumed actors, and Clayton and Manchester. McKenna relates that, privately, Churchill said that "there was not the slightest chance of holding Hong Kong or of relieving it if the Japanese attacked" but that, "rather than risk more of their own troops," the British ask Canada to go to Hong Kong. Canada says yes without analyzing the situation. The Canadian troops identified to go are green and unfit for combat. The costumed actors reappear, and one plays Kay Christie, a nursing sister who accompanied the Canadians. The Christie actor appears on the troop ship en route to Hong Kong and talks about how the Canadian soldiers are undergoing training to learn how to load and use a gun. "Honestly," she says "it's just appalling."

The Japanese take Hong Kong soon after the Canadians arrive, capturing and killing many Allied soldiers. Those murdered and tortured include men hospitalized at a makeshift hospital set up at the British-run St Stephen's College, where the Japanese commit further atrocities on the nursing staff, raping and killing most of them. The Allied troops surrender and the Japanese imprison them. Canadian and other captured soldiers spend three years in the work camps and coal mines where the Japanese work, beat, and starve them. Actors play men who have been imprisoned. Bob Clayton and Bob Manchester visit some of the sites spoken about in the narration and offer their accounts of what had happened to them personally.

One of the scenes with Clayton and Manchester depicts a visit with a Japanese man who was a captain of the guards in one of the camps. The scene turns awkward when the man will not acknowledge the poor treatment of the Allied soldiers in the camps and suggests, through an interpreter, that the opinion Clayton has of it might be due to cultural differences. In a subsequent scene, Manchester goes to a restaurant where he meets four Japanese veterans of the battle. When the conversation gets to what happened at St Stephen's makeshift hospital, Manchester explains to them that Clayton is not present because he is too upset with them over what he experienced at St Stephen's. The Japanese say that they do not know about the incident(s) in question.

The narrative turns back to the wartime events and to a "secret plan" to kill all the prisoners in the camps if the Allies invade. The dropping of the atomic bombs ends that plan. Film footage shows the poor state of the inmates in the camps and prisoner hospitals at war's end. Bob Clayton reunites with the American sailor who was assigned to him on the American ship that took the Canadians back home. The episode ends on a note of betrayal – of the Canadian soldiers by their government. The actor playing Roger Cyr reappears and repeats his claim that the Canadian government knowingly sent its troops to Hong Kong like "lambs to the slaughter." In the narration McKenna states that, in 1952, when veterans were seeking reparations from Japan for what happened, the Canadian government "absolved Japan of any responsibility" and continued to oppose the veterans' rights to compensation.

The second episode, and the target of the most serious post-broadcast criticism, is "Death by Moonlight: Bomber Command," a depiction of the activities of the unit that "area" bombed Germany. The piece begins with the same white text on black background, claiming that the story is true and that there is "no fiction." Right away appear the two featured veterans, Doug Harvey and Ken Brown, each a former member of Bomber Command. They are on location in Yorkshire, England, at the site of a former air base used by Canadians. Actors play out a dramatized scene, and McKenna sets the tone with the following thesis:

> The British high command knew how few bomber crews would survive but deliberately hid the truth. That's not all that was concealed. The crews and the public were told that the bombing targets were German factories and military installations. In fact, in 1942 a secret plan was adopted. Germany would be crushed through the deliberate annihilation of its civilians.

"Death by Moonlight" levels such accusations against those in charge, including the British prime minister, Winston Churchill, and Air Chief Marshal Charles Portal. But the narrator singles out the commander of the unit, Air Chief Marshal Arthur Harris, as the primary villain. Harris appears early and often throughout the episode. The narrator says he is obsessed with "destroying German cities and civilians." The argument overall is that Harris sacrificed his air crews in raids that were not only immoral but also useless with regard to destroying German civilian morale. Wing Commander Mervin Fleming is the second villain. An actor playing Fleming appears and expresses his lack of sympathy for traumatized airmen, later outlining the grim details of how the fire-bombing of German cities actually worked. The portrayals of Harris and Fleming are two of the three that CBC lawyers had earlier flagged as potentially litigious.

Over the course of the episode, the narrator, the veterans, and the costumed actors together provide an outline of the bombing campaign: the targets, the types of raids, the dropping of the bombs, the schedule of the crews, the role of various aircrew members, the risk, the survival rates, the psychology of airmen going out to possible death on their flights. The narrator recounts a sequence on the famous "Dambusters" raid, the 1943 mission that had aircrew in low-flying Lancasters dropping a new type of bomb on the formidable dams in the Ruhr River valley. Ken Brown received a decoration for bravery for the mission, but the narrator explains that now Brown is not so sure it was worth the cost. Although the bombs hit their two targets and caused significant damage to one, nine of the seventeen attacking airplanes and their crews went down.

An actor playing renowned physicist Freeman Dyson appears several times throughout the episode. Dyson was an advisor to *The Valour and the Horror* production team; in 1943 he was a young staffer at Bomber Command headquarters. The narrator describes Dyson as a "brilliant analyst" of the bombing campaign. The actor playing Dyson argues that the campaign was immoral and, at one point, praises the German night fighters, saying they ended the war "morally undefeated." This was because, during the last days of the conflict, they were not fighting for Hitler but only to protect their families, homes, and cities. According to Dyson, this gave them "a clean cause to fight for" – something they had not had at the beginning of the war.

The two veterans in this episode meet some German civilians: the former fire chief and, later, two women from Hamburg, all of whom lived through the bombing of that city. The fire chief shows the veterans photographs of the devastating effects of the bombs on the ground. The women describe to them some of the awful scenes they had witnessed. It makes for some difficult moments when one of the women asks Harvey and Brown how they now feel, given that they were visiting Hamburg in person. As in the Hong Kong episode, the two also meet with their German fighting counterparts and have a conversation over a beer about their days as enemies. The episode ends with Harvey and Brown walking through a Commonwealth graveyard in Yorkshire.

The third instalment of *The Valour and the Horror* is "In Desperate Battle: Normandy 1944." This film deals with Operation Overlord, the Allied invasion of German-occupied France, and one of the missions: the advance on Verrières Ridge. Like the first two episodes, in this one an introductory text appears onscreen claiming that the story ahead is true and there is no fiction in it. The narrator says in voiceover that the true story of "the cataclysms that befell the Canadian army" during that summer, including what happened at Verrières Ridge, "has never really been told." The two veterans this time are (Sydney) Radley-Walters and Jacques Dextraze, who go back to France and talk about the events in which they participated.

The initial focus of the piece is the Allied invasion, including the landing operations in Normandy and the attempt to gain a foothold beyond the beaches. One scenario focuses on the massacre of captured Canadian soldiers at the abbey Ardennes. A subsequent sequence outlines that the Allies, including Canadians, carried out similar atrocities. In contemporary recordings, CBC wartime journalist Matthew Halton praises the landings and overall Allied successes. But the narrator says that Halton's work helped create the myth that the German defences were easily overcome. Scenes show the destruction of the medieval French city of Caen, apparently ordered by General Montgomery for public relations purposes, as he was under pressure to show results. The scenes are accompanied by the voice of Halton, who appears to be a cheerleader for the unnecessary destruction. Halton is the third person, besides Harris and Fleming, whose characterization the CBC lawyers had identified as a potential problem.

The latter part of the episode is mainly about the Canadian series of advances on Verrières Ridge. The narrator explains that the first attack is bungled and the troops incur high losses. Brigadier Ben Cunningham advises his superior, Rod Keller, that the situation is futile and that further attacks should be called off. Cunningham is soon fired. The Black Watch prepare another attack down the ridge, and take more losses as they move past two villages. When they begin to cross an open field in front of the ridge they are trying to take, the Germans quickly and easily mow them down. The production crew filmed the members of the Black Watch re-enacting the event while training. The original battle is referred to by an actor playing a German soldier who witnesses it as "sheer butchery."

According to the account there are several to blame for the disaster. The narrator characterizes top Canadian commanders like Andrew McNaughton and Harry Crerar as inept and incompetent, but, for Verrières Ridge specifically, he deems two men ultimately responsible. One is Keller, drawn as a drinker, who asks to be removed from his post and is refused by his commanding officer, General Guy Simonds. Simonds is the primary target for exposition. The narrator claims the Black Watch were told before the charge that they would be able to take the enemy, while all along Simonds planned to use them as a sacrifice for the allied cause. In the end, "the full extent of the calamity was covered up," and Simonds is decorated.

The first episode garnered almost 2 million viewers, which, according to a CBC research officer, was the largest audience for a documentary in the past four seasons. The following episodes drew equally large numbers.[14] Initial praise from television reviewers was almost unanimous for the "emotionally compelling" and "brilliant" series, which most labelled a documentary. One critic hailed it as "searingly emotional yet ruthlessly unsentimental." Another described it as "the kind of television that should give us hope as we face the current threat to our survival as a nation." And still another commented: "Valour Deserves a Medal."[15]

But there was significant disapproval from one segment of the population. Many Canadian veterans thought the series, especially "Death by Moonlight" and, to a lesser extent, "In Desperate Battle," was biased, inaccurate, and even defamatory. The fallout was almost immediate and gained momentum as the veterans organized. Instrumental in this was Cliff Chadderton, chairman of the National Council of Veteran Associations and CEO of the War Amps of Canada. Chadderton liked the Hong Kong episode but railed against the other two. He bought ads in the print media urging veterans and the public to write letters of complaint.[16] In a repeat airing of the series on CBC *Newsworld* at the end of March, the CBC unsuccessfully attempted to stem the criticism by following "Death by Moonlight" with a panel consisting of Brian McKenna and two Bomber Command veterans.[17]

The production team moved quickly to defend these challenges. Chadderton was dealt with by Galafilm's sending to newspapers across

Canada a response to his ad, accusing him of political correctness and of being opposed to a free press. The news release also pointed out that Chadderton had praised the first episode, about Hong Kong, and suggested his later criticism may have been the result of pressure from his former military superiors.[18] Gelbart also provided to the CBC a list of key informational and talking points, specifically about Bomber Command. Among them was the claim that the history of the bombing campaign and the controversy over Arthur Harris was not new – in fact, it was well known in the United Kingdom.[19]

The affair had come to the attention of Jack Marshall, chairman of the Senate Subcommittee on Veterans Affairs (of the Standing Senate Committee on Social Affairs, Science and Technology). Marshall himself was a veteran not only of the Second World War but also of battles with the media over interpretations of episodes in Canadian military history. In 1985, he led an inquiry into the NFB film *The Kid Who Couldn't Miss* (1983), a work debunking the stellar record and reputation of First World War Canadian flying ace Billy Bishop. The subcommittee charged that one of the problems with the film, also created under the auspices of Adam Symansky, was that, in some cases, words spoken by the actors that were supposed to be authentic were not. Marshall successfully lobbied to get the NFB to attach to the film a disclaimer that it was not a documentary but a docudrama.[20] With *The Valour and the Horror*, the senator declared that his subcommittee would hold similar hearings as to its authenticity. His reasoning was that the CBC had provided to the filmmakers a forum to present their interpretation of the historic events in question, so the veterans and others who opposed the film deserved one too.[21]

The production team members consolidated forces. CBC staff conducted an internal review of the complaints in view of the research and documentation provided by the producers. The CBC and the NFB also hired independent researchers to review the main issues under criticism and to further investigate the most contentious ones. The researchers conducted the work at libraries and archives in Canada and Britain, and they interviewed historians. The results were assembled and given to the senior CBC team to be reviewed with the producers. This information was to be printed in a booklet in which each point of major criticism would be addressed in detail and with documentation, and with a full outline of the original historical research process for the production of the series.[22] In addition, the CBC put in place an "on-going response management group" to coordinate responses and interviews with Galafilm and the NFB, including their responses to the senate subcommittee, the CRTC, and the CBC ombudsman. The group included a staff person responsible for ensuring that all was handled smoothly. A weekly information report and conference call allowed all participants to be updated on new developments and to coordinate next steps.[23]

The production team promptly denounced the Senate hearings, with Galafilm characterizing them as part of the censorship campaign that would result in a chill against similar works.[24] A chorus of media professionals and others joined in the condemnation, some from unexpected quarters. Cliff Chadderton and Jack Granatstein were critical of the series or specific episodes, but they felt that Senate involvement was not appropriate.[25] Chadderton refused an invitation to appear before Marshall's subcommittee, complaining that its investigations would deflect attention from the problems he had outlined in his submission to the CBC ombudsman and the CRTC. Marshall forged on and held two sets of hearings, one each in the summer and fall. The senators heard from an array of witnesses, including veterans and veterans' representatives, Arnie Gelbart and Brian McKenna, and historians both supportive and not supportive of the series.

Chadderton was right: the Senate activities galvanized public discourse, and questions about the series drowned in debates about the roles and responsibilities of the Senate. The hearings and the reaction to them also helped legitimize the filmmakers' claims of censorship. This obscured much of the information that emerged from the hearings about the more complex and nuanced aspects of the production. Communications scholar David Taras has examined the aftermath of *The Valour and the Horror* as a case study in determining who or what has the most influence over media production, and he rightly characterized the senate proceedings as "an exercise in power."[26] But Taras failed to note that the broadcast of a primetime series on CBC television is also an exercise in power. The kind of access, privilege, and support that the CBC afforded the filmmakers brings with it a responsibility that they be as subject to scrutiny as the historical actors covered in the series.

To the surprise of few, Marshall's final report denounced *The Valour and the Horror*. Its two main chapters examined the Bomber Command and the Normandy episodes, and a third outlined the views of the subcommittee on the roles and responsibilities of the CBC and the NFB. Here the subcommittee recommended that the NFB produce and distribute with the series a pamphlet that would provide more accurate information about the featured wartime campaigns. Another recommendation was that, for similar programs in the future, the NFB appoint subject experts to ensure "accuracy and balance." However, for now, the subcommittee called for all videocassettes of *The Valour and the Horror* to carry a disclaimer identifying the series as "a docudrama only partly based on fact."[27]

None of this came to fruition. Indeed, the report got less attention than it might have done because, while the subcommittee was in the throes of the fall hearings, the filmmakers received another, more substantial setback, in the form of a draft report from the CBC ombudsman.[28] Back in May, Gérard Veilleux asked the ombudsman to conduct a review of the series. The task fell to William Morgan, a long-time CBC journalist and the first to hold this new office in Toronto. For his assessment he consulted five historians, including Sydney Wise and David Bercuson, each of whom he asked to write a report on the series. British historian Denis Richards provided a report only on the Bomber Command episode. On the recommendation of the producers Morgan also consulted historians Stephen Harris and Carl Vincent on the Bomber Command and Hong Kong episodes respectively. The filmmakers said later that Harris and Vincent were generally supportive. Morgan, on the other hand, reported that Harris and Vincent agreed with some aspects of the programs but thought others were inaccurate. Wise and Bercuson, in their reports, maintained that the producers excluded important contextual information, ignored evidence and perspectives contrary to the series' main arguments, and allowed imbalance and inaccuracies to go unchecked.[29]

Morgan began his own summary report with definitions of accuracy, integrity, and fairness as laid out in CBC's *Journalistic Policy*. Accuracy meant that neither the language nor the visuals could be misleading or false. It was not a matter of just ensuring that what was onscreen was based on fact, it was also a matter of ensuring that all the pertinent facts were present. Integrity called for the information to be truthful, not distorted or biased. Fairness referred to the balanced and ethical presentation of the relevant facts and points of view.[30] Within the framework of these basic principles, Morgan stated that, while *The Valour and the Horror* was of considerable merit as a whole, it was in some respects "flawed," and it did not meet CBC standards.

Morgan wrote that the stories seemed to have been tailored to fit an already-decided-upon thesis – that the leaders or main decision makers in each episode were incompetents or villains ready to sacrifice those serving under them. There were a number of inaccuracies or misleading inferences throughout the series, and important information and context (e.g., on the bombing campaign and the state of precision bombing at the time) were left out. Another issue was the dramatization, which, in this documentary series, was not properly identified according to CBC policy. Among the most damaging of Morgan's findings was that, in several instances, the words spoken by the costumed actors, as in *The Kid Who Couldn't Miss*, were either taken out of context or not taken verbatim from their real-life counterparts.[31]

Veilleux officially released Morgan's report on 10 November 1992. The filmmakers, who earlier had been given a draft copy, released their response to it the same day. In it they criticized the ombudsman's process and procedures, including his choice of historians as consultants. They countered most of his claims.[32] The two documents, along with a news release from Veilleux with an apology to any offended viewers, triggered a renewed outpouring of opinion from all quarters. This included: a letter from Morgan to Veilleux, reiterating his original conclusions; a petition signed by a thousand-member group of CBC employees, including Mark Starowicz and Peter Mansbridge, that CBC upper management was pandering to the Senate and that the procedures followed by the ombudsman would lead to a "chill on controversial documentary production and journalism in general"; a letter from Veilleux to the *Globe and Mail* and his own staff, defending himself against charges that he had not been supportive of the filmmakers; a letter from Bercuson and Wise to Veilleux, calling on him to release their reports; and a volley of opinion from journalists, veterans, historians, and other members of the public, both supportive and not supportive of the ombudsman and his report.[33]

Ombudsman Morgan found himself vilified by some of his colleagues. Veilleux, supportive of the McKennas in the beginning, was compelled to abide by Morgan's findings. This was especially galling to the filmmakers because the CBC board of directors was mostly critical of the series as well. So, although they enjoyed the support of senior journalists and managers in the corporation, this left them with few allies in the upper echelons of the CBC. Bercuson and Wise, failing to get the CBC to publicly release their reports, published them themselves, together and in book form.[34] As for those in the media, many (but not all) criticized CBC management for succumbing to the pressures of censorship.[35]

The one relevant agency not heard from on the matter was the CRTC, and, in December it awarded to the filmmakers a kind of vindication. The mandate of the commission was to consider complaints only within the terms of the Broadcasting Act and the Television Broadcasting Regulations. From this perspective, its officers examined the three main issues they considered to be the basis of the complaints: historical accuracy, balance, and dramatization. On the question of historical accuracy, the commissioners determined that the competing claims of accuracy (on the part of the filmmakers) and inaccuracy (on the part of their critics) cancelled each other out. Since both sides were able to amass credible evidence, "Some doubts will have to remain unsolved."[36]

Of matters pertaining to balance, the commissioners wrote that the range of CBC programming over the past few years would provide "a constant viewer" with other interpretations on matters similar to those in The Valour and the Horror. This was because, in the few years leading up to 1995, many commemorative pieces about the war were being televised. Therefore, the point of view of The Valour and the Horror would be balanced overall by exposure to similar CBC programs with alternate points of view. Dramatization was a non-issue as the demarcation in the series between the dramatic and documentary portions seemed obvious. In sum, the commissioners noted that their duty was to uphold freedom of expression but that, on the public airwaves, this freedom came with certain responsibilities. In terms of the Broadcasting Act and the Regulations, these responsibilities had not been breached.[37]

The Valour and the Horror: Documentary Sources in Dramatized History

Television production practices and the realities they obscure are not evident to the average television viewer, but there are factors upon which viewers rely and that create trust in the integrity of a documentary or work of journalism. The makers of *The Valour and the Horror* introduced their series as containing no fiction. In other words, they promised that the content was a realistic telling of the events as far as they could be known. Also, audiences would have faith in the content of the series because Brian and Terence McKenna were experienced CBC journalists and producers. Although Brian no longer worked at the CBC, Terence was readily identifiable with CBC news and documentaries. If the McKennas said there was no fiction in their films and that their research was "'bullet proof,'" viewers would be inclined to believe it.[38] Finally, returning to what Bill Nichols has written about the various ways to define a documentary, audience trust in the authenticity of the series rested in part upon the reputation of the CBC as a national public broadcaster, supported by and accountable to the public. The accuracy and reliability of past CBC documentary programming on Canadian history had only rarely been publicly challenged.

By the time *The Valour and the Horror* went to air, CBC documentary programs were subject to pre-broadcast internal reviews based on criteria like controversiality, fairness, and balance.[39] After the broadcast, it was this question of balance that was of special concern to the ombudsman and to the CRTC. The CRTC found that the series satisfied the balance requirement of the Broadcasting Act because its point of view was offset by those of other CBC programming about the war. Yet there had been no recent CBC television programs dealing with the same specific issues as those dealt with in *The Valour and the Horror*. And if any were broadcast afterwards, none was afforded the same prominence in terms of funding, resources, and time slot. The ombudsman's conclusion that the series was faulty, on the other hand, was based on criteria like controversiality, fairness, and balance as outlined in the *Journalistic Policy*. Balance was supposed to be inherent within the work itself: "'Programs dealing with an issue of substantial controversy on a one-time basis should give adequate recognition to the range of opinion on the subject.'"[40]

From the early days of television this very issue, as it pertained to NFB documentaries meant for CBC broadcast, needled CBC staff. Sometimes the response by CBC staff to an NFB documentary they deemed imbalanced was to reject the work outright, but in at least one instance they attached to it a qualifying statement. With *l'Acadie, l'Acadie ?!?* (1971), an NFB film profiling Acadian students in Moncton, the CBC preceded it with a statement that it was not balanced and made "no attempt to show all sides of a complex situation."[41] In 1982, the CBC rejected the NFB short documentary *If You Love This Planet* for the same reason. This film featured physician and anti-nuclear activist Helen Caldicott, and it went on to win an Oscar.[42] Knowlton Nash confirmed that, during his tenure at Information Programming, the CBC was not as enamoured as was the NFB with point-of-view pieces. According to Nash, one problem was that it was often not made evident whether the piece was actually taking a specific point of view.[43]

In fact, after the broadcast of *The Valour and the Horror*, the CBC appointed a task force to review existing policies on the production of documentaries and recommend guidelines for the same, specifically point-of-view documentaries. The team, led by Mark Starowicz, only saw "'point-of-view' advocacy documentaries" as potentially problematic. These were the works, like *If You Love This Planet*, that were contentious and that would mark a departure from regular programming, but they could still be accepted under certain conditions. Among these, the work should be of particular excellence, be accompanied by a statement that it is a work of opinion, and be followed immediately by a presentation showing alternate perspectives. CBC staff should ensure that the work was not financed by special interests and that no CBC employee "normally associated in the public's mind with CBC information programs" was involved.[44]

The task force identified another type of documentary, based on the work of an authority or expert (e.g., Kenneth Clark's *Civilization*), that could be judged on quality and on the merits of the person featured as the recognized authority in his or her field. A third type involved works of a personalized nature ("personalized journalism"), which only had to adhere to the *Journalistic Policy*. According to the task force, these first three categories made up only around 5 percent of the documentaries broadcast. The rest were "journalistic documentaries," which also only had to meet the usual tests of the *Journalistic Policy*, whether they were "investigative, revisionist," or "controversial."[45] This seemed to be the category in which *The Valour and the Horror* would have been classified. But Ivan Fecan, then CBC vice-president of arts and entertainment, suggested that the major reason for the controversy was that "it was never platformed as an essay or a point-of-view piece."[46]

Like the makers of *The Valour and the Horror*, Marcel Ophüls and Claude Lanzmann knew they were disturbing national collective memories with their films. But the French used different presentation methods than the Canadians. Neither Ophüls nor Lanzmann dramatized events with actors. They relied almost entirely on interviews with eyewitnesses conducted in the style of what Bill Nichols has described as the "participatory mode" of documentary. Viewers are always aware of the presence of the camera and of the filmmakers themselves (Lanzmann regularly appears onscreen). They hear the questions put to the interviewees, and, in Lanzmann's *Shoah*, hear even the interpreter's translation of the questions and answers.[47] This lends clarity and context to the accounts as it reveals them as responses to specific questions rather than as unprovoked statements. In *The Valour and the Horror*, the viewer only occasionally hears the questions put to the veterans.

In *The Valour and the Horror* the primary means of telling the story is the narration, supported by the lines of the actors, the words of the veterans, the images, and the sound. Ophüls included some narration, and some period still and moving images, but Lanzmann employed none of these techniques. In *The Valour and the Horror*, the series' dramatic background music, which heightens the emotion and drama, is absent from the French films. The only other method that Lanzmann employed, other than the interview, was to visit the scenes where some of the terrible events took place. Lanzmann, like the makers of *The*

Valour and the Horror, understood that merely showing these locations onscreen lent authority and immediacy to the account.[48] These more basic methods used by the French filmmakers do not preclude distortion of the past; indeed, Ophüls faced criticism for imbalance and omission in his work. But by eschewing heavy narration and overt dramatization, and by conducting the interviews in a more transparent fashion, they at least provided more information to the viewer about the constructed nature of their respective films.

One of the key problems with *The Valour and the Horror* is the dramatization in what the filmmakers claimed was a documentary. A similar issue had come up before. The CBC production of *The Tar Sands* (1977), a docudrama about the negotiations over the tar sands in Alberta, raised hackles over its combination of realism and drama. The premier of Alberta, Peter Lougheed, sued the CBC over his portrayal and won an out-of-court settlement. Another case is *Duplessis* (1978), the serial drama from the French network on the life of the former premier of Quebec. In the House of Commons, the member of Parliament for Richmond called upon the CBC to issue an apology for its errors in interpretation and damage to reputations.[49] And finally *Riel* (1979), a heavily promoted and expensive CBC drama about the titular character, drew scathing criticism from a number of quarters. Reviewers complained about its gross distortion of fact while maintaining pretence to authenticity, having even partnered with the CAAE to produce an accompanying educational pamphlet entitled "Riel: An Experiment in Learning with Entertainment."[50] None of these works were documentaries, yet the dramatization of real people and some blatant departure from known events crossed a line. One scholar has suggested that the type of dramatization in *The Tar Sands* "cast[s] doubt on the rights of journalists to interpret Canada's past and its living history." But if this were true, it had no lasting effect.[51]

For *The Valour and the Horror*, the CRTC examined the use of drama in terms of whether or not the dramatized parts were distinctive enough from the documentary parts. The CRTC determined that they were, and the ombudsman determined that they were not. Most of the scenes with actors are indeed fairly easily distinguishable from the rest of the narrative, and the narrator takes pains in the opening to point out that, in some instances, actors are reading the words of real people. Morgan stressed, however, that the CBC's own policy discouraged drama in journalism because it might make it hard for viewers to assess the nature of the information onscreen, that it might "lend the appearance of reality to hypothesis."[52] This is the main reason dramatization is frowned upon in other forms of journalism (e.g., the news).

Aside from the Senate subcommittee's prescription that *The Valour and the Horror* should carry a docudrama label, the reviewing bodies paid little attention to the soundness of the series overall as a documentary. Although there was supposed to be internal oversight on documentaries regarding journalistic principles, there was no set CBC policy for the categorization of programs as drama, documentary, or docudrama. Dramatization suggests an element of imagination, and depending on the desired effect and audience for a program, sometimes the dramatics were promoted, and sometimes they were downplayed. The CBC and the NFB wanted *Canada's Sweetheart*, for example, to be known not as a docudrama, as some in the press had labelled it despite its documentary elements, but as a drama.[53] Yet the makers of *The Valour and the Horror*, which was also part documentary and part drama, insisted that their work was not a docudrama but a documentary.[54]

Indeed, in the early days of television, both the CBC and the NFB described history programs using techniques similar to those used in *The Valour and the Horror* as dramas, documentaries, or docudramas. The CBC referred to *The National Dream* as a documentary mainly because of the potential problems with the Drama unit and with ACTRA, but Pierre Berton, in his own first episode outlines, called them "dramatized documentaries." Berton did not seem to mind how the series was officially defined as long as the line between drama and documentary was made clear to the viewer. Hence his warning to Jim Murray during the writing phase: "It is essential," he wrote, "that our audience knows exactly what we are doing with the facts: when we are dramatizing from historical evidence and when we are actually using the words that people spoke at the time."[55]

The ombudsman, the Senate subcommittee, and certain veterans' groups paid special attention to this use of real testimony. Morgan found that, with Air Chief Marshal Harris in particular, the producers did not always stick to the historical record.[56] For one statement made by the actor who played Harris, Morgan could only find part of the quote in Harris's memoir. When asked about it, the producers noted that the first part of the quote had been taken directly from Harris's memoir and that the second part was a summary of the text that followed.[57] But the onscreen truncation had somewhat altered the meaning of the written text. Moreover, there was no indication onscreen that the statement had been truncated. Another example is in the chilling scene in the same episode, when the narrator explains that Harris didn't mind killing people. The actor playing Harris appears and says that, when a policeman once pulled him over for speeding with the warning that he could kill someone, he replied, "young man, I kill thousands of people every night." Harris did not actually write or record these words. Rather, one of his crew members recounted it as a rumour about Harris, that he was pulled over and replied to the officer that he killed "hundreds of people every night."[58]

Elsewhere in the episode, the narrator augments Harris's scenes and statements to give them further meaning. One scene has Harris displaying scepticism about the use and precision of the "smart" bombs used in the Dambusters raid. The raid was at night, and since this was a new type of bomb and technique, which required flying at relatively low altitudes, Harris says that the lives of his men were "too precious to be thrown away in this manner." The narrator then offers that the bombs were used anyway because "the public relations side benefits of the plan were undeniable." The potential dangers in thus depicting Harris, though already a figure of some controversy in the United Kingdom, were obvious well before air time and not just to the CBC legal department. A CBC internal document shows that Darce Fardy, noting his approval of a payment for the Bomber Command episode, asked that Arnie Gelbart ensure that the dramatic scenes be identified as such. He wanted claims backed up with solid evidence, especially since Harris was depicted as such an "S.O.B."[59]

In another case, lines delivered by an actor had not been cleared by his living counterpart. Former flight lieutenant Robert Dale, having had no contact with the producers, was surprised to learn there was an actor playing him in "Death by Moonlight." Dale wrote to the CBC that he was very concerned about it because it made him appear to be supporting the attack on Arthur Harris, when he did not.[60] During the Senate hearings, Brian McKenna replied to a question about this by saying that they had not been able to determine whether or not Dale was still living but that his words in the film were taken from quotations in a book by British historian Martin Middlebrook. However, in the book, Middlebrook only briefly described Dale's reconnaissance activities and did not quote him directly.[61]

Kay Christie, portrayed by an actor in the "Savage Christmas" episode, was a nursing sister in Hong Kong during the war. A researcher for the production interviewed Christie about her experiences. But after viewing the series she complained about what she considered to be an inaccurate depiction. The Christie actor appears in the middle of the sequence describing the events at St Stephen's makeshift hospital, where, the narrator and actors explain, the Japanese raped the nursing staff, murdering most of them along with the wounded Allied soldiers. Christie, however, had not worked at St Stephen's.[62]

In other instances the actors make key statements based on scant or somewhat unreliable documentation. In "Death by Moonlight," the actor playing the English girl and WAAF member Mary Moore (real name Dups), nicknamed "Bubbles," tells of her romantic relationship with "Pierre," a doomed French Canadian trapper turned tail-gunner. From the transcript of a pre-broadcast interview conducted with Dups, it appears that Pierre's background was made up of elements of two men with whom she had merely had an acquaintance. The story of Pierre and his dramatic demise in a bomber, which the actor recounts to great effect onscreen as an actual occurrence, appears based on a story and poem that Dups had written and supplied to the production team.[63]

These written accounts and interviews were important supporting documentation used in the creation of *The Valour and the Horror*, although in some instances they were not substantiated by other sources. In the Normandy episode, the depiction of one difficult confrontation, between Brigadier Cunningham and a drinking and agitated General Keller, has the junior officer deploring further attacks as murder. The narrator states that Cunningham is then fired. The scene also stands out because it is one of the few in the series in which the historical characters have any exchange of words (however brief). While it may well have happened as portrayed, the scene is based only on interviews with Cunningham.[64]

Another example of something that was not substantiated by supporting sources is the arresting claim, made in the same episode, by the actor playing Corporal Joseph LeBouthillier. The actor speaks of approaching the beach at Normandy on a landing craft, under orders to shoot anyone who didn't move forward. Veterans later protested that this was not the case. When Morgan requested evidence for this statement, the series' researcher noted that the source for it was an anecdote from Mr LeBouthillier.[65] He was correct, as this veteran had published the same information in a book of memoirs about wartime experiences. Recollections like this were used throughout the series, and, while unlikely, this one may have been accurate. But with other veterans rebutting these recollections, Brian McKenna complained that, even after a half-century, "many people still rely on their anecdotal memories."[66]

Similarly, a CBC internal document shows that, in defence of the criticisms, the CBC publicist wanted to call into question the contention that history could "only be told by people who lived it as is implied by the series' critics."[67] Yet the producers themselves promoted the series on this very premise, and the main role played by the two featured veterans in each episode came from the authority they had derived from having "lived it." A CBC audience survey for episodes 1 and 3 showed that viewers ranked the veterans as the most compelling feature of these episodes.[68] These men willingly participated in the programs, and the words they spoke were their own. It was difficult for anyone, even another veteran, to challenge their accounts as they were their personal, unique memories of a specific time and place. They were the unassailable voices of lived experience that critics of the series were careful to avoid questioning. Historian Edward Linenthal, writing about what happened with the *Enola Gay* exhibition and other attempts at commemorating the Second World War in the United States, has described the sorts of tensions that exist between the commemorative voice, which is often based on "I was there," and the historical voice, which dissects motives and factors only revealed in hindsight.[69] With *The Valour and the Horror* it was not that simple. In this instance there were competing and overlapping versions of both the commemorative voice and the historical voice.

Until the 1970s, eyewitnesses onscreen were uncommon in CBC Canadian history documentaries, but it did happen. One example is from 1959, "Winnipeg General Strike 1919," and from 1962, "Portraits of the Thirties" with Jack Saywell. The increasing use of eyewitnesses onscreen paralleled the growing interest of scholars in oral history both as a field of study and as a practice. In 1969, British sociologist Paul Thompson and his colleagues founded the journal *Oral History*, the first dedicated to the field.[70]

American radio broadcaster Studs Terkel made the practice of oral history famous with his books *Division Street: America* (1967), about a cross-section of people living in Chicago, and *Hard Times: An Oral History of the Great Depression* (1970). Television producers recognized the potential of oral testimony to connect emotionally with audiences. By the 1992 broadcast of *The Valour and the Horror*, interviews with eyewitnesses who had lived through dramatic events had become the gold standard for television histories. It even began to influence the topics chosen for production. In the years following *Images of Canada* and *The National Dream*, CBC television mainly stuck to stories for which eyewitnesses could be interviewed rather than venturing too far into the past.

Eyewitnesses on television speak only about their own experiences, or, because of the selective nature of television production, they can speak for the general experience of a group as well. Thus, they can emit more authority than an individual normally would.[71] By the 1990s, the television journalist, coupled with the onscreen eyewitness, had become the new historical authorities on CBC television. Historian Michael Frisch has commented on this turn in the idea of historical authority in relation to oral history. After the publication of Terkel's *Hard Times*, Frisch noticed that a number of critics wrote positive reviews of Terkel's book, viewing it as a kind of counter-history. The critics seemed to indicate that the interviewees, unlike the work of most historians, provided an unmediated route to the past and told it like it really was.[72]

Like any form of primary source evidence, the context in which oral history is produced is as important as the content itself. But, on television, the context is often not made evident. Frisch has also observed that few of the critics who wrote reviews of *Hard Times* recognized that the interviews reflected not only a personal experience of the past but also the context of the time in which the individual gave the interview. In Frisch's words, it was "the degree to which they [the interviews] involve historical statements rather than, or in addition to, historical evidence."[73] Along with the context, often lost on the television audience is the passage of time and the number of times a recollection is repeated, both of which have a significant impact on the information. Even Terkel wrote that the interviews in his book were "about Time as well as a time."[74]

Complicating matters in *The Valour and the Horror* is the fact that the onscreen eyewitnesses, with the exception of the veterans, are played by actors. Unlike the veterans, who are clearly older men speaking about their past experiences, the actors in the series represent veterans as they appeared in the 1940s. But the words they speak were taken from interviews or written materials often set down long after the events, when memories had been influenced by public discourse. Kay Christie's interview is an example. Onscreen, the Christie actor delivers an excerpt from Christie's interview to great effect. In this interview, Christie talks about how the Canadian soldiers going to Hong Kong had been so poorly trained that they had to be taught how to load a rifle en route. The ombudsman, after reviewing the transcript of this interview, noted that the producers should have included the rest of what Christie had said, which was that the soldiers had not been sent to help fight but merely for garrison duty. The producers replied that Christie meant these comments to be ironic. Morgan responded that he did not pick up this sense of irony from the transcript.[75]

But even if Christie intended the irony, she could only have done so with hindsight, knowing what had happened to the contingent. Over a fifty-year span, memories become distorted by knowledge of what has happened in the intervening years and by the human desire to make meaning out of significant events. As oral historian Alessandro Portelli has observed, the memory of an event and the reasons for its distortion from actual fact are often as meaningful as the event itself.[76] When eyewitnesses are interviewed onscreen, as with Doug Harvey, Ken Brown, and the other veterans, the time gap between the events in question and the interview is obvious given their age and the changed state of the environments where the events took place. Clearly, the words they speak are words that belong to them as aging veterans, not as young men fighting in the war. Similarly, the words Christie spoke as an elderly woman are not the words she could have spoken at thirty years old. Taking her words as an elderly woman and putting them into the mouth of a thirty-year-old actor, in a period setting, obscures this important aspect of oral testimony.

The series has one exception to actors visually depicting people at the age they were during wartime: the physicist, Freeman Dyson. As emerged in the Senate hearings, in 1943 Dyson turned twenty years old and held a junior post at Bomber Command. Yet the actor playing him and delivering his damning analysis appears as a professional of at least thirty-five. While actors play the other witnesses at the age they were during the war, Dyson's portrayal draws upon his later years, after he had become a renowned physicist.[77] Had the producers represented him like the others, as a nineteen- or twenty-year-old, his assessment of the bombing campaign would have come across much differently. It compounded the problem of putting words spoken or written many years later into the mouths of actors situated in historic settings.

Historian Graham Carr has examined the controversy over the broadcast of *The Valour and the Horror* by reviewing who felt they had the authority to say what, and what that authority was based upon. Carr has shown that, before making any claim to authoritative knowledge, all the players had to establish their credentials in some way.[78] The filmmakers did this by drawing on their experience as investigative journalists and by specifically positioning themselves as *not* being historians. "The historians screwed up in telling us about the war," said Brian McKenna, "If you fail to tell the whole story, then you're lying."[79] And "All of us ... are proud of how we told the story, unburied the past, shook up the powerful, and showed historians that journalists and other citizens had not only a right to question the official version of history but a duty."[80] Again, it was the journalist as watchdog, providing a public service on behalf of the people.

McKenna may have been right that the historiography on Canadians in the Second World War was due for some revision. This is the fate of all historical topics. But he seemed to ignore the importance of the means to his end, of the misleading effects of the methods used to present his conclusions. He failed to recognize his own power as a respected member of the media and someone with privileged access to CBC decision makers. Finally, he appeared unaware that historians had already been questioning the "official" history he claimed to have debunked – indeed, he and his colleagues actually used some of their works in order to produce the television series. With *The Valour and the Horror* the precarious relationship between historians and producers of history on CBC television, to that point rarely brought to such public attention, came to be front and centre.

Brian McKenna said to the Senate subcommittee that the controversy over the series was "about history and who gets to tell it," and "about truth and who gets to interpret it."[81] But was it? The filmmakers had ample resources to produce the series, and they enjoyed access to a much wider audience than the typical professional historian. From the beginning, the filmmakers indeed took pains to identify themselves as journalists who would tell "the unvarnished truth": "We were out to do the reporting on World War Two which was never done."[82] It was the journalist speaking as gatekeeper, as someone with a special ability and responsibility to decide what was news and how to report it.[83] It was not about who tells history but about the soundness of the history itself, and how audiences were able to assess it as such. It did not appear to occur to McKenna that reporting in 1992 about events that took place fifty years earlier might involve some different thinking than would reporting on contemporary events. The idea that it was "about Time as well as a time" seemed lost.

The makers of *The Valour and the Horror* defined their methods less by explaining them than by making claims about what historians were not doing. As media historian David Mindich has observed, journalists who claim to be objective and to be simply reporting the facts as they are often do so by claiming bias in others.[84] Although journalism has always been characterized by a range of practices encompassing "'news' to 'views,'" many journalists continued to believe in the possibility of complete objectivity and the inviolability of facts, at least in terms of news reporting.[85] The Canadian historical profession, on the other hand, had long acknowledged not only the impossibility of complete objectivity but also the pitfalls of interpreting the archival record from a much later vantage point.[86]

"Historians don't understand," said McKenna, "what we journalists understand fundamentally, that if you ask the toughest questions everybody will be served and there will be liberation."[87] Yet professional historians were already asking these kinds of questions, and they were increasingly writing about women, Indigenous people, and the rank and file over high-ranking military. They would not have recognized themselves in McKenna's characterizations. The historians especially denigrated by the filmmakers, however, were the "official" and "conservative military" ones, who were guilty of multiple sins, including worrying unduly about "offending sensibilities and ruining reputations." They had done a bad job writing about Canadian involvement in the wars, and those at the Directorate of History at the Department of National Defence took too long to produce the official history of the RCAF.[88]

It was by now the quintessential (albeit, in reality, mythological) stance of the crusading journalist going it alone, à la Woodward and Bernstein. It was the idea of the investigative reporter with a unique responsibility to challenge official stories and to uncover malfeasance wherever it occurred.[89] As journalism scholar Christopher Daly has noted, by the late 1970s, in the Watergate era and with the proliferation of television news, journalists came to believe that politicians were inherently suspect, "guilty until proven innocent."[90] This extended to other authority figures and, for the makers of *The Valour and the Horror*, it seemed to include historians. Some, they claimed, were even party to covering up military secrets. This was the accusation levelled at Charles Stacey and Sydney Wise, and the subject of Brian McKenna's final "shocking story" in his presentation to the Senate.[91] McKenna and his colleagues had actually used Stacey's official history for the main theme of the episode. They praised it in advance of the broadcast as a "pungent assessment of Canadian leadership in Normandy and his critical evaluation of Canadian training."[92] But this new story had Stacey conspiring to hide information related to the same events.

This involved Stacey and Wise in 1972, when Stacey had left the Directorate of History and Wise was his successor. McKenna claimed that the two purposely suppressed a report about Operation Spring, including the events at Verrières Ridge, that had been written soon after they occurred. He based his statement primarily on a letter Stacey had written to Wise, telling him that, after the war, Generals Foulkes and Simonds ordered the report destroyed because they could not agree on its evaluation of what had happened. "All the copies were destroyed," wrote Stacey, "except by some strange mischance, one." He also said that Wise might be able to find that copy in his office at the Directorate. He further advised that, if a brother of Philip Griffin, the leader of the attack at Verrières Ridge, should come to see Wise, Wise should probably not let him see the report. When the series' researchers reviewed the report years later, there was a note on it saying that it was "not to be released to non-DND researchers." This was an example, according to McKenna, of the kind of cover-up that was corrected by *The Valour and the Horror*.

Wise refuted the accusation in letters to the editor of the *Montreal Gazette* and the *Globe and Mail*, and in his later book about the affair. He explained that, while McKenna had interpreted Stacey's actions as part of a conspiracy to suppress the report, Stacey's comment that all the copies but one had been destroyed meant that he had actually saved a copy. On Stacey's suggestion that Griffin's brother should not see the report, Wise surmised that Stacey probably thought it would have been painful for Griffin's family to see since the report inferred that the young major had mishandled the attack. In any case, said Wise, the brother had never come to see him. He added that, although Stacey's report was classified at the time of their exchange, it had long since been freely available to researchers.[93]

The claims of the filmmakers that the series revealed such secrets and cover-ups mirrored the claims made in the series. Morgan wrote in his report that there was no conclusion about secrecy and that where there *were* secrets, in a wartime situation this seemed understandable. And, even of these, most had long since been revealed.[94] Morgan, in order to write his report, had given to the filmmakers a list of questions asking about their sources. One of these questions related to the reason for their claim of "cover-up" concerning the debacle in Normandy. In preparing the responses to Morgan, internal correspondence shows that one member of the production team wondered if the team could really support the claim of cover-up since historian and former lieutenant colonel in the Canadian army, John English, had clearly condemned the Canadian leadership in his book *The Canadian Army and the Normandy Campaign: A Study of Failure in High Command.*

In fact, the production team had listed English in the credits. Yet when he and two other historians later criticized the series to the Senate subcommittee, they became part of "a parade of minor historians, many of them with personal axes to grind against the filmmakers."[95] On the question of the cover-up, the production team researcher proposed that their answer to Morgan could be that English's book was extremely specialized and would be difficult for anyone to locate.[96] Indeed, much of the material identified as evidence in response to Morgan's inquiries was based on the existing work of historians. This work, taken from a number of sources, provided much of the series' foundation.[97]

According to the filmmakers, the significance of the entire controversy lay in journalistic freedom. When the CBC ombudsman issued his report, his findings were merely an example of the new "chill" engulfing documentary filmmakers and journalists in Canada.[98] But if there was a chill, it did not seem to affect the makers of *The Valour and the Horror*. In March of 1993 they were rewarded for their troubles with a round of Gemini awards, among them the prize for best documentary series. Mark Starowicz, who later described Brian McKenna as one of his oldest friends, was appointed in January of that year as executive producer of television documentaries.[99] According to McKenna, Starowicz was supportive of him and his production team in their determination "to continue making war films." He agreed that they should do a new series, this time about the Canadian navy.[100]

It was clear, however, that some lessons had been learned. For the two-hour *War at Sea* project, Starowicz's new documentary unit outlined a set of standards early in the production process. This included directives that the scenes with actors would be clearly distinguishable from the documentary portions, that any edits to the original source material would be made evident ("there should never be an implication of a run-on sentence when there isn't one"), and that consent needed to be obtained from living persons to use excerpts from their memoirs. Finally, both Galafilm and the CBC would engage independent historians as advisors.[101]

For this last purpose the CBC seconded to the documentary unit Gene Allen, a journalist with a PhD in Canadian history. His job was to verify sources, conduct research, maintain editorial standards, and liaise with the independent historians "on issues of interpretation, context and factual accuracy."[102] The pre-broadcast precautions in terms of public relations were substantial. They included an internal circular of twenty possible questions that might arise after broadcast and how they could be answered. All were directly related to *The Valour and the Horror*.[103] One of the advising historians was Marc Milner, an expert on Canadian naval history and professor at the University of New Brunswick. He wrote that the filmmakers had done an acceptable job in interpreting the available scholarship on the subject and that this scholarship was the defence should there be any public complaints about the program.[104] Although the themes and presentation style of the new series were very similar to those of *The Valour and the Horror*, there was little public criticism when *War at Sea* went to air in 1995. Brian McKenna said that now there was a new generation of historians who understood television and what filmmakers were trying to do. But he still needed a nemesis: "We can't leave the history of this country to retired military graduates or members of the Legion."[105]

The Valour and the Horror, unlike most of the previous Canadian history programs on CBC television, challenged instead of reinforced widely accepted and supported notions about the Canadian past. History must be continually revised as new sources and perspectives come to light, and, in this respect, the filmmakers' attempt to reinterpret these wartime events was perhaps a necessary one. With the Allied bombing campaigns especially, the series stimulated important debate in Canada that lasted well into the new millennium. But the means to the end are important. As Pierre Berton had cautioned the production team members of *The National Dream*, it was essential that the television audience understand what they were doing with the historical record. The television audience for *The Valour and the Horror* did not have this same opportunity.

The makers of *The Valour and the Horror* assumed the same role as content authorities that historians had assumed in earlier years. And the antagonistic feeling towards historians on the part of some television journalists, which had come to the surface during the era of *The Days before Yesterday* and *Images of Canada*, was displayed in full with *The Valour and the Horror*. But it belied their reliance on the existing work of professional historians as well as their access to public funding and the continued support of the CBC, which had delivered to them a national television audience. And although the filmmakers promoted their work as a product of journalists and specifically not of historians, it fell short either as a work of journalism or as a work of history.

5 | The One Big Story:
Canada: A People's History

Canada: A People's History

The 1995 referendum on Quebec sovereignty struck fear into the hearts of many Canadians. The first referendum in 1980 had been decisively defeated. But, in the interim, following the failure of the Meech Lake Accord and the Charlottetown Accord, and the creation of the Bloc Québécois, the sovereignty movement had gained momentum. This became starkly obvious to the federal government and the "No" side after Lucien Bouchard, former federal Canadian cabinet minister and charismatic leader of the Bloc, assumed leadership of the growing "Yes" campaign as referendum day approached. Canada ultimately won the day, but the puny margin that allowed the country to stay together created widespread anxiety and uncertainty about Canada's future.

A CBC television series on the history of Canada, produced jointly by the English and French networks, would boost morale and inject into the Canadian psyche a sense of pride and security about the country. As Canadian history programs on CBC television had already shown, nothing speaks to national unity and identity like the idea of a shared past with defining events, heroes, and symbols. The CBC would create the definitive national narrative and wrap it in a compelling television package. It would be a much needed trophy with which to substantiate claims, much as *The National Dream* had done before it, that the CBC was doing its part to "contribute to a shared national consciousness and identity" as it was set out in the new Broadcasting Act, 1991.[1]

Canada: A People's History has generated considerable scholarly review, but none has placed it within the tradition of Canadian history programs on CBC television.[2] Even with the great changes in the written history of Canada, the themes, subject matter, and interpretations show clear continuities with the earliest days of CBC television. Yet the presentation, specifically the dramatic conventions and the use of written and oral testimony, show striking changes. Like the makers of *The Valour and the Horror*, the senior team in charge of *A People's History* stressed their series as a work created by journalists, following a set of principles used in professional journalism. Yet *A People's History* was a linear narrative, beginning in the pre-contact period, with dramatic sequences at its core. It could not and did not always follow journalistic principles, at least as the producers understood them. One member of the executive team further described the series as not a "historians' history" but a "people's history," following the advertisements of the series as told by those "who lived it."[3] But it was not told by those who lived it. *A People's History* was told by the narrator, reading from a script based on secondary sources and only supported by the real words of people who had lived it.

The year 1995 also marked the beginning of another investigation into the fortunes of the CBC. The aim of the Mandate Review Committee (also known as the Juneau Committee), chaired by former CBC president Pierre Juneau, was to review the mandates of the CBC, the NFB, and Telefilm. Among its recommendations were that the CBC gradually eliminate American commercial programming and all commercial activities (except in sports programs) and maintain regional and local programming.[4] In-house talent should be maintained for news, current affairs, and sports programs, but much of the rest should come from independents, with the NFB as a "preferred supplier."[5] The committee acknowledged the difficulties characterizing the past collaboration between the NFB and the CBC but held that the NFB was still a prime producer of quality Canadian content, and it reached audiences mainly through television.[6]

Since the early 1980s, the CBC had become more invested in developing dramatic programming than documentary programming. But according to Slawko Klimkiw, executive director of network programming, with both dramatic and documentary programming, they wanted to create HBO-like "high impact boxed sets" – programs intended to create a buzz and to leave a legacy.[7] *Canada: A People's History* is a great example. It served other purposes too. In addition to its use as a counter to Quebec sovereignty, with the coming of the millennium and the well-worn connection between anniversaries and historical programming, the timing was right. And Canadian history CBC-style also satisfied concerns, like those recently raised by the Juneau Committee, about the role of the CBC as a public service broadcaster. According to the CBC's Harold Redekopp, however, around half of those who had participated in any surveys about the CBC "didn't have a clue what public television was."[8]

Finally, *A People's History* was an answer to increased competition from the now vast array of channels available, for example, the specialty channels carrying the kind of history programming once only produced by public broadcasters. Two of these were the Discovery Channel (the Canadian branch of the American Discovery Channel), launched in 1995, and History Television (the Canadian equivalent of the American The History Channel), launched in 1997. Both employed former CBC executives in top positions: at Discovery Channel, Trina McQueen, and at History Television, Norm Bolen. While much in their lineups turned out not to be Canadian or even history-based, they did run some good-quality history and cultural programs, and provided broadcast outlets for Canadian independent producers. These opportunities saw more independent producers paying attention to history as viable content.

Popular history outside of television, at least the kind with a national focus, was also becoming more prominent. In 1989, the largest permanent museum exhibition on the history of Canada opened at the new Canadian Museum of Civilization in Hull, Quebec. In 1992, the federal government initiated a nationwide celebration of 125 years of Confederation, reminiscent of the centennial and billed as "Canada 125." In 1997, the Dominion Institute was founded with a mission to promote better citizenship "through greater knowledge and appreciation of the Canadian story."[9] And, in 1999, Canadian businessman Charles Bronfman co-founded and endowed the Historica Foundation of Canada (Historica), a non-profit foundation for the promotion of Canadian history. Historica assumed responsibility for *The Canadian Encyclopedia* and *Heritage Minutes*, a series of filmed shorts on Canadian historical events, shown on television and theatre screens since 1991.[10]

Within this context, Mark Starowicz outlined his plan for a CBC television history of Canada. Starowicz was a respected journalist who had landed at CBC radio in 1970 and went on to produce the iconic radio program *As It Happens* and to create *Sunday Morning*. At CBC television he was the first executive producer of *The Journal*, and he remained there until its cancellation in 1992. He then moved to the television documentary unit. Starowicz wrote that the idea of a television history of Canada was not new to him, but his initial plan now was to produce a documentary series, "not intended to be didactic," that would use "conservative re-enactments." In the style of Peter Watkins's *Culloden* and Shelby Foote's *The Civil War: A Narrative* (the basis for American Ken Burns's television documentary series *The Civil War* [1990]), it would unfold in narrative form and highlight the written words of regular people "rather than a diplomatic history."[11] It would be a co-production of the English and French networks. Among other benefits, the series would answer the call from the recent CBC "Repositioning" policy for distinctive programming with branding potential. To that end, the CBC would package the series with related products: a website, a two-volume publication, and the name as a trademark for future use. Unlike *The Valour and the Horror*, there would be no challenge to conventional ideas about Canadian history, so no fear of controversy.

Like the centennial celebrations in 1967 and other big anniversaries, the approach of the millennium prompted mass reflection on the state of the country and gave rise to feelings of national kinship and pride – and not only in Canada. The BBC was producing *A History of Britain* with historian Simon Schama, and its executive producer intended it to be a "Bayeux Tapestry for the 21st Century."[12] Ken Burns felt that his *The Civil War* gave rise to "a kind of emotion and a sympathy that remind us, for example, of why we agree against all odds as a people to cohere."[13] His work helped him to explore the question, "Who are we?"[14] In the same vein, Starowicz suggested that the question "who's the 'we'?" was one of the key themes in *A People's History*: "And the 'we' shifts. In the first episode it's the Aboriginals, then the 'we' becomes the French, then you have the two defeated countries, the Loyalists and the post-conquest Quebec."[15] In neither the American nor the Canadian series was the extent of this concept explored, but both producers seemed to imagine there was a larger "we" who eventually agreed to cohere and that all, in the words of Benedict Anderson, were accepted as members of the national "fraternity."

Closer to home, Télé-Québec was also in production on a major television series, broadcast in 1997 as *Épopée en Amérique: Une histoire populaire du Québec* (Epic in America: A People's History of Quebec). With the referendum in the recent past, Starowicz was compelled to address the coincidental timing of his venture. He was not bothered by the fact that events like the Battle of the Plains of Abraham and the Lower Canada Rebellion would be duplicated in the two series, as this made sense within his centralist position. "Up until the rebellions, he said, the history of Canada and the history of Quebec were essentially the same thing."[16] The comment displays an early foundational bias of the project in that Indigenous peoples, Atlantic Canada, and the Pacific Northwest were not considered central to the early European history of the country.

The production of *Épopée en Amérique* had a bit of a history of its own. When its Quebec producers initially proposed to the NFB that they co-produce the series, the NFB turned them down. So when Film Commissioner Sandra Macdonald approached Starowicz with a $7.5 million co-production offer for his series, accusations (and denials) of federalist collusion were quick to surface.[17] According to Starowicz in his memoir of the making of *A People's History*, Macdonald thought it would be politically unwise for the NFB not to be involved in the CBC series.[18] Starowicz wrote that, over the next months, the two tried to hammer out an agreement, but it fell apart. He wrote that Adam Symansky at the NFB did not like the idea of Starowicz as sole executive producer, and both Symansky and Starowicz knew that NFB staff would not take to the idea of the CBC directing the project. For her part, Macdonald felt she could not overrule her staff on what they thought would be an unequal partnership.[19]

Despite the NFB's withdrawal, the CBC proceeded, now with the participation of Radio-Canada and the securing of Quebec journalist Louis Martin as editorial director. The idea was that the series would be produced in both English and French, and that each episode team would include at least one member from the other network. Starow-icz's early recruitment of staff included Gene Allen as director of research; Hubert Gendron as director of the Montreal-based episode teams; and Gordon Henderson (and later, Kelly Crichton) as director of the Toronto-based episode teams. These five comprised the main senior editorial group. All had worked with Starowicz in the past, as had most of the principal staff members in Toronto. Some of the producers and researchers were permanent CBC staff; others were independents hired solely for the series or for specific episodes. The official projected cost at this time was $20.5 million.[20]

Unlike *Images of Canada*, which was the first attempt at televising the history of Canada, *A People's History* was not a series upon which individual production team members imprinted their unique stamp. Each team, in most cases, consisted of two to five individuals filling the roles of director, producer, writer, and researcher. They received from the senior team a draft outline of what the episode needed to include. They adhered to a common visual style, had their films assessed at regular intervals, and had their scripts doctored and polished by the senior editorial team. Unlike some earlier CBC Canadian history programs, the team did not hire professional writers solely for that purpose, nor did they hire historians as writers or as onscreen commentators.

Deciding on the style of the series started with the senior group viewing popular works of history for television. These included *The Civil War*; *Liberty! The American Revolution* (1997); *Épopée en Amérique*; and *Culloden*.[21] The senior team decided that one person in each language would narrate the entire series. For the depiction of the time period before the age of photography, the team adopted the technique of costumed actors speaking direct to camera that appeared in *Culloden*, *Liberty!*, and *The Valour and the Horror*. For dramatization, one of the standards was *Culloden*. Starowicz admired *Culloden* and planned to use Watkins's work as the model for the central scene of the series: a re-creation of the Battle of the Plains of Abraham, which he himself would write.[22] Another model, especially useful for the depiction of the time period after the advent of photography, was *The Civil War*, which was one of the most important media events of the 1990s.[23] For visuals, *The Civil War* relied almost exclusively on period photographs, with actors in voiceover reading from original documents.

On the structure of the series, the team initially decided to break up the content into sixteen two-hour episodes. Like *The Civil War*, each episode would then be divided into "chapters."[24] Preliminary ideas for effective ways to open the series included depictions of the Battle of the Plains of Abraham and Confederation. The team eventually concluded that, since the series would be mostly chronological, the two events should occur where they did naturally in the historical timeline.[25]

After the fallout from *The Valour and the Horror* it was risky not to seek advice from professional historians. Historian Christopher Moore has described attending a planning session for the series in the spring of 1997, and a further discussion with Starowicz in which the latter suggested that he could not get anything from having a professional historian on his team that he could not get from having a discussion with one "over a beer or two."[26] Nevertheless, the team members determined that counsel would be needed. Allen contacted Ramsay Cook and Jean-Claude Robert, a historian at the Université du Québec à Montréal. He asked the two historians to submit a breakdown of how they would envision a television series of approximately sixteen two-hour episodes, roughly chronological, with the basic necessities: "Each episode needs to focus on one central event or theme ... Ideally, the central event will involve a dramatic story that can be told in narrative form, through the eyes (and in the words) of a central character or characters." Allen also wanted the historians to suggest "4 or 5 subsidiary events, themes and characters that are thematically related to the central event. One of the challenges," Allen wrote, "is to find ways of integrating 'social history' material and themes in what is essentially a narrative and character-based structure."[27]

Cook submitted an outline, roughly chronological, beginning with the diversity of cultures in the pre-contact period. Following the European arrival were themes on exploration and settlement, politics and economics, and region, class, gender, and ethnicity, the latter most evident in his suggestions for the post-nineteenth century. Here he recommended pieces dealing with regionalism and multiculturalism, the farm movement and unionism, women's fight for equality, English-French relations within Canada and Canada's relationships abroad, the welfare state, and the evolution of policy relating to Indigenous peoples. The last episode he called "The Great Debate," indicative of the "new history," which would amass all the strands.[28]

According to Allen, the outlines from Cook and Robert were valuable as general guides in making the initial content choices, but the team adopted neither in detail.[29] This was because they were not exactly chronological and would "lose a lot of narrative tension." Nor were they stories of individuals, to which the team thought television audiences would more easily relate.[30] Individuals and their stories, as in novels and reportage, often provide the basis of history on television as they are thought to more easily evoke emotion and engage the audience. In *A People's History*, these were the individuals of the imagined "we," whom Starowicz sought as representatives of the national community.

The team then in charge of CBC documentaries, unlike during the experimental era from the 1950s to the mid-1970s, now had more fixed notions about what made good history on television. Good history on television was a chronological presentation. It was told in a linear narrative and supported by the words of people who had lived through historical events. It featured combinations of film-like dramatizations and archival footage. Bad history on television was non-linear modes of presentation, complexity and detailed explanation, and historians onscreen. Yet these were all characteristics of previously successful CBC television productions, such as the *Explorations* programs, *Images of Canada*, and even, to a certain extent, *The National Dream*. This dichotomy parallels cultural theorist Stuart Hall's observations, made in 1976, on television in general: "It is 'good television' if there are no breaks or discontinuities ... 'Good' television visualizes wherever it can, never uses a word when it can supplant it with an image or an illustration, and is constantly beset by people who do not understand its visual mysteries ... 'Good' television is visually dramatic, the pictures are full of incident. 'Bad' television is static, talking heads, long camera takes, pictures which do not 'move.'"[31]

According to the senior producers of *A People's History*, bad history on television also meant historians onscreen, but they were still needed as advisors. In addition to Cook and Robert, based in Toronto and Montreal, respectively, the team hired Olive Dickason, a historian of

First Nations and Métis peoples who was professor emeritus at the University of Alberta and then teaching at the University of Ottawa. These three, as Starowicz later wrote, covered "the three great currents of Canadian history," with the immigrant perspective being equally valid.[32] The team eventually hired additional experts, but Cook, Robert, and Dickason were to read and comment on scripts, view rough cuts, and be available when needed. While Allen assured the historians that their comments would be taken into account, he explained that the production team alone would make the decisions.[33] Cook recalled that, even though what was shaping up was a traditional narrative history, the team seemed interested in integrating social history and that, in Allen, the consultants had a guarantee of sorts that they would be taken seriously.[34] Allen noted that the historians did not have much of an impact on the overall structure of the series but, rather, served to point out big problems, omissions, or imbalanced emphasis.[35]

One of the early discussions was about the onscreen time allotted to New France. The Battle of the Plains of Abraham and the Seven Years' War (of which it was part) would have its own two-hour episode, but initial discussions involved only one more hour on the French regime. Both Hubert Gendron and Ramsay Cook reported having to argue to get it more screen time; one opposing argument was that anglophones would dislike the abundance of French accents (Starowicz later noted having been relieved that there was no backlash to having "too much French history").[36] In the end, the era of New France, comprising over 150 of four hundred years of European-based history in Canada, received only five hours of the total thirty-two. With regard to the major choices like these, Henderson said: "The main thing is, we approached this as journalists ... We focus on what are the most important stories the most interesting stories, human stories ... and then politics don't matter and agendas don't matter."[37]

The presentation style of A People's History was unusual but not unique. Like Images of Canada, A People's History featured an original musical score. The depiction of the era before photography and moving images was part documentary, with the usual array of paintings, maps, and other archival visuals; and part drama, with costumed actors speaking direct to camera and in non-speaking dramatized scenes. Computer-generated imagery (CGI) simulated and amplified images of things like ships in a harbour and soldiers on a battlefield. Starowicz felt that, since the photographic record did not exist during this period, he had no choice but to dramatize in this manner.[38] As Stuart Hall observed, by this time television producers required visuals to be dramatic, full of incident, and quickly changing. The speaking actors, limited to a maximum of fourteen per two-hour episode, spoke the real words as written by the people portrayed.[39] In the later episodes, the costumed actors disappeared and the recreated scenes diminished due to the existence of photographs and moving images. Words spoken by the onscreen actors in the earlier periods were, in these later instalments, spoken in voiceover to a photograph or other type of image.

The practice of using a wide range of actors to read the real words of people as written in memoirs, diaries, and letters had been used before in CBC television histories, but it became ubiquitous after *The Civil War*. It gives voice to eyewitnesses no longer living and helps to create intimate connections between the onscreen characters and the audience. It also provides an opportunity to showcase regular people like foot soldiers and domestic servants, in addition to the more commonly seen military and political leaders. And, in *A People's History*, it accounted for the use of the titular phrase "people's history." The phrase was used to describe *War at Sea* as well, and now, with this new series, it framed the work overall as being told by those "who lived it."[40]

The phrase "people's history," however, has a different genesis than its use in *A People's History* suggests. People's history emerged in the United Kingdom and the United States at the end of the 1960s (Starowicz even wrote that they had to change the original name of the series, *A People's History of Canada*, because to some people, including CBC president Perrin Beatty, it sounded a bit Marxist).[41] The movement aimed to uncover and popularize the history of workers in order to gain and promote a deeper understanding of the labour past and to better inform contemporary labour issues. Historians and labour activists encouraged workers to conduct the research and writing themselves, partly through workshops designed for this purpose.[42] People's history came to refer to a progressive, often oppositional kind of history, one that challenged received wisdom and emphasized the process of constructing history rather than just the final product.[43] One of the best-known works published on this premise is historian Howard Zinn's *A People's History of the United States*, a perennial bestseller that interrogates the way American history had been written to support the status quo.

Thus, the use of the phrase in *Canada: A People's History* did not at all reflect its original meaning; rather, it represented the fact that the actors were playing real people from the past and reading actual words from the historical record. Throughout the production process, the team maintained the validity of the approach, with Starowicz saying that, if all the individual stories together were told properly, "the history will emerge."[44] Even though with this premise someone still had to make choices about which stories were the important or interesting ones, implicit within it is the notion that the series would not reflect any subjective or ideological position on the part of the producers. It seemed to indicate that, as a team of journalists, they comprised an objective party, providing only the vehicle for the actors to transmit personal testimony to the audience and thereby avoiding mediation so as to present a more democratic type of history.[45]

But these personal stories were not applied to a neutral canvas that could have been interpreted by the audience in any number of different ways. The producers wrote a narrative into which these stories would fit. It was this narrative, the basic structural elements of which were established long before the idea of producing a series on the history of Canada occurred to anyone, that did more to determine which stories were in and which were out. National narratives conform to established models, and, as historian Lyle Dick has pointed out, in *Canada: A People's History* we have the outlines at least of a national epic.[46] Similar to *The National Dream* there is the great unifying story, opposing forces, setbacks and defeats, but with a plot nevertheless marching towards the apex. This is a history leading to an inevitable destiny, constantly foreshadowed: "he would become one of the most powerful men"; "it would be the greatest naval invasion"; it "will become the most destructive conflict" or "change the course of history."[47] The part on the construction of the CPR – again, similar to the depiction in *The National Dream* – presents the railway as something that will see "the rise and fall of political and financial fortunes" and "determine the destiny of the nation."

So the use of multiple voices in *Canada: A People's History* must be understood simply as a means to support the narrative. Even the actors representing living people reflecting on relatively recent events, as featured in the last episodes, recount only their personal experiences of those events and generally do not reflect on the larger narrative. The use of multiple voices does allow for the possibility of conflicting or even opposing viewpoints, but in a nationalist perspective such as this one, even if they do appear they are typically subsumed within an underlying consensus.[48]

The use of multiple voices over a vast span of time can be misleading in other ways. Inclusion of a wide range of people and the presentation of their testimony in exactly the same manner implies that, throughout Canadian history, all opinions were considered equal, when we know they were not. In attempting to project modern ideals of equality and inclusiveness, without providing an explanation of the nature and use of the source material, the CBC created a history based on present-day norms rather than on a more realistic past. In *A People's History* viewers saw articulate people like themselves, with neat clothing, good teeth, and similar ways of speaking. It was a comforting and less jarring depiction than the more realistic portrayals of the past as "a foreign country," of which novelist L.P. Hartley wrote, and that Peter Watkins created in *Culloden*.

The attempt at diversity also met with only limited success. The archival record simply does not preserve a widely diverse range of voices before the mid-nineteenth century. So from the time of first European contact, the written words of explorers, military men, and politicians are relatively abundant, but those of women, people of colour, Indigenous peoples, and the poor are as scarce as the former are abundant. This is due not only to low levels of literacy but also to the fact that the low social status of these people meant that anything that they did write was not likely to be retained. In the first season, for example, after the first episode, in which anonymous Indigenous men and women recount various legends from oral history, those few who feature as speaking characters are legendary male chiefs like Joseph Brant and Tecumseh. During the same period the voices of women are also relatively rare, and even well into the nineteenth century they are mainly white and were either born or married into wealth and status. Episode 5, on the American Revolution and the War of 1812, is the first to include women in any numbers, but these are exceptional accounts, or voices of upper-class or literate women. Until relatively recently, to be part of the archival record was to be a person of some kind of privilege, distinction, or exception.

Exacerbating the problem was the producers' emphasis on "through" characters. These are the characters who were able to represent multiple storylines over time, like explorer and mapmaker David Thompson, who appears throughout episode 6, and Pierre Trudeau and René Lévesque, who appear throughout the last three episodes. This was the main reason, Starowicz explained, they omitted Laura Secord from the sequence on the War of 1812. The impact of Secord's actions on wartime events remains debatable, but this was not the reason for her absence in *A People's History*. Starowicz said that, since she did not speak to any of the other themes in that episode, to include her for only a few minutes would not be good documentary structure.[49] But Secord did not speak to the other episode themes because the producers focused on subject matter related to the military and politics, from which women were excluded for most of Canadian history. So the choice of subject matter, coupled with a presentation style that emphasized real words and "through" characters, helped to silence and to perpetuate the overall paucity of women in the early episodes.

For the executive team, the use of people's voices was part of the argument for not having historians onscreen. The team members made this decision early on, based partly on two of the model series they viewed in the pre-production phase – *The Civil War* and *Liberty! The American Revolution*. Although the two series had successfully combined the words of historical people with those of historians, the team felt that it was not a good combination as the historians "broke the bubble," in Gendron's words.[50] According to Allen and Starowicz, it disrupted the flow of the narrative overall.[51]

Gordon Henderson claimed: "this is the people's history of Canada, not the historians' history of Canada."[52] And: "We keep driving the narrative and don't stop to look at a person in a tweed suit with a bookcase behind, who'll give you his or her analysis. We let you choose what you think, we let you the viewer pull your stories out."[53] Nor was Starowicz interested in having "a floating Supreme Court of historians passing judgments on events."[54] The producers were not only ignoring their own role as decision makers and interpreters, they were also discounting the labour of professional historians whose judgments on Canadian history actually *were* incorporated into the series. This included the work of historians who contributed directly to the content of the series as well as the many upon whose written work the producers relied. Since the 1970s, this negativity from some journalists about historians and Canadian history on television had been building in the background, but, with *The Valour and the Horror* and now *A People's History*, it was now laid bare.

Early in the fall of 2000, the media event of the year was fast approaching. For months the press and the public had been duly primed by the CBC promotional machine. In addition to television commercials heralding the upcoming broadcast, members of the production team gave interviews, spoke to interested parties, and catered to other journalists visiting their sets and looking to write stories about the production. The promotional video featuring the dramatization of the Battle of the Plains of Abraham played across the country in various venues, including some movie theatres, where it appeared before the main feature. The communications manager for the series noted that this was part of the strategy to market to the coveted twelve-to-thirty-four age demographic.[55] CBC staff worked tirelessly to ensure that *A People's History*, like *The National Dream*, would be a nation-binding media event, a legacy project to be talked about for years to come.

The CBC followed through on a companion book and hired two writers, one to write a text in English and the other to write a text in French. A vast website was in the works. There were press kits, videos, and compact discs for sale. The CBC made announcements about a teacher resource package to be released in 2001, including lesson plans and discussion ideas, in both English and French, for Grades 5 to 9, and 10 to 12.[56] For the first season, Sun Life Financial paid around $2 million for a thirty-second spot every half-hour, but, for the second season, the CBC managed to entice only one other main sponsor – Bell Canada Enterprises (BCE).[57] So for all of this as well as the actual production of the series, Canadian taxpayers bore most of the financial burden.

On 22 October 2000, *Canada: A People's History* opened with "When the World Began." Recalling *The National Dream*, the series opener begins with a scene of a steam locomotive rolling towards the camera. This first episode is the story of Indigenous peoples before the coming of Europeans (the first hour) and at the time of first contact(s) (the second hour). The account begins in the early nineteenth century with Shawnadithit, the last of the Beothuk people of Newfoundland, who is taken in at St John's by a William Cormack. Using words from Cormack's book about the Beothuk, a costumed actor playing him tells Shawnadithit's story. From there, the narrative attempts to outline the history of the Indigenous peoples of Canada, beginning with the migration over the ancient land bridge connecting Asia and North America, and ending the first hour back with Shawnadithit.

Since no written records exist from this period, the producers relied for the basis of the presentation on the archaeological and pictographic record, and on oral history. A range of individual Indigenous men and women recount various creation myths and legends. Narrator Maggie Huculak, in a departure from the narrative form in the rest of the series, comments on some areas in which information is scant or unknown. This type of commentary on the reliability of the evidence never accompanies the following episodes, which are based on the textual record. One of the most dramatic effects in this first hour is a map of what is now Canada showing the approximate geographical borders of the many groups of Indigenous peoples before the time of contact with Europeans. This map, accompanied by the narrator reading aloud some of the names of these nations, simply but effectively transmits an idea of their numbers and distinctiveness.

The second hour starts with the voyages of John Cabot and Jacques Cartier in the late fifteenth and early sixteenth centuries, and ends with eighteenth- and early nineteenth-century British Columbia and the encounter between British explorers and the Nuu-chah-nulth (Nootka). The depiction of these different meetings reveals that first contacts between Europeans and Indigenous peoples happened in many places across Canada and over a great span of time. In this second hour, reliance on the archaeological record and Indigenous oral history diminishes in favour of the written word. This sets the tone for the rest of the series, in which lines are delivered and scenes dramatized from memoirs, letters, and other textual records. Since these sources provide the bases for the narrative and the visual scenes, the viewpoint correspondingly shifts from Indigenous peoples to Europeans, telling us as much about Jacques Cartier and John Jewitt as it does about the subjects of their documents: the First Nations leaders Donnacona and Maquinna. With this move into the realm of written history, the story also relies on European-based assumptions about these encounters – a pattern that was mostly absent in the first hour.[58]

Episodes 2 to 4, "Adventurers and Mystics," "Claiming the Wilderness," and "Battle for a Continent," focus on the founding of New France, its expansion in North America, its struggle with Great Britain, and, finally, its demise. "Adventures and Mystics" starts with Martin Frobisher's search for the Northwest Passage in the 1570s, the exploitation of the Grand Banks fishing grounds, and John Guy's establishment of a settlement in Newfoundland. Champlain is the main champion of this episode and the story follows him, not from Port Royal in Nova Scotia (where he and others founded a settlement that would mark the beginning of permanent European presence in Canada) but from Tadoussac and Quebec, on the St Lawrence. The European craze for beaver skins leads to an intensified fur trade and the forging of alliances between the French and the Huron against the Iroquois. With the French come the Jesuits and other missionaries. The Huron suffer from exposure to their illnesses as well as from increasing attacks by the Iroquois. King Louis XIV finally declares New France a Crown colony under the administration of Intendant Jean Talon. The French *filles du roi* arrive, and the colony prospers.

"Claiming the Wilderness" is the first one-hour episode. It covers the expansion of New France, beginning with the claiming of Louisiana by the French explorer René-Robert Cavalier de La Salle. The fur trade network grows, and this trade, as well as conflicts between the French and the English, largely define their relationships with Indigenous peoples. These conflicts play out both in Europe and North America, including in the English colonies to the south. The Great Peace of Montreal (1701) brings peace between New France and its Indigenous allies, and their enemies the Iroquois. The eighteenth century sees the growth of the colony, and the episode portrays daily life in the small settlements. The last part of this episode finally turns to Acadia, or Nova Scotia, where the French first settled in the beginning of the seventeenth century and where French and Acadians were still living. As in *Images of Canada*, the Acadian Deportation that follows centres on those living in Grand Pré, Nova Scotia, who are deported in 1755. The events are a precursor to renewed and full-blown war between the French and the British.

The fourth episode, "Battle for a Continent," is about the Seven Years' War, the Quebec Act, and the lead-up to the American Revolution. The focus of the episode is a dramatization of the Battle of the Plains of Abraham. Though it was directed by Serge Turbide, Starowicz was the real master. In his memoir, he explained that the reasons for his involvement in the episode were both personal, especially in the battle dramatization, and political caution. Being of neither English nor French descent, he wrote the script himself in order to avoid arguments in favour of either side.[59]

Unlike the 1959 depiction of the battle in "The Fall of Quebec," where Charles Stacey merely points out battle locations on a map, the scenes in *A People's History* entailed thorough planning, with great attention paid to the particulars of costumes, props, and environment. Starowicz complained that, somehow, the exact time that the British and French had fallen to fighting was not known (was it nearer to nine o'clock or ten o'clock?), and he blamed this on historians and their lack of attention to detailed storytelling, on their "narrative cleansing" of the past.[60] Professional historians were again guilty of bad history, this time for ignoring details that made no difference to the outcome of the original event and would not have been noticed by a television audience. Yet journalist Charlotte Gray (soon to become known as a popular historian and biographer) shared Starowicz's concern. Gray wrote in a pre-broadcast essay in *Saturday Night* magazine that Starowicz had to get the timing of the battle just right because this would be discernible from the shadows cast on the field.[61]

Starowicz referred to the dramatization of the Battle of the Plains of Abraham as a "reconstruction." Any event is difficult to truly reconstruct in a completely different context and with a completely different mindset. Starowicz himself realized the difficulties associated with merely determining the exact timing of the battle, of trying to reconstruct or re-enact something neither seen nor experienced by any living person. Nevertheless, with a hundred professional re-enactors and computer-generated imaging, the new Battle of the Plains of Abraham, the original version of which was over quickly, took place over the space of a couple of days in a farmer's field near Ottawa.

Starowicz noted that his copying of *Culloden* was not done cinematographically but by attempting to capture the "sense of fate and chance" – something that Peter Watkins had brought to his work.[62] The visual styles of the two television battles are similar, and the narration is more so, particularly at the point in *A People's History* at which the narrator introduces individual members of the fighting units.[63] But *Culloden* is essentially a critique of the memory and the conventional interpretation of that battle as well as a statement about the nature of television itself as mediator. *A People's History*, while presenting material most likely unknown to most viewers, reinforces both the accepted version of events and the dominant televisual form for docudrama. The CBC battle, with no contemporary elements such as *Culloden*'s reporter, aimed to entirely erase the distinction between past and present. Watkins, for his part, was not happy about the imitation. In reference to *A People's History* overall, he criticized the rigid uniformity in which all the time periods, cultures, and languages are portrayed. He felt that the series, among other things, displayed "a cynical relationship towards history and the audience."[64]

Starowicz wanted his team to produce the series not in the style of dramatic filmmakers but in the style of documentary filmmakers. So, in a directive to the production team, he wrote that, with the dramatizations, the camera should record the action spontaneously, as if simply documenting it as it happened rather than as something that was planned. The contrived footage was to act as archival news footage in that one would not expect it to have all the best clips.[65] As director of photography Michael Sweeney put it, "We tried to recreate the look of a documentary unit out in the field in 1759."[66] Dramatization detracts from the perception of authenticity typical of a documentary or of a work of journalism, and the team did not want questions of this sort to arise in the minds of viewers.

But to recreate the appearance of a documentary is not to create a documentary. The effort to treat the past no differently from the present applied not just to the look of the series but to the content too. From the beginning, Starowicz told the team members to proceed according to CBC journalistic policies and to treat the past as they would the present.[67] It was reminiscent of Brian McKenna's statement about *The Valour and the Horror*, that they were doing the reporting in 1992 that had not been done earlier. It seemed that this was a way to overcome any argument or ambiguities that existed in the historical record or in accounts written by professional historians. With this approach, at least the journalists of *A People's History* themselves would be in accord with each other: "a French and an English journalist will come from two different worlds," said Starowicz, "but will agree on a certain number of things – that there's two witnesses to an event, corroborating evidence ... when it comes down to 'did the French run or did the French not run?' you can actually settle the damn thing by journalistic rules."[68]

Although there are primary and secondary accounts of the Battle of the Plains of Abraham from which answers to these questions could have been drawn, some of the dramatization in *A People's History* was based on the account of just one person. This is because, in the historical record, particularly in the more distant past, there is often no corroborating testimony, no "two witnesses." Such is the nature of historical evidence and it presents problems for anyone attempting to reconstruct the past. It accounts for the standard in professional history to provide context and transparency pertaining to sources, much as Jack Saywell and Pierre Berton attempted to do in their television projects. But in *A Peoples History*, aside from the very first episode about pre-contact Indigenous peoples, for which there are no traditional written sources, the narrator never strays from simply telling a story. So, despite statements by Starowicz and others about adherence to journalistic standards and principles, it is not always clear exactly which standards and principles were being adhered to.

That these unique accounts must be used with a critical eye is illustrated by the scenes in the first episode, which portrays the Nuu-chah-nulth abduction of John Jewitt in 1803. Historian Jonathan Vance has pointed out that Jewitt's account of his experiences, originally written in simply styled journal entries, was superseded by a book ghostwritten by a Richard Alsop. The later work is a colourful and lively rendition of Jewitt's adventures, and it proved much more effective in gripping the imaginations of its nineteenth-century readers. Although parts of Alsop's tale are not in Jewitt's original, Alsop's was the basis of much of the television dramatization.[69] Presenting scenes like this as factual, with no qualification, is an approach more consistent with docudrama or feature films than with a work of journalism.

Some scholars writing about *A People's History* have questioned these claims about journalistic practice.[70] Any narrative – historical or journalistic – is equally open to distortion. As Howard Zinn has suggested, "the historian's distortion is more than technical, it is ideological," meaning that selection and emphasis are necessary in order to present any account of the past, but that these are always the result of "some kind of interest."[71] Other reviewers of the series have accepted as credible the beliefs of the producers regarding their journalistic approach.[72]

Charlotte Gray, in the *Saturday Night* piece, claimed that the production could possibly save Canadians from a history made boring and confusing due to "academic infighting and political caution."[73] Accompanying this essay is a cartoon depicting two historians arguing while a battle rages in the valley below them. The senior team preferred narrative accounts of history rather than having to deal with historical complexities and contested interpretations such as those suggested in the cartoon; however, in earlier programs (like "The Fall of Quebec" and the last episode of *A War for Survival*), these formed the core of the presentation. The political caution described by Gray might well have applied to *A People's History*, with its traditional take on Canadian history and its avoidance of differing perspectives and interpretations. In this respect it did not seem to accord with a journalistic approach to content.

The first part of the fifth episode, "A Question of Loyalties," covers the American Revolution, the Loyalist migration, and the division of Quebec into Upper and Lower Canada. The second part is an interpretation of the War of 1812. Like the earlier treatment of the conflict in Jack Saywell's *A War for Survival*, it covers the events mainly as they play out in Upper and Lower Canada. There was little mention of the Atlantic colonies or of the maritime aspects of the war on the Atlantic coast, which Saywell barely mentioned either, and which were important to the outcome of the actual conflict. This interpretation focuses on the exploits of de Salaberry, Brock, and Tecumseh, who are painted as the heroes of the conflict. Saywell had purposefully avoided the latter two.

After episode 5, the series broke for December and reappeared in January 2001 for episodes 6 through 9: "The Pathfinders," on the fur trade and the exploration of the Northwest; "Rebellion and Reform," on the rebellions in Upper and Lower Canada and the struggle for responsible government; and "The Great Enterprise" and "From Sea to Sea," on the Confederation era. The Pathfinders highlights adventurers like Pierre Esprit de Radisson, Pierre Gaultier de Varennes et de laVérendrye, and David Thompson as the main "through" character. It is unique in that it breaks from the chronological treatment of the rest of the series. Hubert Gendron reported that the principal reason for it was the pressure the team felt to include western Canada, which to that point had appeared only in the first episode.[74] "The Pathfinders" spans the second-longest period of time in the series.

The next entry, "Rebellion and Reform," produced in Montreal, paid special attention to the rebellions in the Canadas and their leaders, William Lyon Mackenzie and Louis-Joseph Papineau. Gendron considered the events in Lower Canada, if compared to the importance placed by the English network on the Battle of the Plains of Abraham and Confederation, at least as important to the Montreal team.[75] This was primarily because of the significance in Quebec attached to the Lower Canada Rebellion and its hero, Papineau, and the consequences and aftermath of the rebellion: the Durham Report, the union of Upper and Lower Canada, and the Baldwin-LaFontaine alliance – some of which Jack Saywell had also covered in *Durham's Canada*. Unlike in the Saywell series, in "Rebellion and Reform" Joseph Howe appears as representative of the Atlantic reformers and as leader of the first colony in the British Empire to achieve responsible government.

The following two episodes (three hours) on Confederation cover the threat of the American Civil War, Confederation, and the first few years of the new Dominion. Along with the Battle of the Plains of Abraham, Confederation is the centrepiece. The presentation style changes at the age of photography, so here photographs begin to replace the actors onscreen. "The Great Enterprise" opens with the American Civil War and the threat it poses to Canada. One of the first characters to appear is one of the main heroes of the series, John A. Macdonald. The narrator describes him in a manner similar to that used by Pierre Berton in *The National Dream*: "Even when at play, Macdonald is always at work." One of Macdonald's colleagues supports this depiction, but the narrator also describes Macdonald as calculating for he was concerned mainly with getting himself re-elected, starting by forging an alliance with George-Étienne Cartier from Canada East. The gaining of responsible government in Nova Scotia is followed by Confederation and, in "From Sea to Sea," the entry of British Columbia into the union. This last part introduces Louis Riel, the armed resistance to the new Canadian government, and the birth of Manitoba and its entry into the union. It sets the stage for the continuing tensions between Indigenous peoples and the Canadian government. The end of this episode concludes the first season.

The immediate print reviews of the series were overwhelmingly positive, describing it as "gold," an "epic docudrama," and "Canada's remarkable story."[76] The ratings bore out these reviews. To maximize viewing potential, on the English network each episode had been rebroadcast twice in the same week, and on the French network, once in the same week. For the first episode in the first week, according to the CBC, these broadcasts together drew just under 3 million viewers. The following episodes over the first season averaged 1.2 million viewers each on the English network, and on the French network, 360,000 viewers each.[77]

Several daily newspapers sought reviews from historians. Those reporting in the Halifax *Daily News* and the *Vancouver Sun*, commenting on the first four episodes and the fourth episode, respectively, in general applauded the CBC's efforts and found the content factually correct but the episodes either boring or lacking in context and critical examination.[78] The *National Post* invited four historians – Michael Bliss, Jack Granatstein, David Bercuson, and Jonathan Vance – to comment on the first season. Three of them had expertise in military history; three had also been publicly either for or against *The Valour and the Horror*. Three historians commented on two episodes each, while one, Granatstein, commented on three episodes. Two found theirs very well done and had few or no serious criticisms regarding accuracy, though more than one remarked on the boring sequences, superficiality, and slow pace.[79] Vance, Bercuson, and Granatstein noted that ordinary people were ignored in favour of leaders and the elite. To Granatstein, this made the series "a constitutional/political/military tale that gladdens the heart of this unreconstructed historical reactionary, no matter the array of social historians marshalled as advisors and consultants."[80]

Less analytical but more consistently laudatory were the emails from viewers that poured in to the CBC throughout the broadcasts. Students in a public history class at Carleton University in Ottawa analyzed these submissions. They found that most emails expressed more of an emotional reaction to the series – a sense of pride and wonder at the history viewers had not known about – than any substantial discussion of it.[81] As Michael Sweeney said of the Battle of the Plains of Abraham sequence, this emotional reaction was just the kind of effect that the producers were after, and the actors were especially important in it.[82] Similar to *War at Sea*, in which the actors were meant to "convey emotion rather than straight information," the actors in *A People's History* made the issues brought forward by the narration more intimate.[83]

Episodes 10 through 17 were broadcast from the end of September to the end of November 2001, with the last repeated episode on the French network on 6 January 2002. Due to the existence of still images and moving images, the instalments assume a more traditional documentary style than did those of earlier episodes. Although period settings and simple dramatizations are still included, gone are the elaborate dramatizations and the reliance on costumed actors speaking direct to camera. These elements, which had characterized the first season, are in the second season replaced by still images and film and video excerpts. In the last episodes the form again shifts to include personal recollections from living people, given by actors in voiceover, rather than just accounts from historical people.

The first episode in the new season is "Taking the West," about the North-West Resistance, and the completion of the CPR. The negotiation of the numbered treaties has begun between the Plains Indigenous peoples and the Canadian government. It sees the reappearance of Riel as the leader of another resistance. This one does not end as well for Riel and his supporters. Unlike the depiction of these events in *The National Dream*, a lengthy sequence covers the details and injustices of Riel's trial and death. The portrayal of John A. Macdonald and his government in the treatment of Riel and the Indigenous peoples, in their neglect, starvation, and removal of their children to residential schools, is not flattering. Yet, in the end, similar to how he was characterized in *The National Dream*, the narrator claims that Macdonald "helped forge a country, from a continent-sized wilderness and a handful of disparate colonies." The tragedy and losses are acknowledged but it is pointed out, in rather purple prose, that the goal has been attained: that the plains and valleys "have been taken at great cost, but now stand ready to play their part in a country that stretches from sea to sea."

Compared to most of the episodes in the first season, the episodes in the second season cover very short time periods, from as few as six to a maximum of twenty-three years. In the first season, only the episode depicting the era just after Confederation spans such a short time. This could have allowed for a fuller treatment of the stories in the second half; however, as the time period approaches the present, each episode treats a much greater number of not necessarily connected stories. The narrative becomes less sweeping, which allows for a greater diversity of material but also emphasizes the selective nature of the events depicted in the first season. With the decades that take place within living memory of the television audience, the producers had less creative leeway to impose a unified, dramatic story.

As it moves into the twentieth century, the series highlights the massive influx of immigrants to western Canada, women and their politicization, the Depression, and the long-standing tensions between English and French Canada. The latter theme emerges with the government of Wilfrid Laurier, his relationship with Henri Bourassa, and the reorientation of French Canadian nationalism under Bourassa. The two world wars and the Cold War are also prominent, with the Great War accompanied by an account of its overall futility and of the major battles in which Canadians participated. The home front receives the standard coverage of the conscription crisis and the damage it causes to English-French relations in Canada. The interpretation of the Winnipeg General Strike bears some similarity to the 1959 CBC version, though in *A People's History* is presented as a narrative film whereas the earlier piece presents the opposing viewpoints of actual participants in the strike events as well as commentary on the various scholarly perspectives.

The episode on the Second World War, along with the one on Confederation, covers the shortest time period in the series, with the fighting in Europe and the Atlantic displayed in fact-based accounts showing the usual archival footage. Historian Veronica Strong-Boag, reviewing a draft script, suggested that there be some attempt to compare "area bombing" to the Blitz.[84] But as area bombing had been central to *The Valour and the Horror* controversy, the producers steered well clear of any detailed interpretation. A brief scenario devoted to this topic lasts for only one minute. Strong-Boag also noted the overwhelming emphasis on males and the male perspective, but the end result is at least less traditional in its coverage than were most of the previous CBC productions on the subject, with the home front and the role of women receiving comparatively more attention.[85] Experiences of people on the home front include the story of a group of Tlingit in the Yukon and the Dene in the Northwest Territories mining uranium ore.

The postwar period brings *A People's History* into the era of television and thus begins the use of CBC television clips for illustration. The coming of television itself receives star treatment, and the clips are a self-referent for the glory days when CBC news had little competition. They refer to the nation-building project that was the foundation of the CBC itself, a unifying medium of communications comparable to the building of the CPR. The cult of (political) personality, evident from the beginning of the series, becomes increasingly obvious with the succession of premiers and prime ministers, including Joey Smallwood and Maurice Duplessis, and René Lévesque and Pierre Trudeau, as key characters. These last episodes address some of the recommendations made by Ramsay Cook in his original draft outline, including the battle for women's rights, the rise of Indigenous peoples as a political force, and English-French relations. Throughout the series, the narrator constantly refers to the precarious nature of English-French relations in Canada, the tension always building. It culminates in these last episodes with the Quiet Revolution and the growing vitality of Quebec nationalism, the Trudeau/Lévesque battles, and, finally, the first referendum on Quebec sovereignty and the failure of the Meech Lake Accord.

In the postwar episodes the producers use recollections of living persons in addition to archival sources. It is the same strategy used in *The Valour and the Horror* except that, in *A People's History*, the actors represent the individuals only in voiceover, not onscreen. Ramsay Cook, commenting earlier on a draft script, recommended caution: "Do we automatically accept as 'fact' or accurate reconstruction an individual's memories of his or her heroic actions in the past? As an historian, I don't. Why not, for example, try to find what Jim Laxer actually said in the late sixties and early seventies rather than take at face value what he says he was doing and thinking?"[86] Cook was questioning the practice of basing scenes on information derived from memories recounted well after the event, with no transparency pertaining to that fact. He was urging the producers to at least question the accuracy of human memory and to consider what might have happened to it since the event being recalled had taken place.

The standardization of the voiceovers further obscures the informational sources. Whether the sources are documents contemporary to the time period depicted, or interviews conducted long afterwards, perhaps even specifically for the broadcast, is not made clear to viewers. And, like *The Valour and the Horror*, the age of the actor presenting the testimony enhances the uncertainty. Examples occur throughout the series. In the final episode, a James Schmaltz talks about getting an early home computer. The year is 1980, he is twelve years old, and he speaks in a boy's voice in the past tense: "They saw it as something complex to learn from, an educational type of thing. We were looking at it for fun games to play, and making our own games, which we did." A later voiceover from an actor playing Schmaltz, depicting a time in his life after he has graduated from university, has him speaking in an older voice. In episode 5, from the first season, an actor portraying Hannah Ingraham, daughter of Loyalists from New York, talks about boarding the ship that will take them to Nova Scotia. Ingraham appears onscreen and in voiceover as a young woman of eleven, but her words were taken from reminiscences she dictated when she was an elderly woman.

The final episode ends the series on a high note. There were the requisite setbacks and defeats, but, overall, gains were made in the rights of women and Indigenous peoples, and in the growth of immigration from all parts of the world. If there was ever a doubt about the narrative arc of the series, the finale removes it: from "the first travellers" who came to this continent fifteen thousand years ago, to "the next journey of adventurers" four hundred years ago, and ending with families searching for opportunity and sanctuary. It is an epic drama that we are still living, and it is about "the homelands of the First Peoples, the future of the French and the English, the newcomers who have shaped our century, the eternal dynamic with the United States."

Indeed, the central ideas in *A People's History* are that Canada is a land of immigrants (often referred to throughout the series as "the dispossessed"), a land where the English and the French are in a constant state of tension, and a land that is emphatically not the United States. During the production and in his memoir of the making of the series, Starowicz made much of his status as a product of Polish postwar immigrants and of the immigrant experience as one that bound together all Canadians, though they may have arrived at different times. He explained the chronological approach to the series in the following terms: "because the central unifying idea of Canadian history is once there was nothing here ... that's why we chose to do it as the growth of an entire united nations of peoples."[87]

While the initial hour of the first episode does focus on the presence of Indigenous peoples in North America long before European contact, this explanation of the chronological approach recalls the idea of an empty land waiting to be populated by newcomers. It ignores the vastly dissimilar circumstances of the Indigenous migration and non-Indigenous colonization and immigration, and it also suggests a homogeneity in the cultures and identities of Indigenous peoples and in the nature of their contacts with settler colonists. In terms of immigrant groups, it stresses a unity and sameness that obscures vast differences among and within later groups as well as how they were treated by the host populations. Finally, it belies the fact that the immigrant experience in the series was represented in general terms. Even after the massive influx of immigrants to Canada beginning in the late nineteenth century, few of the immigrant personalities speak of their long-term or unsuccessful immigrant experience.

Reference to Canada as a land of immigrants had become increasingly prominent on television screens since the introduction of official multiculturalism and the creation of the new Broadcasting Act. It joined two more traditional ideas, represented repeatedly in the CBC's Canadian histories: (1) the vulnerability of Canadian unity to Quebec and (2) the vulnerability of Canadian identity to the United States. Charles Stacey claims in *A War for Survival* that an outside threat is always good for nationalism, and clearly, throughout *A People's History*, Americans play a key role as antagonists. One newspaper reported that Starowicz had an idea for a promotional trailer that would begin with a clip from actor and director Mel Gibson's big-budget movie on the American Revolution, *The Patriot* (2000). The clip would cut to a black screen with white text reading "Had Enough?...Our Turn," followed by highlights from *A People's History*.[88]

Allen recounted how forcefully one production team member had pushed the importance of the War of 1812 as the trial that defined Canadian nationalism and made Canadians distinct from their neighbours to the south.[89] As the narrator states at the end of that episode: "In its determination not to become American, Canada has drawn closer to Britain than ever, and has seen a glimmer of its own identity." This American threat, described by one commentator on the first season as a shark circling each episode, had for a long time been manifest in the discourse of CBC broadcasting itself and was something familiar to Starowicz and other Canadian cultural nationalists.[90] *A People's History* would be an antidote to this American force and a counter within Canada to the regional, ethnic, and racial "'segmentation and isolation'" that, according to Starowicz, were subversive of the Canadian political system, progress, and democracy.[91]

As for regional divides, a long-time problem for the CBC, reviews on the series again raised the issue. Historian Margaret Conrad has complained that the national history in *A People's History* was presented at the expense of Atlantic Canada in particular. Conrad wondered why Champlain first appeared as the founder of Quebec and not Port Royal, which he helped found three years earlier and that marked the beginning of permanent European presence in Canada. Where were the Mi'kmaq and the Maliseet (Wolastoqiyik), and the Acadians (before the Deportation)? Why was the significance of Newfoundland not brought forth? Why did the fortress of Louisbourg first make an appearance only on the eve of its destruction? And why did Prince Edward Island not seem to exist until Confederation?[92] These and other contexts were not only important to the history of the region and to Canada in general, they were also full of the drama and conflict that characterizes much of the first season.

For *A People's History* a production team member had assembled material for a potential segment on the unique and acrimonious leasehold tenure system that plagued Prince Edward Island until the Confederation era. The segment was dropped, even though the activities of the island's Tenant League constituted a popular protest with some foundational parallels to the contemporary Red River Resistance, an event ingrained in the national narrative and one receiving good coverage in *A People's History*.[93] As Conrad pointed out, the Atlantic provinces, at least before Confederation, must be central to any discussion of the history of the country.[94] That this was not so in *A People's History* is largely because of the tendency of national narratives to present the past in light of present realities, hence the long-standing focus on central Canada in CBC television histories. Historian David Frank has observed that, in the post-Confederation episodes, the Atlantic provinces did appear, but it was within "an implied narrative of exploitation, disaster and failure."[95] These were the segments on the human consequences of coal mining, Africville, and the "Goin' Down the Road" exodus of Atlantic Canadians to other parts of Canada.

Even Allen acknowledged that one of the things he lost out on was the prominence of Atlantic Canada.[96] He reported having had to convince a Montreal director that it was essential to include in his piece some treatment of the Nova Scotian anti-Confederate leader and advocate for responsible government Joseph Howe, who was actually a featured character of Canadian history on CBC radio and television from the 1940s to the 1960s. Allen said that one of the overall difficulties in producing the series was that some of the team members had set-in-stone ideas about Canadian history, and, in retrospect, they might have had a better grounding in the subject before beginning work.[97] Although reports suggest that between sixty and one hundred historians were consulted during production, it was clear that the historians as advisors to *A People's History* did not have the same kind of involvement they had enjoyed in the days of *Explorations* or *Images of Canada*.[98]

One of the provinces that was well represented in *A People's History* is Quebec, which is not surprising not only because of its relatively long European-based history but also because the relationship between the English and the French in Canada has been a traditional theme in Canadian history on CBC television. On the interpretation of Quebec history, however, Hubert Gendron felt in some instances a disconnect between how it was understood by members of the Montreal production team and how it was understood by members of the production team who were not from Quebec. Gendron noted being uncomfortable, for example, with the inclination by some to romanticize James Wolfe.[99] Commenting on a draft manuscript of the book that accompanied *A People's History* he cautioned about the biased treatment of the French in New France in general: "The chapter is told solely from the British, and particularly, Wolfe's point of view ... First, the Canadiens are virtually absent ... Instead we get those old chestnuts (not in the TV episode) Bigot and his mistress, pandering to the prejudice that the French were unusually corrupt etc."[100]

One of the biggest problems for the team members in Montreal was the attitude by some in the Quebec media, even by some within Radio-Canada, who believed that, by co-producing a history of Canada with the English network, they were supporting the federalist cause. The series did not get the same attention from the French network or from the francophone press that it got from the English network and the anglophone press, and what notice it did receive was often uncomplimentary.[101] Although the proportion of the French-speaking audience watching the series was similar to the proportion of the English-speaking audience, the relative audience numbers were low in terms of comparable popular programming in Quebec.[102] Gendron said that, if able to do it again, he would include more historical voices and less political history: "But now we can talk about something different, because that exists."[103]

CBC producers designed *Canada: A People's History* to be entertaining and not to be overtly educational, although it was packaged, marketed, and sold to schools and other libraries. *A People's History* also served national and cultural aims by promoting nation building and Canadian content as one big narrative, with expected content and accepted interpretations. Mark Starowicz said to an audience of history teachers in 2004 that, unlike the programming on the History Channel and its nineteen branch networks around the world, his series had not been produced to sell pop or soap.[104] But *A People's History* sold something else – the idea of an old/new national dream that ostensibly left no one out. With apprehension abounding about the fitness of the CBC as a national public service broadcaster, on the eve of the new millennium it offered up *A People's History* as its most prominent exemplar.

Independent producers worked on *A People's History*, but, unlike *Images of Canada,* which also had different producer/directors for individual episodes, they worked under the control of a senior editorial team that streamlined each piece and removed any evidence of individuality. Rather than disturbing popular conceptions about Canadian history, the producers of *A People's History* delivered the broad outlines of what most Canadians expected to see, and from the perspective from which they expected to see it. Many stories in the series were undoubtedly new to viewers, and there is evidence – for example in the portrayal of Indigenous peoples in the first season, of women as important historical actors in the second season, and of immigration as an important theme throughout – that more recent historiography, such as that suggested by Ramsay Cook, was taken into account.

But the larger narrative into which these stories fit does not stray too far from the nation-building narratives of old. It depicts Canada as a predetermined nation, created through economics, politics, and war, and, especially in the first season, with politicians and military men as the heroes. Allen said that the criticism of the series as an old-fashioned account with great men was in some ways fair but that at least the information it contained was accurate.[105] For this the producers had historians to thank, but opposition to their deeper involvement was unmistakable. It was history as one big story, created by professional journalists, with dramatizations and personal testimony in supporting roles. For the audience there was little evidence of sources, conflicting interpretations, or even alternate perspectives. And it formed the new standard for Canadian history on CBC television.

Conclusion

From *Explorations* to *Canada: A People's History*, a pattern emerges in Canadian history documentaries and docudramas on CBC television. The content in these programs aimed to define Canada as a nation, unique and separate from the United States, a nation unified, despite the long-standing tensions between English and French Canada, and a nation glorified through its national heroes and exemplary moments. These were the programs on the building of the Canadian Pacific Railway and Confederation, the periods of conflict and reconciliation between English and French Canada, and the wars: the Seven Years' War, the American Revolution, the War of 1812, and the First and Second World Wars. This nationalist perspective highlighted as the important force in history the male explorer, military leader, and politician. Its focus was central Canada and its ideology, the march of progress. The CBC promoted these programs to Canadians across the country as something important to watch and to Parliament as proof that the CBC was doing its job.

Until the late 1960s, nationalism also characterized the writing of Canadian history, so professional history and history on CBC television were compatible. But Canadian historical writing has changed dramatically since then, and while the more recent television programs incorporated some elements of the new historiography, the principal themes, subjects, and interpretations remained the same. Given the long-standing importance of nation building to the CBC, this focus is not surprising. But altogether, and with few alternatives, it overwhelms any interpretation of Canada's past other than the development of the nation, and any identity other than the national. With some exceptions we have not seen treatments of the larger social, cultural, or regional histories of Canada explored on their own terms and not just as part of the national story. We have seen little of the social forces behind the actions of the heroes (and the villains), of the political unions and conflicts, of the wars and the railways, and even less of their social consequences. And CBC television versions of the national past that have challenged rather than repeated those already widely accepted have been equally rare. In addition to the pattern in what appeared on television, there was a pattern in what got left out.

These television histories were examples of the corporate commitment to building national unity and identity, but for a time they also supported the idea of the CBC as a public service broadcaster. Until the 1970s, public service broadcasting at the CBC also meant educational programming. This was evident in the early output of the corporation and it was one of the reasons federal policy makers saw the National Film Board, with its strengths in documentary and educational film, as a fundamental component of CBC programming. The producers of the Canadian history programs in *Exploring Minds* and *Explorations* treated them as educational vehicles and regarded many of them as just that: explorations, queries, probes. They were first concerned with finding effective ways to present Canadian history on television in order to make it educational, and then they were concerned with creating entertaining television.

Canadian history programs also helped define the CBC as a public service broadcaster by providing what was considered to be quality television. This was linked to its educational role as well as to its distinctiveness from American offerings. In the 1950s, it was actually not very difficult for CBC shows to be distinctive from American fare. On American network television at the time there were some public affairs programs, but what most Canadians saw were comedy and variety shows, all with advertising. So programs like *Explorations* were different from others on the schedule as Canadian content, and as informative, thought-provoking, and ad-free. Later, with the overwhelming resources behind American productions and their inroads into Canada, quality programming at the CBC came to mean *imitating* American television. When the CBC's strategy during the 1980s and early 1990s of becoming more distinctive by increasing its output in drama did not pan out, it still sought to produce HBO-like branded series with "high impact." One example, *Canada: A People's History*, was unique as Canadian content but was otherwise not distinct from American offerings in the same genre.

Regional production of Canadian history programs for national consumption was rare because it was not conducive to the centralized structure that the CBC has maintained. Although *Explorations* included many pieces from the regions (since regionally produced shows were part of its raison d'être), much of its history programming was produced in Toronto. With the exception of the piece on the Winnipeg General Strike and the regional contributions to the centennial programming, producers in Toronto, Ottawa, and Montreal produced all of the programs covered in this book, even the episodes on Canada's regions in *Images of Canada*. Over the years some regional offices created their own Canadian history programs, but not much of it appeared on the national network.

The pressure at the CBC to generate commercial revenue has been a factor in all of its programming, including Canadian history documentaries and docudramas. Commercialism affected choices regarding CBC program output, content, presentation, and scheduling. Similar to the conflict inherent in a public service broadcaster with nation building at its core is the conflict of a public service broadcaster with an audience of consumers rather than citizens. As far back as 1961, one CBC official observed that *The Nature of Things* did well when originally scheduled in prime time, but because it was not a commercial program, it was relegated to Sunday afternoons. He further noted that, if it hadn't been for these kinds of commercial pressures, viewers would see "more programs of this kind in prime time."[1] From then on, the pressures only intensified.

Similarly, the first seasons of *Explorations* and *Images of Canada*, neither of which carried advertising, were televised on Tuesday nights at 10:00 p.m. – within prime time, though a poor slot. The producers of *Explorations* compensated with various strategies, such as creating programs to coincide with anniversaries, juxtaposing pieces in order to maximize the effects of opposing personalities and ideas (Creighton and Underhill), and taking advantage of other popular offerings on the schedule. One manager noticed that general audience numbers for

Explorations seemed to rise when its episodes were preceded by episodes of *The Valiant Years*, a popular British-American series about Winston Churchill.[2] The absence of commercials also freed the producers to experiment. Commercial programs call for consistency in order to meet the perceived expectations of the audience and advertisers, but it can also lead to homogenized programming. The producers of *Explorations*, with the Canadian history content alone, freely tested, adapted, and combined many different styles of presentation, thereby avoiding prescriptive formulas.

Connected to commercialism was the changing attitude towards television audiences. CBC staff had always been concerned with audiences, and managers took quantitative and qualitative audience research seriously. But by the early 1970s, if judging only by the discourse on the CBC licence renewal hearings, efforts to capture mass audiences had become a source of major criticism. There were lots of in-house complaints about this as well. The program proposal form that concerned Vincent Tovell called for proponents to define, among other things, program "objectives" and a "target audience." The two choices on the form for the question on target audience, for example, along with questions about targets connected to audience age and education, were "'a general mass audience'" or "'a more sharply defined audience.'" Staff usually selected the former even if the project was clearly more for special interest.[3] Nash said later that, at the time, he was concerned about audience but not *just* audience, and not necessarily how to get the biggest audience.[4]

Expectations in terms of audience size were lofty for *The National Dream*, but they were balanced out with other programs not necessarily expected to draw large audience numbers, like *Images of Canada*. Although this too may have been a negotiation, as it was also in 1974 that CBC president Picard defended the quest for a mass audience and denigrated elitist-type broadcasting, a description that, for him, might have applied to *Images*. In 1978, the CRTC criticized the continued pandering to mass audiences overall. It counselled the CBC to be content with producing quality programming even if it attained only moderate viewer numbers. The fear of attracting only "PBS-like" audiences was one of the reasons the CBC did not follow this path.

In terms of the presentation strategies in the Canadian history programming, the conventions did not change as much as did the specific techniques. Docudramas like some of the episodes of *Explorations*, and *Durham's Canada*, followed the *You Are There* model. The nonlinear approach to history aimed to explain and inform as well as to entertain. Rather than blurring the line between drama and documentary, by juxtaposing historical characters with modern-day reporters, and thereby making clear that the dialogue was an interpretation constructed many years after the fact, the line was made more evident. Film and television scholar Colin McArthur, reviewing Peter Watkins's *Culloden*, which was also produced *You Are There* style, thought it progressive because it highlighted the televisual processes of constructing events rather than simply recording them.[5] McArthur had some reservations about the attempt by Watkins to impart to the viewer a sense of actually witnessing the battle as well about as the limited historical context in which the battle was placed. But these limitations are actually compatible with the imagined television news format that the filmmaker had created.

Much of the more recent docudrama has focused on making the dramatized parts like a commercial film and, even with the documentary portions, erasing all evidence of contemporary influence. A comparison of the treatments of the War of 1812 in *A War for Survival* and forty years later in *Canada: A People's History* serves to illustrate these differences. The earlier series has Jack Saywell directing a group of actors in a series of theatrical scenes. The actors are dressed in street clothes and the sets are sparse. Before each scene plays out, Saywell answers questions from the actors about the motivation of their characters and occasionally mentions where there are gaps in the historical record. In the final episode the historians debate various aspects of the war. In *A People's History* much of the event is dramatized, lavishly produced to voiceover narration and dramatic background music. The documentary portion shows period paintings with the same voiceover narration and music. This creates an intimacy and continuity with the past, but it disguises the present. This was deliberate. As Mark Starowicz explained, the goal was to get viewers firmly ensconced in the past: "and when you get there you can't break that."[6]

With the dramatization in *A People's History* and other more recent works of history, producers tended to over-authenticate small details in an attempt to recreate the past and to avoid anachronism. The trouble taken with small particulars, irrelevant to the causes or consequences of an event, seemed to supersede the need to provide fuller historical context. Reconstructing a landscape or replicating the exact timing of an occurrence became a way to display the authenticity and authority that, in other history productions, like *A War for Survival*, came from context, explanation, and dialogue between characters.[7] In dramatizing the Battle of the Plains of Abraham Mark Starowicz lamented not knowing exactly what time the fighting began.[8] In *A War for Survival*, on the other hand, this type of detail was unimportant. An actor about to play out an impressment scene, for example, put on a ship captain's hat made from a newspaper.

The over-attention to minor detail reflected an idea that the past is accessible and knowable as long as the characters are in the right costumes and are performing in settings reproduced exactly from the original. In terms of creating realism it was also a way to mitigate the fictional aspect of drama as compared to documentary. It was for this reason that the makers of *The Valour and the Horror* and *Canada: A People's History* expressly avoided the label of docudrama. Yet at the time these two series were produced, viewers knew and accepted docudrama as a form of history programming within the traditions of CBC television.[9]

Compared to the 1950s and 1960s, a focus on relatively recent events distinguishes the more recent Canadian history programs on CBC television. While most of *Images of Canada*'s *The Whitecomers* covers the period before the twentieth century, the last seven episodes of *A People's History* depicts the last hundred years. In other words, *A People's History* highlights the era of film and television, yet there are over four hundred years of Canadian history based on textual documents – thousands of years if the archaeological record and oral history is taken into account (which it was in this series). One explanation for this is that audience members are believed to recognize and connect more easily with history that is familiar to them; another is that events already recorded by CBC television (and other media organizations) are readily available for use. In *A People's History* these events include Pierre Trudeau's "just watch me" comment, made in 1970 during the October Crisis, and Paul Henderson's winning goal in the 1972 hockey series between Canada and Russia. These incidents, originally captured on television, now form part of the national narrative. The reliance on first-person testimony further encouraged a focus on recent history.

The producers of *The Valour and the Horror* and *A People's History* also used first-person testimony presented by actors as a way to make emotional connections to the audience. This allowed the characters to explain how larger historical events affected them personally while also supporting the perspective of the narration. In the *Explorations* docudramas, in the absence of narration, actors playing historical people provide alternate perspectives on events. But in the more recent series, the first-person testimony supports only one larger narrative perspective. The producers of *The Valour and the Horror* and *A People's History* framed the actors' statements as an unmediated window on the past, with little explanation of the context within which the testimony was recorded and no challenge to the testimony itself. In the *Explorations* docudramas, and even in *The National Dream* to a certain extent, the mediation is more evident.

One of the changes in the presentation of Canadian documentary and docudrama history on CBC television has been the removal of references to history as a process of inquiry. In *Explorations*, in some episodes of *Images of Canada*, and even in *The National Dream* to varying degrees, hosts and narrators refer to the realities of historical evidence and interpretation. With the dramatization they sometimes reveal the historical sources used as its basis, and mention gaps in the record or other problems with sources and interpretation. Much of this early work, especially in *Explorations*, also allows for multiple and opposing points of view, interviews, debate, role-playing, and even non-specialist opinion. In short, up until the mid-1970s, the programs often give some indication of history as an incomplete or contested form of knowledge rather than as just a straight narrative of events. Earlier producers made attempts to better inform audiences on the historical nature of what they were seeing and hearing.

As Donald Creighton put it in his "Long View of Canadian History" interview, historians should engage the public not only with the "end products" of history but also with the process. In "The Fall of Quebec," Charles Stacey uses his pointer and map to show the battle positions. Various scholars and members of the public give their views on the historical events as well as their contemporary implications. Where we encounter these multiple views, in this and other programs, they are sometimes even left as such with no correct version given. The host of *A War for Survival*, for example, ends the historians' debate by cutting off Jean-Pierre Wallot in mid-sentence. "Winnipeg General Strike 1919," also presents various and opposing opinions.

In *A People's History*, only in the first episode on the pre-contact Indigenous peoples, where the narrative relies on oral history and the archaeological record, does the narrator hint that our knowledge of the past is imperfect. This is an uncertainty not afforded the following episodes for which there are written records or first-person testimony. Lyle Dick has written that *A People's History* shared with *The National Dream* a similar combination of narrative and fictional techniques.[10] But aside from this combination they are not so similar. With Berton, even though his was an authoritative voice, the audience at least knows that *The National Dream* is only his interpretation of events. This is not so with the unseen narrator of *A People's History*.

In the *Explorations* programs too, the variety of presentation strategies, including multiple and opposing perspectives, and reference to incomplete evidence, conveys to the viewer some of the challenges of arriving at historical knowledge. Even in *Durham's Canada*, the *You Are There* device serves to highlight different viewpoints on the same events. The journalists' questioning of Durham suggests that there were contemporaneous challenges to Durham, even if, in the end, the ideas of the television writers emerge as the most relevant. Later television histories rarely allowed opposition to the narrative perspective. Altogether the presentation of history as contested, or at least as not always fully knowable, distinguishes some of the earliest programs from the more recent ones.

Connected to the one big story approach of *A People's History* is the diminished role of professional historians. After *Images of Canada*, historians disappeared from the screen and, except for the role of consultant or advisor, from behind the screen as well. But until then some historians had been very involved. With *Explorations*, Eric Koch admitted not being much conversant with Canadian history but said that Jack Saywell had been very helpful to him.[11] In Koch's time not just Saywell but also historians like Donald Creighton, Charles Stacey, and Kenneth McNaught played important roles in CBC productions, including those based on their own publications. Ramsay Cook, later recalling his experience in *Images of Canada*'s "The Craft of History," said he had "a very free hand" in the production, and the producers encouraged him to choose his interview subjects, devise his own questions, and fully participate in the editing.[12] Saywell had a similar experience working with Koch. Creighton too, in "Heroic Beginnings," seems to have worked relatively unrestricted.[13] After this era, producers still used historians' written works, but the scholars themselves were rarely involved in the same way. In *The Valour and the Horror* they were clearly unwelcome and in *A People's History*, at least by some on the executive team, only welcomed as advisors.

The reasoning on the part of the makers of *The Valour and the Horror* seemed to be that, as journalists, they were more objective than historians and better equipped to get at the truth of history. The senior team of *A People's History* felt they could better present history to the public. First-person testimony in all its forms was also seen as an authoritative and unmediated route to arrive at what really happened, which was something historians could not provide. Thus the combination of journalist-written narrative and first-person testimony helped to justify the exclusion of historians onscreen. Jack Saywell (in *A War for Survival*) and Donald Creighton (in *Images of Canada*) do put forward their ideas relatively unchallenged. And, although interviewers Paul Fox and Ramsay Cook, in the two "Long View[s] of Canadian History" and "The Craft of History," pose some difficult questions to their historian subjects, the scholars are allowed to expound upon their ideas at some length. But this is no different than the narratives in *The Valour and the Horror* and *A People's History* and the selected first-person testimony that support them. Even the old-school historians like Creighton and Arthur Lower were at least aware of their own subjectivities: in "The Craft of History," Creighton says to Cook that, in terms of making value judgments, he was only human. And Lower says, "What's a man amount to who hasn't got some bias, who doesn't stand for anything?"[14] They were conscious of the personal values and viewpoints they brought to their work.

The challenges of *The Valour and the Horror* show what can happen when assuming a stance of complete objectivity while clearly professing a point of view. Producers of *A People's History* were more subtle in their approach, but striving to avoid controversy by reserving judgment and attempting to be neutral is also a problem. Historian Patrice Groulx has noted that, in *A People's History*, the conquest of Quebec is treated as a contest that nobody won.[15] It is the same kind of interpretation offered at the end of "The Fall of Quebec" some forty years earlier, where, despite the fractious symbolism of the Battle of the Plains of Abraham and its role in the continuing tensions between English and French Canada, Georges-Henri Lévesque ends with the idea that somehow "both sides won." At least in that program a range of historians express various opinions on the meaning and significance of the event.

The move in Canadian historiography away from nationalist histories was not central to the move away from the involvement of professional historians in Canadian history programming at the CBC. Historians specializing in the history of Canadian national development have always been active. Certainly there was a growing emphasis at the CBC on entertainment over the educational and informational values with which historians had traditionally been associated. But more important is the fact that the producers of Canadian history on CBC television were no longer the program organizers, producers, and directors who once worked collaboratively with the scholars. They were journalists, who declared their professional standards and practices to be at odds with those of professional historians. They used historians' written material to create the television narratives but presented works of "people's history" that were undisturbed onscreen by imperfect knowledge or messy debate.

This book begins and now ends with *Canada: The Story of Us*, the first major CBC television documentary or docudrama series on the history of Canada since *Canada: A People's History*. It was also the second such work on Canadian history to prompt the CBC president to issue an apology to viewers. The series was produced "under the guidance of" experts, by a company led by former CBC executive and self-described producer and journalist Julie Bristow.[16] Yet the nature and extent of the expert input was limited before production even began, as the model for the series had been established with *America: The Story of Us* and *Australia: The Story of Us*, which featured twelve and eight episodes, respectively. The Canadian version had ten, each with one theme, five stories, celebrity commentary, and extensive CGI. According to Bristow, it was "history for a new generation."[17] But after the first few episodes it was clear that, at least in terms of content themes and presentation, it was not new history.

Documentaries and docudramas on CBC television have been an important source of knowledge about Canadian history. As such, these works can be critiqued in terms of content and of the means provided to the audience to assess the nature of what they were seeing and hearing. But in order to understand why this programming took the shape it did, it must be understood within the many contexts of television production. It was not simply a result of choices made by television producers based on popular ideas about Canadian history. It was more a reflection of governmental and institutional policy, trends in the television industry, and institutional and professional practice. Television mirrors the society in which it operates, but it also helps to shape it. The CBC has helped to shape how and what we know, as well as what we do not know, about the Canadian past.

Notes

INTRODUCTION

1 Eric Koch, interview by author; Vincent Tovell, interview by author; George Robertson, interview by author.

2 A critical political economy approach to studying cultural products involves examining these products in light of their specific contexts of production and consumption. See Golding and Murdock, "Culture, Communications, and Political Economy."

3 Golding and Murdock, "Culture, Communications, and Political Economy," 77.

4 Nichols, *Introduction to Documentary*, 6.

5 Canadian Media Fund, app. A (2018–19) "Definitions and Essential Requirements," 2–7, https://cmf-fmc.ca/getattachment/a092a446-be 98-4503-add8-f8bb058da775/Appendix-A-Definitions-and-Essential-Requirements.aspx (viewed May 2018).

6 Nichols, *Introduction to Documentary*, 14–41.

7 Ibid., 7.

8 *Broadcasting Act* (S.C. 1991, c. 11), 3 (l), http://laws-lois.justice.gc.ca/eng/acts/B-9.01/ (viewed June 2017).

9 See Raboy, *Missed Opportunities*, for a thorough discussion of national broadcasting policy from the Aird Commission in 1929 to the late 1980s.

10 See Vipond, *Listening In*, and "The Beginnings of Public Broadcasting," 151.

11 Canada, Parliament, House of Commons, *Debates*, Parliamentary Session 17/3, 18 May 1932, 3035.

12 See Vipond, "Beginnings of Public Broadcasting in Canada." This model eventually extended to television and became the lasting standard for broadcasting in Canada.

13 Canada, Royal Commission on National Development in the Arts, Letters and Sciences, *Report*, xi.

14 Ibid., 23–49.

15 CBC, *Annual Report, 2001–2002,* 20–1.

16 Carvalho and Gemenne, "Introduction," 1.

17 Anderson, *Imagined Communities,* 7.

18 See ibid., 5–12, and chapter 11.

19 Smith, *Nationalism: Theory, Ideology, History,* 126–7.

20 See Anderson, *Imagined Communities,* esp. chap. 11.

21 See Gordon, *Hero and Historians,* for how Jacques Cartier was used to help construct English and French Canadian nationalisms in similar ways.

22 Breuilly, "Nationalism and the Making of National Pasts," 10. See Neatby and Hodgins, "Introduction," 3–8; Vance, *Death so Noble,* 3–11; Smith, *Nationalism,* 126–7.

23 On the role of historians in the production and sustaining of silences about the past, see Trouillot, *Silencing the Past.*

24 CBC Public Affairs Department, "A War for Survival," 28 September 1962 [VTR date], CTASC, F0402, file 2001-015/001 (09), 29; Saywell, "Documentary Dramas–Broadcast on CBCTV 1960–66, CTASC, F0402, file 2004-015/001 (02)."

25 Martin, *Past Futures*; also see White, *Metahistory,* introduction.

CHAPTER ONE

1 "Report on Television by Director General of Programmes of the Canadian Broadcasting Corporation on a Visit to The United Kingdom from May 20th to June 14th – 1949 by E. L. Bushnell," 47, LAC, RG 41, vol. 338, file 14-4-7.

2 Some involved historians, for example, *Canada as a Nation* was a four-part series on important Canadian statesmen from the past that featured historians Frank Underhill, Donald Creighton, Arthur Lower, and Gordon Rothney. CBC, *Annual Report 1950–51,* 15; QUA, Arthur Lower Fonds, box 21, file B571.

3 The departments were Talks and Public Affairs, News, Drama, Music, Farm and Fisheries, Religious, Children's, School and Educational, and Outside Broadcasts.

4 CBC achieved this by combining owned-and-operated stations with privately owned affiliated stations, making them part of the longest microwave network in the world by 1958. Peers, *Public Eye,* 44–7.

5 Some examples were variety fare with Ed Sullivan, Milton Berle, and Jackie Gleason. Similar Canadian offerings were *Showtime, Juliette,* and *Holiday Ranch,* but the schedule also included lots of drama in CBC *television Theatre, General Motors Theatre,* and *Folio,* and in public affairs shows like *Tabloid.*

6 The meaning of "adult education" programming was not internally uniformly understood. It referred to shows like *Explorations* as well as to more formal educational programs. After the late 1960s, to lessen confusion, Eric Koch proposed that only those programs actually produced in collaboration with a university or organization like the CAAE be referred to as such, and programs (like the former *Explorations*) were referred to as "enrichment." "Arts and Sciences, Eric Koch, n.d.," LAC, RG 41, vol. 593, file 280.

7 This file is dated 1959 but noted as based on an earlier document. See "Public Affairs Broadcasting in the CBC," 4, 7, 11, LAC, MG 30, E 481, vol. 41, file "Program Policy 1959."

8 On *Radisson*, see E.L. Bushnell, Management Memo No. 65, 6 March 1957; E. H. Hausmann, "Radisson," *Star TV Week*, 8 August 1970; Barbara Moon, "How They're Making a Hero Out of Pierre Radisson," *Maclean's*, 19 January 1957, 14–16, 46. All at CBCRL, Production File "Radisson."

9 Hallman to Jennings, 2 November 1955, LAC, RG 41, vol. 206, file 11-18-11-68; Hallman to McDonald, 28 December 1956, LAC, RG 41, vol. 484, file 11-18-11-108.

10 D.E. Lytle and Pierre Juneau, "Draft Report on Study of CBC/NFB Relations," 1 March 1966, including "Appendix A," A.D. Dunton, "Joint report dated Ottawa, October 23, 1952 [...] on the degree and nature of cooperation which should exist between the CBC and the NFB on television matters," LAC, RG 41, vol. 596, file 319, pt. 2.

11 Hallman to Graham, 20 July 1956, LAC, RG 41, vol. 249, file 11-38-4, pt. 1.

12 Hallman to Whalley, 18 May 1956, LAC, RG 41, vol. 249, file 11-38-4, pt. 1.

13 Koch described the role of program organizer, in his day, as a cross between today's executive producer and producer. Producer was the equivalent of a later director. Eric Koch, interview by author; CTASC, Inventory F0472, fonds-level description.

14 Koch to Peers, 9 May 1956; "Explorations: Tentative Plans," 27 August 1956. Both in LAC, RG 41, vol. 249, file 11-38-4, pt. 1.

15 Kemp to Koch, 21 September 1956, LAC, RG 41, vol. 249, file 11-38-4, pt. 1.

16 CBC press release, November 1957, CBCRL, Production File "Explorations 1957–58."

17 "New Horizons/On Television: TV Documentaries A Bold New Series," *CBC Times*, 21–27 October 1956, in CBCRL, Production File "Explorations 1956–57."

18 Hallman to McDonald, 28 December 1956, LAC, RG 41, vol. 484, file

11-18-11-108; Hallman to Graham, August 1956, LAC, RG 41, vol. 249, file 11-38-4, pt. 1.

19 NFB, *Annual Report* (1960–61), 8, 9; NFB, *Annual Report* (1961–62), 7; Catherine McIver, 30 March 1962, 2 October 1962. All in LAC, RG 41, vol. 250, file 11-38-4, pt. 8. See also CBC, "CBC-TV Network 1962–63," 33; CBCRL, T170, CBC/CC, 1961, 4. These were part of the larger *The History Makers* series produced by the board. See National Film Board, *Annual Report* (1962–63), 10, (1963–64), 8.

20 Hallman to McDonald, 28 December 1956, LAC, RG 41, vol. 484, file 11-18-11-108; CBC press release no. 398, 27 November 1957, CBCRL, Production File "Explorations 1957–58." *Explorations* producers had to find a different production studio than the one planned, so they were forced to use a mobile crew and equipment that year.

21 Hallman to Asst. Director of Program Planning and Production, 2 April 1957, LAC, RG 41, vol. 250, file 11-38-4, pt. 3; CBC press release, November 1957, CBCRL, Production File "Explorations 1957–58."

22 McDonald to the regional producers, 30 May 1957, LAC, RG 41, vol. 250, file 11-38-4, pt. 3; CBC press release, November 1957, CBCRL, Production File "Explorations 1957–58."

23 Koch to Patchell, 14 August 1957, LAC, RG 41, vol. 250, file 11-38-4, pt. 4; Koch to Hallman, 6 February 1957, LAC, RG 41, vol. 250, file 11-38-4, pt. 3.

24 Koch to Hallman, 6 February 1957, LAC, RG 41, vol. 250, file 11-38-4, pt. 3. Study bulletins accompanied some of the programming run by CBC radio Talks and Public Affairs.

25 Duke was in the film department. Duke to Koch, 6 September 1957, LAC, RG 41, vol. 250, file 11-38-4, pt. 4.

26 Emphasis in original. Koch to Duke, 16 September 1957, LAC, RG 41, vol. 250, file 11-38-4, pt. 4.

27 From the Massey Commission, for example. See Canada, Royal Commission on Broadcasting, *Report*, 33.

28 Patchell to Koch, 13 December 1956, LAC, RG 41, vol. 249, file 11-38-4, pt. 2.

29 Peers to Patchell, 20 December 1956, LAC, RG 41, vol. 249, file 11-38-4, pt. 2.

30 Nixon to Peers, 27 December 1956, LAC, RG 41, vol. 249, file 11-38-4, pt. 2.

31 Koch to Cowan, 12 September 1958, LAC, RG 41, vol. 250, file 11-38-4, pt. 6.

32 Cowan to Koch, 28 August 1958, LAC, RG 41, vol. 250, file 11-38-4, pt. 6.

33 Koch to Cowan, 12 September 1958, LAC, RG 41, vol. 250, file 11-38-4, pt. 6.

34 Cowan to Koch, 24 September 1958, LAC, RG 41, vol. 250, file 11-38-4, pt. 6.

35 Forbes, "In Search of a Post-Confederation Maritime Historiography," 4.

36 Koch to Gray, 18 February 1959, LAC, RG 41, vol. 250, file 11-38-4, pt.7; Tovell to Kemp, 17 November 1959, LAC, RG 41, vol. 250, file 11-38-4, pt. 8.

37 Ouimet to Peers, 3 October 1960, LAC, RG 41, vol. 484, file 11-18-11-108.

38 Mann, *Dream of Nation,* 300.

39 Nelles, *Art of Nation-Building,* 122–40.

40 Powley to Ouimet, 29 April 1959, LAC, RG 41, vol. 482, file 11-39-29.

41 Morton, "Historical Societies and Museums," 254.

42 Stacey, "Canadian Archives."

43 Moore to Koch, 28 November 1958, LAC, RG 41, vol. 250, file 11-38-4, pt. 7.

44 Stacey, *Date with History,* 266.

45 Powley to Nixon, 18 February 1959, LAC, RG 41, vol. 482, file 11-39-29.

46 Bushnell to Pearkes, 4 June 1959, LAC, RG 41, vol. 482, file 11-39-29.

47 Ibid.

48 McArthur to Major-General Allard, 5 August 1959, LAC, RG 41, vol. 482, file 11-39-29.

49 Koch to Stacey, 30 April 1959, LAC, RG 41, vol. 250, file 11-38-4, pt. 7.

50 Steinhouse to Koch, 23 June 1959, LAC, RG 41, vol. 250, file 11-38-4, pt. 7.

51 The French version aired on Radio-Canada in *Premier Plan* on the same night. Peers to Ouimet, 20 August 1959, LAC, RG 41, vol. 484, file 11-18-11-108.

52 See Rudin, *Making History,* chaps. 2 and 3.

53 Ibid., 52.

54 Neatby, "National History," 211–12.

55 Koch to Steinhouse, 15 September 1959, LAC, RG 41, vol. 250, file 11-38-4, pt. 7.

56 Peers to Jennings, 5 August 1959, LAC, RG 41, vol. 484, file 11-18-11-108.

57 McNaught, *Conscience and History,* 81.

58 *Winnipeg Tribune* and *Winnipeg Free Press* clippings, both 9 July 1959, LAC, RG 41, vol. 484, file 11-18-11-108.

59 *Winnipeg Tribune,* 29 July 1959, LAC, RG 41, vol. 484, file 11-18-11-108.

60 Brown to Finlay, 13 July 1959, LAC, RG 41, vol. 484, file 11-18-11-108.

61 Finlay to Jennings, 16 July 1959, LAC, RG 41, vol. 484, file 11-18-11-108.

62 Peers to Jennings, 5 August 1959, LAC, RG 41, vol. 484, file 11-18-11-108. Jennings had initially pointed out to Peers the mistake about the ad, 27 July 1959, LAC, RG 41, vol. 484, file 11-18-11-108.

63 McArthur to Finlay, 7 August 1959, LAC, RG 41, vol. 484, file 11-18-11-108.

64 Ouimet to Alphonse Ouimet, 21 August 1959, LAC, RG 41, vol. 484, file 11-18-11-108.

65 "Winnipeg General Strike 1919."

66 Peers referred to the interviewing of Charles Simonte, also a member of the Committee of One Thousand, who does not appear in the final program. It's possible his clips were cut for balance. Peers to Jennings, 5 August 1959, LAC, RG 41, vol. 484, file 11-18-11-108.

67 See, for example, Kealey, "1919"; McKay, "Strikes in the Maritimes"; Reilly, "General Strike in Amherst."

68 McKay, "Strikes in the Maritimes," 10. This is a statistic McKay believes to be comparatively high in the national context.

69 See Reilly, "General Strike in Amherst."

70 Kealey, "1919," 15; Historian Kurt Korneski, reviewing the film *Prairie Fire* (1999), noted that its interpretive framework was this idea of "western exceptionalism." See Korneski, "Prairie Fire," 259.

71 Kealey, "1919," 14–15.

72 CBC, *Long View of Canadian History*, 7.

73 Neatby to Underhill, 25 August 1957, 17 September 1958, LAC, MG 30 D 204, vol. 11.

74 Possibly rivalled by the two volumes by Richard Gwyn, published in 2007 and 2011.

75 CBC, *CBC Times* (10–16 February 1957), 4–5. For example, "Canada as a Nation," with Lower and Underhill; the radio docudrama "The Honourable Member from Kingston," also for *Wednesday Night*; and the television drama "John A. of the Double Wedding," for *Folio*.

76 The above from CBC, *A Long View of Canadian History*, 1–7.

77 Wright, *Donald Creighton*, 168–9.

78 "Outlines of Thirteen Television Programmes in the History of Canada from Earliest Times to the End of the 19th Century," LAC, MG 31 D 77, vol. 34, file "History of Canada TV Series."

79 "A Long View of Canadian History, with Professor Frank Underhill."

80 Donald Wright, "Creighton, Donald Grant"; Francis, *Frank H. Underhill*, 160.

81 Stacey, *Date with History*, 228, 247; Francis, *Frank H. Underhill*, 160. Ramsay Cook, a student and later colleague of Creighton's, agreed that "crusty" might be a good term for him but that there was much more to Creighton than that. The CBC's George Robertson, who worked with Creighton on *Images of Canada*, thought him a sentimental man and noted that he had a humorous side. Ramsay Cook, interview by author; George Robertson, telephone communication with author.

82 See Francis, *Frank H. Underhill*.

83 On Underhill's early years, see Francis, *Frank H. Underhill*, esp. chaps. 5, 8–10.

84 He stressed the similarities between the two within the British liberal-democratic tradition. Francis, *Frank H. Underhill*, 168; "A Long View of Canadian History, with Professor Frank Underhill."

85 Francis, *Frank H. Underhill*, 75.

86 Fox to Underhill, 12 May, 17 June 1960, LAC, MG 30 D 204, vol. 11.

87 Also see Berger, *Writing of Canadian History*, 200.

88 "Prof. Underhill Speaks on Confederation at Banquet," Saskatoon *Daily Star*, 2 July 1927, LAC, MG 30 D 204, vol. 17, file "Canadian Confed, July 1, 1927," 2–3, quoted in Francis, *Frank H. Underhill*, 70–1n19.

89 Pat Pearce, "History Is Ours," 10 June 1960, and "Provocative Show Stars Professor," 16 June 1960, both in the *Montreal Star*, CTASC, F0472, file 2004-047/010 (14).

90 Creighton to Crysler, 23 June 1959, LAC, MG 31, D77, vol. 9, file "Television Broadcasts June 16 and June 30, 1959."

91 Fairley to Underhill, 5 July 1960, LAC, MG 30 D 204, vol. 10, file "CBC pt. 1." See CBC, Publications Branch, *Long View of Canadian History* and *Radical Tradition*.

92 King to Koch, 10 July 1958; Koch to Partridge, 24 October 1958. Both in LAC, RG 41, vol. 250, file 11-38-4, pt. 6.

93 Wright, *Professionalization of History in English Canada*, 169–70.

94 The three other series were *Portraits of the Thirties*, a documentary on the 1930s in Canada, on Premiers Maurice Duplessis, Mitch Hepburn, and Bill Aberhart; *The Fourteenth Colony*, a docudrama on the invasion of Quebec by the Americans during the American Revolution; and *Reluctant Nation*, a drama on the one-hundred-year period after Confederation.

95 Jack Saywell, interview by author.

96 Jack Saywell, "Documentary Dramas – Broadcast on CBCTV 1960–1966," CTASC, F0402, file 2004-015/001 (02); "Durham's Canada," pts. 1–3, *Explorations*.

97 Tovell to Kemp, 17 and 23 November 1959, LAC, RG 41, vol. 250, file 11-38-4, pt. 8; "Durham's Canada," CBC *Times*, 10–16 December 1960, 13.

98 Craig, *Lord Durham's Report*, 13.

99 The published script refers to *Durham's Canada* as "A Play for Television." Koch, Tovell, and Saywell, *Success of a Mission*.

100 National Public Radio, interview with Walter Cronkite, 27 October 2003, http://www.npr.org/news/specials/cronkite/ (viewed April 2018).

101 Craig, *Lord Durham's Report*, 104.

102 Ibid, 16.

103 "Durham's Canada," CBC *Times*, 10–16 December 1960, 13.

104 Pat Pearce, "CBC 'Explorations' Fascinating Series," *Montreal Star*, 29 December 1960, 6, CTASC, F0402, file 2004-015/001 (01).

105 Bob Burgess, *Ottawa Journal*, 22 December 1960; Phil Lee, *Victoria Daily Times*, 30 December 1960, both in CTASC, F0402, file 2004-047/017 (04).

106 R.H. Roy, "Historic Drama Invites More of Its Type," [unsourced newspaper review], CTASC, F0402, file 2004-015/001 (01).

107 Bob Blackburn, *Ottawa Citizen*, 22 December 1960, CTASC, F0472, file 2004-047/017 (04).

108 McIlhagga to Hallman, 8 December 1961, LAC, RG 41, acc. 86-87/031, box 198, file 18-16-A-2 to P-18.

109 CBC Public Affairs Department, "A War for Survival," 28 September 1962 [VTR date], CTASC, F0402, file 2001-015/001 (09), 29; Saywell, "Documentary Dramas–Broadcast on CBCTV 1960–66, CTASC, F0402, file 2004-015/001 (02)."

110 William Morton on R.G. Trotter, "Aims in the Study and Teaching of History in Canadian Universities To-day," in *Annual Report*, Canadian Historical Association, Annual Report (1943), 61, quoted in Berger, "William Morton," 23n27.

111 Catherine McIver, 2 October 1962, LAC, RG 41, vol. 250, file 11-38-4, pt. 8.

112 See Kuffert, *Great Duty*, 198–238.

CHAPTER TWO

1 McArthur to list, 6 December 1961, LAC, RG 41, acc. 86-87/031, box 198, file 18-16-A-2 to P-18.

2 Robert Fulford, "Canadian Cultural Nationalism," in *1974 Britannica Book of the Year* (Toronto: Encyclopedia Britannica, 1974), 171, quoted in Bruce McKay, "CBC and the Public," 136.

3 Powley to Nixon, 3 October 1960, LAC, RG 41, acc. 86-87/031, box 198, file 18-16-A-2 to P-18.

4 Powley to Nixon, 9 November 1960, LAC, RG 41, acc. 86-87/031, box 198, file 18-16-A-2 to P-18.

5 Powley to Nixon, 3 October 1960, LAC, RG 41, acc. 86-87/031, box 198, file 18-16-A-2 to P-18.

6 Powley to Nixon, 20 October 1961, LAC, RG 41, vol. 728, file 51.

7 Canada, Federal Cultural Policy Review Committee, *Report*, 278–9; CRTC, "Decision: Renewal of the Canadian Broadcasting Corporation's Radio and Television Network Licences, 52–5, 30 April 1979, CBCRL.

8 CBC, "Regionalization in the CBC," October 1976, LAC, RG 41, vol. 979, file 9. p. 1.

9 Picard to CBC staff, 25 March 1970, CBCRL, CBC-Policy [fiche].

10 Knowlton Nash, interview by author.

11 Nash, *Prime Time at Ten*, 65.

12 Hogarth, *Documentary Television in Canada*, 92–6.

13 Ibid., 94.

14 Eric Koch, interview by author; Vincent Tovell, telephone interview by author.

15 Barry to Nixon, 3 August 1966; Raymond to Nixon, 3 November 1967. Both in LAC, RG 41, vol. 726, file 16.

16 On the entrance of the CTV, see Rutherford, *When Television Was Young*, 108–22.

17 Swan, "Educative Activities," 3, 5.

18 "Arts and Sciences, Eric Koch," n.d., RG 41, vol. 593, file 280.

19 "Educational TV – Informal," 14 November 1966, LAC, RG 41, vol. 865, file PG 4-3-1; "Canadian Broadcasting Corporation Adult Education Programming," n.d. [c. 1964–65], LAC, RG 41, vol. 865, file PG 4-3-1.

20 "CBC Position on Educational Television," February 1967, 6, LAC, RG 41, vol. 865, File PG -4-3-1.

21 The Quebec Broadcasting Bureau (1969), the Ontario Educational Communications Authority (1970), and the Alberta Educational Communications Corporation (ACCESS) (1973). See Swan, "Educative Activities," 3, 5.

22 Swan, "Educative Activities," 3, 5.

23 One example that annoyed CBC management for this reason was a Channel 19 show fittingly entitled, "The Crisis in Education," which aired during prime time on a Sunday night in December 1974. Munro to VP Corporate Affairs, 7 January 1974, LAC, RG 41, vol. 774, file GM 7-2-16.

24 Canada, *An Act Respecting Broadcasting*, 1958.

25 Stewart and Hull, *Canadian Television Policy*, 29–37; McKay, "The CBC and the Public," 331–3. Regarding the Commonwealth productions, this was due to the fact that, for its quota system, the Independent

Television Authority in the UK awarded to Canadian productions a 100 percent rating and wanted the same for its productions in Canada. See Canada, Parliament, Standing Committee on Broadcasting, *Minutes of the Proceedings and Evidence*, no. 3, 20 February 1961, 83–4, cited in Edwardson, *Canadian Content*, 88. For Commonwealth and French-language productions this calculation was valid up to one-third of total broadcast time over every quarter. Canadian content was part of a larger project of Canadianization. See Edwardson, *Canadian Content*.

26 "The Tenth Decade, 1957–1967," file "The Tenth Decade," CBCRL.

27 "King-Bennett-Meighen-St Laurent Program Proposal," 15 October 1971, LAC, RG 41, vol. 827, file 134.

28 The clips, along with other material, comprised thirteen half-hours of television for each series. CBC press release, May 1973, LAC, RG 41, vol. 249, file 11-38, pt. 3; CBC, "One Canadian: The Political Memoirs of John Diefenbaker," CBCRL.

29 The Canadian content quota for Commonwealth and French programs previously in effect was restricted in 1970 with new CRTC regulations. In 1972 the restriction was abolished. See Canada, Federal Cultural Policy Review Committee, *Report*, 287.

30 Nash, interview by author; CBC, "Regionalization in the CBC," 1 October 1976, LAC, RG 41, vol. 979, file 9, p. 1.

31 Nash to Koch and Tovell, 16 March 1971, LAC, RG 41, vol. 827, file 134.

32 Tovell to Nash, n.d.; Koch and Tovell to Nash, 10 November 1970. Both in LAC, RG 41, fol. 827, file 134.

33 Nash to Garriock, 14 October 1971, LAC, RG 41, fol. 827, file 134. Other ideas were to base the series on the history of particular Canadian cities and to include four episodes of biographies. Tovell, "Canadian Civilization," n.d., LAC, RG 41, vol. 827, file 134.

34 Tovell, telephone interview by author.

35 Koch and Tovell to Nash, 10 November 1970, LAC, RG 41, vol. 827, file 134.

36 Tovell to Patchell, 21 September 1971, LAC, RG 41, vol. 827, file 134.

37 Tovell, "Canadian Civilization," n.d., LAC, RG 41, vol. 827, file 134.

38 PGR Campbell to Nash, 27 January 1971, LAC, RG 41, vol. 827, file 134.

39 Koch to Nash, 22 December 1970; Tovell, "Canadian Civilization," n.d. Both in LAC, RG 41, vol. 827, file 134.

40 Tovell, "Canadian Civilization," n.d.; "Images of Canada" program proposal, 21 September 1971. Both in both in LAC, RG 41, vol. 827, file 134.

41 See Berger, *Writing of Canadian History*, 259–320.

42 Cook, "Canadian Centennial Cerebrations," 663; Careless, "'Limited Identities' in Canada."

43 Robertson to Nash, n.d., LAC RG 41, vol. 827, file 134.

44 On the goals of the episode: Robertson to Nash, n.d.; Robertson to Nash et al., 20 December 1971; Tovell to Kerr, 25 June 1971. All in LAC, RG 41, vol. 827, file 134. See also Cook, *Craft of History*, introduction; CBC press release, 25 August 1971, LAC, RG 41, vol. 827, file 134.

45 Lower also read French and corresponded with francophone historians in Canada (see Wright, *Donald Creighton*, 272), but he also had an overall sentimental and romantic view of the French Canadian people (see Berger, *Writing of Canadian History*, 127).

46 Lower, *History and Myth,* 122. On Groulx, who worked with the CBC French language service (Radio-Collège) on discussions and dramatized pieces on the history of Quebec, see Bilodeau, "L'Histoire Nationale," 228.

47 On the scholarly thinking of historians of Quebec about the history of the province Quebec throughout the twentieth century, see Rudin, *Making History in Twentieth-Century Quebec.*

48 Wright, *Donald Creighton*, 306.

49 *Conversation with Professor Donald Creighton.*

50 On Creighton's attitude towards Riel, see Wright, "Donald Creighton, John Gray, and the Making of Macdonald."

51 "Audience Reactions to English Television Network Programs" (17–23 March 1972), 8, in CBC, Research Department, "Performance of CBC English Television Network Programs" (Fall–Winter 1971–72), UTRL. These figures were almost identical for its repeat showings. See "Audience Reactions to English Television Network Programs" (23–29 March 1973), 10, in CBC Research Report No. 23, CBC, Research Department, "Performance of CBC English Television Network Programs" (8 September 1972–24 May 1973), UTRL.

52 L. Ian MacDonald, "Images of Canada: A Mirror in the Tube," *Montreal Gazette*, 17 February 1973 [written a year after "The Craft of History" first aired], 27–8, LAC, RG 41, vol. 827, file 134; Blaik Kirby, "CBC vs. Canadian Complex," *Globe and Mail*, 21 March 1972, CBCRL, Production File "Images of Canada"; Sheila McCook, "Historians Almost Upstaged History," *Ottawa Citizen*, 22 March 1972, in *Canada in Perspective*, 20, CBCRL, Production File "Canada in Perspective."

53 Ted Ferguson, *Vancouver Sun*, 22 March 1972, in CBC, *Canada in Perspective*, 21, CBCRL, Production File "Canada in Perspective."

54 Kerr to Nash, 12 February 1971; Nash to Koch and Tovell, 16 February 1971. Both in LAC, RG 41, vol. 827, file 134.

55 Tovell to Kerr, 25 June 1971, LAC, RG 41, vol. 827, file 134.

56 Quoted in L. Ian MacDonald, "Images of Canada: A Mirror in the Tube," *Montreal Gazette*, 17 February 1973, 27–8, LAC, RG 41, vol. 827, file 134.

57 "Audience Reactions to English Television Network Programs" (23–29 March 1973), 10, in CBC Research Report No. 23, CBC, Research Department, "Performance of CBC English Television Network Programs" (8 September 1972–24 May 1973), UTRL.

58 CBC press release no. 87, 9 February 1973, CBCRL, Production File "Images of Canada."

59 In 1974 Creighton's expanded story was published in book form by Macmillan of Canada in cooperation with the Department of Indian and Northern Affairs (which then governed Parks Canada and the National Historic Parks and Sites Branch).

60 Ronald Way, "Recommendations Concerning the Louisbourg Project," quoted in Taylor, *Negotiating the Past*, 180n38 (see also 169–90).

61 Vincent Tovell on "Images of Canada," a series "unique in television," CBC press release no. 12, 4 March 1974, CBCRL, Production File "Images of Canada, 1973–1977."

62 MacNutt, *New Brunswick*; and MacNutt, *Atlantic Provinces*.

63 See Reid, "Writing about Regions," 71–5. Atlantic myths and stereotypes have been dissected by scholars like Ian McKay, who writes about Nova Scotia in this respect. See, for example, McKay, *Quest of the Folk*; McKay, *In the Province of History*; and his articles in *Acadiensis*.

64 The Prairie region later split into Manitoba and Saskatchewan, while the Maritimes (Atlantic) continued to be combined.

65 See Forbes, "In Search of a Post-Confederation Maritime Historiography," 12. The works were MacKinnon, *Government of Prince Edward Island*; Beck, *Government of Nova Scotia*; Thorburn, *Politics in New Brunswick*.

66 Bill Musselwhite, *Calgary Herald*, 20 March 1974, [press clippings "Images of Canada (The Promised Land – March 18)"], LAC, RG 41, vol. 814, file T-1-3-10, pt. 4.

67 For example, Joan Irwin, "Images of Canada Portrays our Past with High Artistry," n.d., *Montreal Star*, LAC, RG 41, vol. 827, file 134; and excerpts in "Images of Canada (The Promised Land – March 18)," LAC, RG 41, vol. 814, file T-1-3-10, pt. 4.

68 Also noted by Tovell, telephone interview by author.

69 "Audience Reactions to English Television Network Programs" (23–29 March 1973), 10, in CBC Research Report No. 23, CBC, Research

Department, "Performance of CBC English Television Network Programs" (8 September 1972–24 May 1973), UTRL.

70 Although a CBC press release stressed that the two foreign series were personal statements, while *Images* consisted of "interpretive essays on the background of modern Canada." CBC press release No. 126, 4 March 1974, CBCRL, Production File "Images of Canada 1973–77."

71 It was the last essay in Klinck, *Literary History of Canada*.

72 "Wednesday Special on Inuit Art, People," *Regina Leader Post*, 22 October 1976, http://news.google.com/newspapers?id=XElVAAAA IBAJ&pg=3878,2076964 (viewed June 2018).

73 *Images of Canada* brochure, LAC, RG 41, acc. 86-87/C31, box 152. Tovell had originally wanted to follow these two episodes with two more on the northern links between the Soviets and Canada. Tovell, telephone interview by author.

74 "Program Production Costs Estimates," [for 1973–74], LAC, RG 41, vol. 827, file 134.

75 Tovell, preface, in Cook, *Craft of History*.

76 Quoted in L. Ian MacDonald, "Images of Canada: A Mirror in the Tube," *Montreal Gazette*, 17 February 1973, 27–8, LAC, RG 41, vol. 827, file 134.

77 Bob Blackburn, *Toronto Sun*, 7 December 1973, 28, quoted in McKay, "CBC and the Public," 121.

78 CBC, *Canada in Perspective*, 2, in CBCRL, Production File "Canada in Perspective."

79 "CBC Television Presents: The National Dream: Building the Impossible Railway," LAC, MG 31 D 196, vol. 250, file 7.

CHAPTER THREE

1 Rudyard Griffiths, "*The War on History*: An Interview with Pierre Berton by Rudyard Griffiths." 2002. https://www.chapters.indigo.ca/en-ca/books/marching-as-to-war-canadas/9780385258197-item.html (viewed June 2018).

2 "CBC television Presents: The National Dream: Building the Impossible Railway," LAC, MG 31 D 196, vol. 250, file 7.

3 Koch to Nash, 23 June 1970, LAC, RG 41, vol. 810, file T-1-3-2-5, pt. 1.

4 Tovell to Patchell, 30 May 1972, LAC, RG 41, vol. 827, file 134.

5 Laird to Nash, 4 October 1973, LAC, RG 41, vol. 805, file T-1-3-1-1, pt. 9.

6 Quoted in McKay, "CBC and the Public," 190–1; "Selected excerpts from the CRTC announcement in regard to renewal of CBC licenses" (1978), 11, LAC, RG 41, vol. 942, file 882.

7 [CBC] "Selected excerpts from the CRTC announcement in regard to renewal of CBC licences," 1978, 11, LAC, RG 41, vol. 942, file 882. On the 1974 hearings, see Hardin, *Closed Circuits*, 116–22; Committee on Television, "Saving the CBC," February 1974, LAC, RG 41, vol. 944, file 946, pt. 1; Robert Lewis, "Pierre Juneau's Spectacular Leap of Faith," *Saturday Night* (August 1974), 16, LAC, RG 41, vol. 67, file 2-3-18, pt. 6; Anon., "The CRTC Reports on National Broadcasting," *Montreal Gazette*, 5 April 1974, LAC, RG 41, vol. 67, file 2-3-18, pt. 6.

8 The commercials eventually disappeared only from radio.

9 CBC, "Touchstone for the CBC," June 1977, CBCRL. Johnson noted that the CBC report was deliberately advanced in order to precede the CRTC document. "The CBC Underwhelms Its Critics," *TV Guide*, 16–22 July 1977, 1–2, CBCRL, CBC-Policy [fiche].

10 The document also concluded that the CBC was "caught between its [public service] mandate and its commerciality." CRTC, "CBC television: Programming and Audiences – The English Language Service," Committee of Inquiry into the National Broadcasting Service, a background research paper, 4–6, 36, CBCRL.

11 CBC, "The CBC: A Perspective," vols. 1–3, 150–2, CBCRL.

12 Reported by Julianne Labreche, "Wasn't Louis Riel the Guy who Built the Alamo?" in Michael Posner, "The CRTC Gong Show Presents … The CBC!" *Maclean's* (23 October 1978), 21, LAC, RG 41, vol. 67, file 2-3-18, pt. 6.

13 Nash to Hallman, 27 September 1971, LAC, RG 41, vol. 805, file T1-3-1-1, pt. 5.

14 Nash to Norn Garriock, 5 February 1973, LAC, RG 41, vol. 810, file T1 3-2-6, pt. 2.

15 CBC, "Material in Support of CBC Applications for Renewal of Network Licences: English Language Television" (November 1973), 33, quoted in McKay, "CBC and the Public," 138.

16 Bob Patchell to Joe Doyle, 28 June 1973, LAC, RG 41, vol. 805, file T1-3-1-1, pt. 10.

17 Charland, "Technological Nationalism." Although, as Charland notes, unlike the railway, Canadian broadcasting was compelled to operate within the American model of cultural production.

18 Only his voice was heard, off-screen. See CBC press release no. 144, "Special Drama-Documentary, Mackenzie the Firebrand on CBC-TV March 17," 2 March 1971, LAC, RG 41, vol. 807, file T1-3-1-11, pt. 2.

19 Koch to Nash, 9 February 1971; Nash to Koch, 11 February 1971. Both in LAC, RG 41, vol. 810, file T1-3-2-5, pt. 1.

20 Nash to Sinclair, 19 May 1972, LAC, RG 41, vol. 840, file 311.

21 Sinclair to Nash, 28 September 1971, LAC, RG 41, vol. 840, file 311.

22 "The Great Railway," LAC, MG 31 D196, vol. 63, file 8.

23 Re Klondike, WRDARC, Pierre Berton Fonds, box 156, file 4; Production File "Klondike," CBCRL.

24 Berton to Norman Griesdorf, 2 February 1972, WRDARC, Pierre Berton Fonds, box 236, file 13.

25 Berton to Sinclair, 28 August 1974, WRDARC, Pierre Berton Fonds, box 236, file 13.

26 Ken Black to Nash, 18 October 1971, LAC, RG 41, vol. 840, file 311.

27 Thom Benson to Garriock, 24 November 1971, LAC, RG 41, vol. 840, file 311.

28 Nash to Garriock, 2 December 1971, LAC, RG 41, vol. 840, file 311.

29 "I recognize also that this department has had it's [sic] failures as well as its successes," Patchell to Nash, 26 November 1971, LAC, RG 41, vol. 840, file 311.

30 On the technicians' strike and the Whiteoak family tree, see Kenter, TV North, 197.

31 L. Ian MacDonald, Montreal Gazette, 26 May 1972, WRDARC, Pierre Berton Fonds, box 332, file 1.

32 Timothy Findley's diary entry, 20 March 1972, LAC, MG 31 D 196, vol. 58, file 2.

33 Ibid., entries 20 and 25 March 1972.

34 Hallman to Munro, 2 April 1970, LAC, RG 41, vol. 608, file 4.

35 Eldon Wilcox to Paul Siren, 21 April 1972, LAC, RG 41, vol. 840, file 311.

36 John Grenville to Wilcox, 24 May 1972, LAC, RG 41, vol. 840, file 311.

37 Wilcox to Stanley Cox, 29 May 1972, LAC, RG 41, vol. 840, file 311.

38 Peter Russell to Cox, 31 May 1972, LAC, RG 41, vol. 840, file 311.

39 Nash, Prime Time at Ten, 68.

40 Nash to Patchell, 12 June 1972, LAC, RG 41, vol. 840, file 311; "The National Dream: Notes on the First Outlines, April 7th, 1972," LAC, MG 31 D 196, vol. 58, file 9. "Preamble to Outlines," n.d., LAC, MG 31 D 196, vol. 58, file 8.

41 Berton to Murray, n.d. [comments on drafts for the first four episodes], LAC, MG 31 D 196, vol. 58, file 13; Berton to Murray, n.d. [comments on draft for episode one], LAC, MG 31 D 196, vol. 59, file 9.

42 Michael Bliss to Pierre Berton, 24 January 1970, with attachment: "The Great Railway, vol. 1: The National Dream. Specific Comments," 1–10, WRDARC, Pierre Berton Fonds, box 1, "Bliss, Michael" file, in McKillop, Pierre Berton, 489n21, 490n22.

43 For example, Nelles, "Ties That Bind: Berton's CPR," Canadian Forum 50, November–December 1970, 270–2, outlined in McKillop, Pierre Berton, 508–9.

44 Berton to Murray, n.d. [comments on drafts for the first four episodes], vol. 58, file 13; Berton to Murray, 23 February 1973 [comments on drafts, episodes 5 and 8], vol. 61, file 23; Berton to Murray, 23 February

1973 [comments on draft, episode 6], vol. 61, file 45; Berton to Murray, 27 February 1973 [comments on draft, episode 2], vol. 59, file 35; Berton to Murray, 27 February 1973 [comments on draft, episode 3], vol. 60, file 14; Berton to Murray, 9 March 1973 [comments on draft, episode 4], vol. 61, file 5. All in LAC, MG 31 D 196.

45 Berton to Murray, 12 March 1973 [comments on draft, episode 7], LAC, MG 31 D 196, vol. 61, file 45.

46 This may have been because *The Tenth Decade*'s focus was on the very recent past, but *The Days before Yesterday* featured no historians other than Dale Thomson, a former politician, and Laurier LaPierre, a historian better known at the time as a television personality. And most of the episodes for *Days* were written by Newman, a journalist and, like Berton, later a writer of popular Canadian history.

47 Quoted in L. Ian MacDonald, "The CBC Takes Another Look at Our Past," *Saturday Gazette* (Montreal), 3 November 1973, WRDARC, Pierre Berton Fonds, box 332, file 9.

48 See, for example, Mindich, *Just the Facts*; and Deuze, "What Is Journalism."

49 See Knowlton, "Into the 1960s," 223, 229.

50 Deuze, "What Is Journalism," 447.

51 Granatstein, *Who Killed Canadian History*, chap. 3.

52 The film was not made. Berton to Richard Parker, 3 December 1971; Berton to Armando Ammendola, 17 July 1972, and other correspondence in this file. Both in WRDARC, Pierre Berton Fonds, box 202, file "Railway Movie – Ammendola."

53 See Francis, *National Dreams,* 15–28.

54 Powley to Nixon, 3 May 1962, LAC, RG 41, vol. 728, file 51.

55 Creighton to Findley, 1 April 1973, LAC, MG 31 D 196, vol. 2, file 94-3.

56 McKillop, *Pierre Berton*, 529–34.

57 Berton to Murray, n.d., WRDARC, Pierre Berton Fonds, Box 236, file 13.

58 Berton, *My Times*, 342–3, in McKillop, *Pierre Berton*, 495n33.

59 CBC, "The CBC: A Perspective," 366–7, CBCRL.

60 Granatstein, *Who Killed Canadian History?*, 71.

61 Black to Nash, 18 October 1971, LAC, RG 41, fol. 840, file 311.

62 Nash to Patchell, 29 March 1972, LAC, RG 41, vol. 840, file 311.

63 Nash to Sinclair, 19 May 1972, LAC, RG 41, vol. 840, file 311.

64 Nash to Patchell, 12 June 1972, LAC, RG 41, vol. 840, file 311.

65 Patchell to Nash, 12 June 1972, LAC, RG 41, vol. 840, file 311.

66 Berton to Murray, 2 October 1972, WRDARC, Pierre Berton Fonds, box 236, file 13.

67 Berton to Murray, 23 February 1973, WRDARC, Pierre Berton Fonds, box 90, file 7.

68 Berton to Murray, 9 March 1973, WRDARC, Pierre Berton Fonds, box 90, file 7.

69 L. Ian Macdonald reported that Christopher Plummer had expressed an interest in or had been approached for the role of Van Horne. *Montreal Gazette*, 9 September 1972 and 25 October 1972, both in WRDARC, Pierre Berton Fonds, box 332, file 1. At the other extreme, many were non-actors from the ranks of the CPR staff and from some First Nations reserves in the Prairies. See Maureen Jamieson, "Filming 'The Dream,'" *Lethbridge Herald*, 9 June 1973, 26–7, WRDARC, Pierre Berton Fonds, box 332, file 4.

70 Nash to Peter Campbell, 17 June 1970; Nash to Garriock, 7 July 1970; Kerr to Nash, 18 June 1970; Campbell to Nash, 23 June 1970. All in LAC, RG 41, vol. 840, file 295, pt. 1.

71 The *Winnipeg Free Press* indicated that this amounted to $250,000. See also "CBC Television Presents: The National Dream, Building the Impossible Railway," *Winnipeg Free Press*, 13 February 1974, LAC, RG 41, vol. 249, file 11-38-3. L. Ian Macdonald said it was $350,000 (see *Montreal Gazette*, 13 March 1973, same file).

72 Hubert Bauch, *Globe and Mail*, "A Spike in the Coffin of the Van Horne Mansion," 7 August 1973, 4, quoted in L. Ian Macdonald, "Berton Never Dreamed of Sponsor's Other Role," *Edmonton Journal*, 27 October 1973, 71, WRDARC, Pierre Berton Fonds, box 332, file 8.

73 Berton to Murray, n.d., WRDARC, Pierre Berton Fonds, box 236, file 13.

74 On Wayne and Shuster, *TV Times*, 23 February 1974, WRDARC, Pierre Berton Fonds, box 332, file "February"; *Globe and Mail* and *Saskatoon Star Phoenix*, [March?] 1974, WRDARC, Pierre Berton Fonds, box 134, file "National Dream TV letters."

75 Blaik Kirby, "National Dream: CBC at Its best," *Globe and Mail*, 1 March 1974.

76 Bill Musselwhite, *Calgary Herald*, February 1974, WRDARC, Pierre Berton Fonds, box 332, file "February 1974."

77 Basil Deakin, "CBC Took Two Years to Make National Dream...," *Mail Star* (Halifax), 6 February 1974, WRDARC, Pierre Berton Fonds, box 332, file "February 1974."

78 [Editorial], "History Can Be Theatre," *Ottawa Journal*, 16 February 1974, 6, WRDARC, Pierre Berton Fonds, box 332, file "February, 1974."

79 Dennis Braithwaite, "Make Berton Give Us Back Our History," *Toronto Daily Star*, 6 March 1974, CBCRL, Production File, "The National Dream."

80 Urjo Kareda, "The CBC's National Dream Goes Highballing into Boredom," *Toronto Star*, 20 April 1974, LAC, RG 41, vol. 249, file 11-38-3.

81 CBC, Audience Research Report, 1, LAC, RG 41, vol. 840, file 311.

82 CBC, Audience Research Report, 2–3; "Audience Reactions to English Television Network Programs," 29 March–4 April 1974, 10, 4–18, in CBC Research Report No. 22, "The Performance of CBC English Television Network Programs," 11 September 1973–11 April 1974, UTRL.

83 Blaik Kirby, "Lost: 800,000 National Dreamers," *Globe and Mail*, 8 April 1974, CBCRL, Production File "National Dream"; Jack Miller, "National Dream Slips," *Toronto Star*, [8?] April 1974, CBCRL, Production File "National Dream."

84 CBC, Audience Research Report, June 1974, 4, LAC, RG 41, vol. 840, file 311.

85 Blaik Kirby, "Lost: 800,000 National Dreamers," *Globe and Mail*, 8 April 1974, CBCRL, Production File "The National Dream."

86 CBC, Audience Research Report, June 1974, 4, LAC, RG 41, file 311.

87 Mel Hurtig to Berton, 26 April 1974, WRDARC, Pierre Berton Fonds, box 134, file "National Dream TV Letters."

88 See Daschuk, *Clearing the Plains*.

89 "Klondike, Outlines for Twelve One-Hour Drama-Documentaries for CBC-TV, from Pierre Berton," 1974, WRDARC, Pierre Berton Fonds, box 189, file 3.

90 "Vimy: A Television Proposal from Pierre Berton," n.d., WRDARC, Pierre Berton Fonds, box 378, file 24.

91 Quoted in Zena Cherry, "Six Buy a Place in the Sun," *Globe and Mail*, 1 March 1974.

92 Berton to George McAfee, 1 December 1972 and 5 November 1973, WRDARC, Pierre Berton Fonds, box 236, file 13; Nash to George Desmond, 13 March 1972, LAC, RG 41, vol. 840, file 311.

93 "Vimy: A Television Proposal from Pierre Berton," n.d., WRDARC, Pierre Berton Fonds, box 378, file 24.

94 Various documents in WRDARC, Pierre Berton Fonds, box 236, file 15.

95 Berton likely would have agreed. Garriock to Nash, 24 January 1972, LAC, RG 41, vol. 840, file 311.

96 "Klondike, Outlines for Twelve One-Hour Drama-Documentaries for CBC-TV, from Pierre Berton"; "Klondike: A Pseudo-Documentary," 1975. Both in WRDARC, Pierre Berton Fonds, box 189, file 3. See also Whitehead to Berton, n.d., WRDARC, Pierre Berton Fonds, box 110, General Correspondence, 1975–76.

97 See also Nash to Berton, 19 February 1974; Nash to Berton and McCartney-Filgate, 14 July 1978; Nash to Berton, 24 August 1978. All in WRDARC, Pierre Berton Fonds, box 236, file 13; Nash, *Prime Time at Ten*, 69–70.

98 Berton to Bill Armstrong, 23 June 1983; Berton to Michael McLear, 18 June 1984. Both in WRDARC, Pierre Berton Fonds, box 244, file 33.

99 Berton to McLear, 18 June 1984; McLear to Berton, 4 July 1984. Both in WRDARC, Pierre Berton Fonds, box 244, file 33.

100 Contract signed by Berton, 31 October 1990, WRDARC, Pierre Berton Fonds, box 347, file 21.

101 "CBC Television Presents: The National Dream: Building the Impossible Railway," LAC, MG 31 D 196, vol. 250, file 7.

CHAPTER FOUR

1 Canada, Department of Communications News Release, 24 October 1983, CBCRL, file "CBC Policy."

2 Roman Jarymowycz is credited as an additional co-writer of the Normandy episode.

3 Quoted in Ted Shaw, "Canada at War: Repentant Reporter Seeks Terrible Truth," *Vancouver Sun*, 10 January 1992, CBCRL, Production File "World War II Programming – The Valour and the Horror."

4 For example, Carr, "Rules of Engagement"; and Taras, "Struggle over *The Valour and the Horror*." However, Sloniowski, "Popularizing History," examines the conventions of historiography and the presentation of history in the series in the context of other popular forms of contemporary television programming, including documentaries, docudramas, reality television, and movies of the week. Bercuson and Wise published their reports, written for the CBC ombudsman, on the historical accuracy and interpretation of the series. See Bercuson and Wise, *Valour and the Horror Revisited*. And Dick, "History on Television," looks at the use of archival documents in the series.

5 Anon., "Procedures for Approval," in Anon., "The Valour and the Horror" (n.d.), CBCRL, Production File "World War II Programming – The Valour and the Horror."

6 Section 4.03 and section 5.02b of contract dated 14 December 1990, "Excerpts from 'The Valour and the Horror' Contract," in Anon., "The Valour and the Horror," n.d., CBCRL, Production File "World War II Programming – The Valour and the Horror."

7 Pennefather also testified that the board's participation with projects under the Independent Co-Production Program was as a facilitator and as a provider of technical services. See Canada, Parliament, Standing Senate Subcommittee on Social Affairs, Science and Technology, *Proceedings of the Standing Senate Subcommittee on Veterans Affairs*, 2 November 1992, 5, 5: 16–17, 20–1.

8 In the end, the lawyers were satisfied that the portrayals were supportable. "Procedures for Approval."

9 "Procedures for Approval," and "Activities and Strategies after Airing of

the Programs" in Anon., "The Valour and the Horror," CBCRL, Production File "World War II Programming – The Valour and the Horror."

10 The style of *Culloden* was to be followed mainly in the Black Watch's re-enactment of the action at Verrières Ridge. See "The Valor [*sic*] and the Horror: Canada and the Second World War, October 8, 1989," CULSC, P112/G6, box HA 1346, file "Valour and the Horror Transcripts, Additions: Hong Kong."

11 Cook, "Making the Past Present," 224–5.

12 "*The Valour and the Horror*: Canada and the Second World War," 1, CBCRL, Production File "The Valour and the Horror."

13 For example Neatby and Hodgins, "Introduction," 7.

14 This came to 1.792 million viewers according to Ivar Kangur to Nancy D'Anunzio, 17 February 1992, CBCRL, Production File "The Valour and the Horror." A Galafilm press release on 25 June 1992 suggests that the series had been seen by 6 million viewers since it first aired. See Galafilm press release, 25 June 1992, and NFB news release, same day, CBCRL, Production File "The Valour and the Horror."

15 Lois Legge, "War Series Emotionally Compelling," *Halifax Herald*, 11 January 1992, B9; John T.D. Keyes, "In Review," *TV Guide*, 11 January 1992: 28. Both in CBCRL, Production File "World War II Programming – The Valour and the Horror." Peter Trueman, "CBC Does Itself Proud…," *Starweek*, 4–11 January 1992, 11, CBCRL, Production File "World War II Programming – The Valour and the Horror." See also John Haslett Cuff, "Debunking the Official War Line," *Globe and Mail*, 11 January 1992, A2; Ian Johnston, "Valour Deserves a Medal," 19 January 1992. Both in CBCRL, Production File "World War II Programming – The Valour and the Horror."

16 The ad, "An Invitation to the Public," the *Toronto Star*, 15 April 1992, CULSC, P112/G6, box 1154, file "War Amps Attack."

17 The two veterans were Lionel E. Hastings and Donald Elliot, *CBC Newsworld*, 28 March 1992, 8:00 p.m., CUML, Newsworld Archives.

18 Brian McKenna and Arnie Gelbart, 22 April 1992, CBCRL, Production File "The Valour and the Horror." The CBC public relations staffer wrote that the letter was sent to "100 major dailies and 800 weeklies and regional dailies across the country." Ginny Bellwood to Trina McQueen et al., 24 April 1992, CBCRL, Production File "The Valour and the Horror."

19 Gelbart to Bellwood, 30 April 1992, CBCRL, Production File "The Valour and the Horror."

20 Canada, Parliament, Senate, *Report of the Standing Committee on Social Affairs, Science and Technology*, "Production and Distribution of the National Film Board Production 'The Kid Who Couldn't Miss,'" 9–17, 19–20.

21 Canada, *Debates of the Senate*, 18 June 1992, 1784.

22 "Activities and Strategies after Airing of the Programs," in Anon., "The Valour and the Horror," CBCRL, Production File "World War II Programming – The Valour and the Horror." Another part of this larger document, "Independent Research," 9 May 1992, app. 4, indicates that some of the historians whom the researchers were attempting to contact were British scholars Noble [Frankland], John Keegan, R.J. O'Neill, and D.E. Greenwood. The booklet is also noted in Gelbart to Bellwood, 30 April 1992, and Bellwood to McQueen et al., 24 April 1992. Both in CBCRL, Production File "The Valour and the Horror." Bellwood indicates that the booklet was being prepared by the series' researcher D'Arcy O'Connor. It does not appear to have been made publicly available in that form.

23 "Activities and Strategies after Airing of the Programs," in Anon., "The Valour and the Horror," CBCRL, Production File "World War II Programming – The Valour and the Horror."

24 Gérard Veilleux, "Open Letter from the President and CEO," 25 June 1992, CBCRL, Production File "The Valour and the Horror." On censorship see, for example, Gelbart to Bellwood, 30 April 1992, CBCRL, Production File "The Valour and the Horror," and Gelbart and McKenna quoted in Mike Boone, "CBC Film-maker on Senate Hot Seat," *Montreal Gazette*, 10 June 1992, C10, CBCRL, Production File "Productions – The Valour and the Horror – 1992."

25 From the media, see, for example, Boone, "CBC Film-maker on Senate Hot Seat," *Montreal Gazette*, 10 June 1992, C10, CBCRL, Production File "Productions – The Valour and the Horror – 1992"; Pierre Berton, "Valour and Horror: Not Politically Correct?" *Toronto Star*, 30 May 1992, J3, CBCRL, Production File "World War II Programming – The Valour and the Horror"; Jack Granatstein, letter to Terence McKenna quoted in "The Valour and the Horror, Comments from Historians and Writers," CBCRL, Production File "The Valour and the Horror"; War Amps News Release, "Veterans' Representative Not to Appear at Resumption of State Hearings," 22 October 1992, at http://www.waramps.ca/newsroom/archives/valour/1992-10-22.html (viewed August 2018).

26 Taras, "Struggle over the Valour and the Horror," 737.

27 Canada, Parliament, Standing Senate Committee on Social Affairs, Science and Technology, no. 10, "The CBC Series *The Valour and the Horror*," 4 February 1993, 10:6–10:66.

28 The Ombudsman's position at the CBC was a result of a recommendation by the Caplan/Sauvageau Task Force and was less than a year old.

29 Wise, "Valour and the Horror"; and Bercuson, "Valour and the Horror."

30 Morgan to Veilleux, [Report on *The Valour and the Horror*], 5–6. CBCRL, Production File, "The Valour and the Horror."

31 Ibid., 8–13.
32 "Response to the CBC Ombudsman," 10 November 1992, CBCRL, Production File "Productions – Valour and the Horror –1992," reprinted in Bercuson and Wise, *Valour and the Horror Revisited*, 73–88.
33 [Morgan to Veilleux], "Comments on Nov. 10 Galafilm Response," CBCRL, Production File "The Valour and the Horror"; [Staff], "1,000 CBC Employees Sign Petition," *Globe and Mail*, 21 November 1992, C8; Veilleux to the Editor of the *Globe and Mail*, "Note to Staff," 23 November 1992, CBCRL, Production File "The Valour and the Horror"; Bercuson and Wise, "Introduction," in Bercuson and Wise, *Valour and the Horror Revisited*, 7. Examples of public and media response include: Geoffrey Chambers, "The Power of the Press," *Montreal Gazette*, 14 December 1992, B3; Stephen Godfrey, "Doctoring the Line between Docu and Drama," *Globe and Mail*, 21 November 1992, C8; Peter Worthington, "The CBC Deserves a Cheer or Two," *Toronto Sun*, [November] 1992; Christopher Harris, "Caplan, Sauvegeau Urge Restructuring of Ombudsman Role," *Globe and Mail*, 25 November 1992, C3; Desmond Morton, "Hell Hath No Fury Like the Media Scorned," *Toronto Star*, 19 November 1992, A25. All in CBCRL, Production File "Productions – The Valour and the Horror – 1992."
34 Wise, "Valour and the Horror"; Bercuson, "Valour and the Horror."
35 One journalist called the board "utterly hypocritical" for accepting the ombudsman's criticism about the line between documentary and drama, and another referred to Veilleux in particular as "crude." See Stephen Godfrey, "Doctoring the Line between Docu and Drama," *Globe and Mail*, 21 November 1992, C8, CBCRL, Production File "Productions – The Valour and the Horror – 1992"; Lysiane Gagnon, "Valour Debate Reveals Crude Style of Veilleux," *Globe and Mail*, 5 December 1992, D3, CBCRL, Production File "Productions – The Valour and the Horror – 1992." Someone who expressed more of an understanding of the actions of the ombudsman and CBC management was Jeffrey Simpson, "Looking Back in Anger, The Pitfalls of Interpreting History," *Globe and Mail*, 20 November 1992, A26, CBCRL, Production File "The Valour and the Horror."
36 Allan Darling [CRTC] to Veilleux, "Re: The Valour and the Horror," 17 December 1992, CBCRL, Production File "The Valour and the Horror." Darling indicated that the response was also sent to most of those who had written in to the CRTC about the series.
37 Darling [CRTC] to Veilleux, "Re: The Valour and the Horror," 17 December 1992, CBCRL, Production File "The Valour and the Horror."
38 Quoted in Galafilm press release, "Historians Agree with Filmmakers 'The Valour and the Horror' is Bullet-Proof," 25 June 1992, CBCRL, Production File, "The Valour and the Horror."

39 Hogarth, *Documentary Television in Canada*, 94–6.

40 Morgan to Veilleux, [Report on *The Valour and the Horror*], 6, CBCRL, Production File "The Valour and the Horror."

41 The full statement: "'L'Acadie, L'Acadie' is not a quiet, balanced documentary narrative. The film makes no attempt to show all sides of a complex situation. It is rather a passionate, and sometimes bitter statement about being young and French Canadian at a certain time in a certain place in this country, and that is why we present it to-day." See Eugene Hallman to Norn Garriock, 10 January 1972, LAC, RG 41, vol. 773, file GM 7-2-10, pt. 1. For more see *Moncton Times* articles of 12, 13, and 15 January 1972, also in this file.

42 Gary Evans gives the following explanation of why the CBC rejected *If You Love This Planet*: "because it takes a strong position on nuclear arms and does not give a balanced and objective view of the subject" and because it would likely not be able to find a pro-nuclear war panel to counter its thesis. See NFB, *Minutes*, 18–19 June and 17–18 September 1982, and James de B. Domville, interview by Gary Evans, 9 June 1988, quoted in Evans, *In the National Interest*, 283n92. The program eventually aired on CBC.

43 Nash, interview by author.

44 Mark Starowicz et al., "Final Report of Task Force on Point of View Documentaries," April 1993, 17–19, CBCRL.

45 Ibid., 8.

46 Quoted in Nash, *Microphone Wars*, 532.

47 Nichols, *Introduction to Documentary*, 31.

48 Sloniowski, "Popularizing History," 162.

49 Canada, House of Commons, *Debates*, 30th Parliament, 3rd Session, 5 (1978), 4825–6.

50 Documents in CBCRL, Production File "Riel."

51 Hogarth, *Documentary Television in Canada*, 87.

52 Morgan to Veilleux, [Report on *The Valour and the Horror*], 12, CBCRL, Production File "The Valour and the Horror."

53 *Canada's Sweetheart*: "This is first and foremost a *drama*, based on a true experience and interspersed with documentary style vignettes. A catch-all description like docudrama, re-creation or something similar is really not an accurate representation of this unique program form. Therefore we will not seek to characterize it in this way." Emphasis in original. Susan Jones [CBC] to Hanna Acemian [NFB], 27 May 1985, CBCRL, Production File "Defence of Canada."

54 Brian McKenna, "A Word from the Director," n.d., 4, CBCRL, Production File, "The Valour and the Horror." See also Bellwood to McQueen et al., 24 April 1992, CBCRL, Production File "The Valour and the Horror."

55 Berton to Murray, [1972], WRDARC, Pierre Berton Fonds, box 236, file 13.

56 Morgan to Veilleux, [Report on The Valour and the Horror], 12–13, CBCRL, Production File "The Valour and the Horror."

57 "Response to Bill Morgan Queries," n.d., CULSC, P112/G6, box 1155, file "V&H/ Ombudsman – Questions." In the film, Harris says: "In spite of all that happened at Hamburg, bombing proved a relatively humane method. There is no proof that most casualties were women and children." In his memoir, Harris writes, "In spite of all that happened at Hamburg, bombing proved a comparatively humane method." He then cites the much higher number of casualties caused by the blockade of Germany during the First World War and compares it with the casualties caused by the Allied bombing of the whole of Germany during the Second World War, ending with: "There is no estimate of how many of these were women and children." Besides the different meaning caused by word changes in the last sentence and the removal of the reference to Germany, in the original there are sixteen full lines of text between the two sentences. See Harris, *Bomber Offensive*, 176–7.

58 Recounted by Ken Tweedie, a No. 460 squadron navigator, quoted in Neillands, *Bomber War*, 405.

59 Darce Fardy to DiNunzio, 9 July 1991, CULSC, P112/G6, box 1152, file "V&H CBC 'Vetting.'" Fardy wrote that he was satisfied with the assurances of the production team that the depiction of Harris and the other characters was accurate. On requests and assurances, see Fardy, "Notes from Darce Fardy, Former Area Head ..." n.d., in Anon., "The Valour and the Horror," CBCRL, Production File "The Valour and the Horror."

60 Robert Dale to Robert O'Riley, 17 March 1992, reproduced in Canada, Parliament, Standing Senate Committee on Social Affairs, Science and Technology, *Proceedings of the Subcommittee on Veterans Affairs*, no. 7, "The CBC Series *The Valour and the Horror*," app. VA-7C, 4 November 1992, 7A:10.

61 Canada, Parliament, Standing Senate Committee on Social Affairs, Science and Technology, *Proceedings of the Subcommittee on Veterans Affairs*, no. 9, "The CBC Series *The Valour and the Horror*," 9:88. Middlebrook did quote a weather forecast from another officer, seemingly based on Dale's description of what he saw, but there was no direct quote from Dale. See Middlebrook, *Nuremberg Raid*, 101–2; and Middlebrook, *Berlin Raids*, 304–5.

62 K. G. Christie to [?], reproduced in Canada, Standing Committee on Social Affairs, Science and Technology, *Proceedings of the Subcommittee on Veterans Affairs*, no. 7, "The CBC Series *The Valour and the Horror*," app. VA-7B, 7A:9. See also ibid., no. 8, 5 November 1992, 8:46, 8:112; O'Connor to Gelbart, 10 September 1992, CULSC, P112/G6, box 1155, file "V&H/ Ombudsman – Questions."

63 She was called Mary Moore in the film. Mary ("Bubbles") Dups interview by [member(s) of *The Valour and the Horror* production team], 25
September 1990; short story entitled "Mushroom Territory" and unti-
tled poem. All in CULSC, P112/G6, box HA 1152, file "Mary Bubbles
(Moore) Dups." The Bomber Harris Trust statement of claim stated
that the poem was entitled "The Trapper." See Bomber Harris Trust,
Battle for Truth, 11, 127, 128.

64 Puchniak to [Gelbart?], 24 July 1992, CULSC, P112/G6, box 1155, file
"V&H/Ombudsman – Questions"; [Morgan to Veilleux], "Comments
on Nov. 10 Galafilm Response," 7, CBCRL, Production File "The Valour and the Horror." Keller is shown in the scene as edgy and drinking.
Morgan wrote that some of what Cunningham said "and the depiction
of a fearful Keller, run directly counter to what the late Brigadier
Cunningham had said" in his pre-broadcast interview. Historian Terry
Copp also noted, in a submission as part of the senate proceedings,
that there was no evidence that drinking was connected to Keller's
actions during that operation. And, in Copp's own interview with
Cunningham, Cunningham described Keller during the confrontation
as "calm and determined." See Canada, Parliament, Parliament,
Standing Senate Committee on Social Affairs, Science and Technology,
Proceedings of the Subcommittee on Veterans Affairs, no. 3, 25 June
1992, app. 3A, 20.

65 Puchniak to [Gelbart?], 24 July 1992, CULSC, P112/G6, box 1155, file
"V&H/ Ombudsman – Questions." When two other veterans questioned LeBouthillier on his comment, he wrote to them that "there must
have been a misunderstanding" between him and the filmmakers. To
the Senate, Brian McKenna replied (correctly) that LeBouthillier was
on record saying this in a book entitled *J'ai vecu la guerre*. Canada,
Parliament, Standing Senate Committee on Social Affairs, Science and
Technology, *Proceedings of the Subcommittee on Veterans Affairs*, no.
9, "The CBC Series *The Valour and the Horror*," 6 November 1992,
9:95–9:96. See Cormier, *J'ai vécu la guerre*, 130. English translation:
Cormier, *Forgotten Soldiers*, 89.

66 Quoted in Christopher Guly, "Debate Rages on over CBC War Series,"
Today's Seniors, December 1992, P7, CBCRL, Production File "Productions – The Valour and the Horror – 1992."

67 Bellwood to McQueen et. al., 24 April 1992, CBCRL, Production File
"The Valour and the Horror."

68 Dick, "History on Television," 216n17.

69 Linenthal, "Anatomy of a Controversy," 9–10.

70 Oral History Society, at http://www.ohs.org.uk/journal/ (viewed May
2018).

71 Bell, "Beyond the Witness," 77, and citing Gray, "Learning from

Experience: Cultural Studies and Feminism," in *Cultural Methodologies*, ed. J. McGuigan (London: Sage, 1997), 100.

72 Frisch, *Shared Authority*, 7.

73 Ibid.

74 Terkel, *Hard Times*, cited in Frisch, *Shared Authority*, 9.

75 Morgan to Veilleux, [Report on The Valour and the Horror], 9–10, CBCRL, Production File "The Valour and the Horror"; [Morgan to Veilleux], "Comments on Nov. 10 Galafilm Response," 14, CBCRL, Production File "The Valour and the Horror."

76 Portelli, *Death of Luigi Trastulli*, 1–26.

77 This also came up during the senate proceedings. See Canada, Parliament, Standing Senate Committee on Social Affairs, Science and Technology, *Proceedings of the Subcommittee on Veterans Affairs*, no 9, "The CBC Series *The Valour and the Horror*," 6 November 1992, 9:75.

78 Carr, "Rules of Engagement."

79 Quoted in Ted Shaw, "Canada at War: Repentant Reporter Seeks Terrible Truth," *Vancouver Sun*, 10 January 1992, CBCRL, Production File "World War II Programming – The Valour and the Horror."

80 Canada, Standing Senate Committee on Social Affairs, Science and Technology, *Proceedings of the Subcommittee on Veterans Affairs*, no. 9, "The CBC Series *The Valour and the Horror*," 6 November 1992, 9:73.

81 Canada, Standing Senate Committee on Social Affairs, Science and Technology, *Proceedings of the Subcommittee on Veterans Affairs*, no. 9, "The CBC Series *The Valour and the Horror*," 6 November 1992, 9:61.

82 Quoted in Shaw, "Canada At War: Repentant Reporter Seeks Terrible Truth," *Vancouver Sun*, 10 January 1992; Anon., "Notes on the Valour and the Horror," *The Weekender* [St John's], 12 January 1992, 2. Both in CBCRL, Production File "World War II Programming – The Valour and the Horror."

83 See Vos and Finneman, "Early Historical Construction of Journalism's Gatekeeping Role."

84 Mindich, *Just the Facts*, 141.

85 Daly, *Covering America*, 411, 413.

86 See Martin, *Past Futures*.

87 Quoted in Shaw, "Canada at War: Repentant Reporter Seeks Terrible Truth," *Vancouver Sun*, 10 January 1992, CBCRL, Production File "World War II Programming – The Valour and the Horror."

88 Brian McKenna, "History of Project," [n.d.], CULSC, P112/G6, box HA 1346, file "Valour – History of Project"; Boone, "CBC Film-maker on Senate Hot Seat," *Montreal Gazette*, 10 June 1992, C10, CBCRL,

Production File "Productions – The Valour and the Horror – 1992"; Gelbart to Bellwood, 30 April 1992, CBCRL, Production File "The Valour and the Horror"; Mike Boone, "Canada's War: Montrealer's Documentary Series Recalls Valor and Horror of World War II," CBCRL, Production File "World War II Programming – The Valour and the Horror"; *Montreal Gazette*, 10 January 1992, C1, C6, CBCRL, Production File "World War II Programming – The Valour and the Horror"; McKenna, "A Word from the Director," n.d., 4–5, CBCRL, Production File "The Valour and the Horror."

89 On the "mythic" aspects of Watergate, and Woodward and Bernstein, see Schudson, *Power of News*, 142–65; Matheson, "Watchdog's New Bark," 82–92.

90 Daly, *Covering America*, 393.

91 Canada, Standing Senate Committee on Social Affairs, Science and Technology, *Proceedings of the Subcommittee on Veterans Affairs*, no. 9, "The CBC Series *The Valour and the Horror*," 6 November 1992, 9:71–9:73.

92 [Roman Jarymowycz] to Gelbart and McKenna, 27 May 1992, CULSC, P112/G6, box 1154, file "War Amps Attack"; McKenna, "Word from the Director," n.d., 5, CBCRL, Production File "The Valour and the Horror."

93 Letter reproduced in Bercuson and Wise, *Valour and the Horror Revisited*, 89–91. McKenna responded in the *Globe and Mail*, 18 November 1992.

94 Morgan to Veilleux, [Report on The Valour and the Horror], 8, CBCRL, Production File "The Valour and the Horror."

95 Canada, Standing Senate Committee on Social Affairs, Science and Technology. *Proceedings of the Subcommittee on Veterans Affairs*, no. 9, "The CBC Series *The Valour and the Horror*," 6 November 1992, 9:70.

96 [Puchniak] to [?], "Tom's observations on Normandy Response," 26 August 1992, 1, CULSC, P112/G6, box 1155, file "V&H/Ombudsman – Questions."

97 CULSC, P112/G6, box 1155, various files.

98 Gelbart to Bellwood, 30 April 1992, CBCRL, Production File "The Valour and the Horror"; Gelbart quoted in Mike Boone, "CBC Film-maker on Senate Hot Seat," *Montreal Gazette*, 10 June 1992, C10, CBCRL, Production File "Productions – The Valour and the Horror – 1992"; Brian McKenna quoted in Rudy Platiel, "Filmmaker Warns of Libel 'Ice-Age,'" *Globe and Mail*, 13 July 1993, CBCRL, Production File "Productions – The Valour and the Horror – 1993." The Senate proceedings were considered part of the chill. See Canada, Standing Senate

Committee on Social Affairs, Science and Technology. *Proceedings of the Subcommittee on Veterans Affairs*, no. 9, "The CBC Series *The Valour and the Horror*," 6 November 1992, 9:61.

99 Starowicz, *Making History*, 53.

100 Brian McKenna, 25 November 1996, CULSC, P112/G6, box HA 1346, file "CBC, Politics of Post Valour Films."

101 Marie Natanson to Gelbart et al., 7 November 1994, CULSC, P112/G6, box 1346, file "CBC, Politics of Post Valour Films."

102 [The CBC Documentary Unit], n.d., CBCRL, Production File "War at Sea."

103 Soles, "War at Sea Briefing Notes," CBCRL, Production File "War at Sea."

104 Marc Milner to Starowicz, 16 September 1995, CBCRL, Production File "War at Sea." One reviewer called the new series "a lobotomized sequel." See Tony Atherton, "The War at Sea Lacks Passion," *Ottawa Citizen*, 7 October 1995, p. H4, CBCRL, Production File "War at Sea."

105 Playback staff, "Quebec Scene: Galafilm, McKenna Brothers," *Playback*, 19 June 1995, at http://playbackonline.ca/1995/06/19/4412-19950619/ (viewed June 2018).

CHAPTER FIVE

1 http://www.cbc.radio-canada.ca/en/explore/mandate/ (viewed June 2018).

2 See Côté, *Construire la nation au petit écran*; West, "Selling Canada to Canadians"; Frank, "Public History and the People's History." Scholars have also evaluated *A People's History* from perspectives that place less emphasis on the factors of production and reception and more on its visual and aural representations and narrative grammar. See Dick, "Saving the Nation through National History"; and Brook, "Picturing an Experience of the Past."

3 Gordon Henderson quoted in Friesen, "'Canada: A People's History' as 'Journalists' History,'" 190.

4 Canada, Mandate Review Committee, *"Making Our Voices Heard,"* 101–2.

5 Ibid., 102.

6 Ibid., 175–6.

7 Bugailiskis, "Programming CBC television," in "CBC Television – Celebrating Fifty Years," Canadian Broadcasting Corporation, [2002], 16, CBCRL, General File "CBC History."

8 Ibid., 15.

9 http://www.dominion.ca/Downloads/newdibrochure.pdf (viewed June 2018).

10 In 2009, Historica and the Dominion Institute amalgamated to become the Historica-Dominion Institute; in 2013 it became Historica Canada.

11 Starowicz, *Making History*, 28–9.

12 Quoted in Bremner, "History without Archives," 75.

13 Edgerton, quoted in Ken Burns's "Rebirth of a Nation," 125.

14 Ken Burns, "Ken Burns and the Historical Narrative on Television," the Museum of Television and Radio University Satellite Seminar Series, 19 November 1996, quoted in Edgerton, "Mediating *Thomas Jefferson*," 174n19.

15 Quoted in Friesen, "Canada," 201.

16 Quoted in Anon. [Bell Globe Media], "Montcalm and Wolfe Haunt Series," *Globe and Mail*, 20 February 1997.

17 Ibid.; Starowicz, *Making History*, 39.

18 Starowicz, *Making History*, 38–9.

19 Ibid., 55–8.

20 The above details from Hubert Gendron, interview by author; Catherine Dawson, "The Next Chapter," *Globe and Mail*, 29 September 2001; Martin Knelman, "Charge of the CBC Marketing Brigade," *Toronto Star*, 15 October 2000. Starowicz reported that $25 million was the estimate initially arrived at with the NFB. Starowicz, *Making History*, 59–60. The final costs were between $25 and $30 million.

21 Gendron, interview by author; Gene Allen, interview by author.

22 Starowicz, *Making History*, 144–7, 156.

23 Gendron, interview by author; Starowicz, *Making History*, 147–8.

24 Allen to Cook, 5 June 1977 [*sic*] [1997], Ramsay Cook private papers.

25 Gendron, interview by author.

26 Moore, "Coffee with Mark Starowicz," 54–5.

27 Allen to Cook, 5 June [1997]. Ramsay Cook private papers.

28 Cook to Allen, 16 June 1997, Ramsay Cook private papers.

29 Allen, "Professionals and the Public," 382.

30 Allen, interview by author.

31 Hall, "Television and Culture," 250, quoted in McArthur, *Television and History*, 12.

32 Starowicz, *Making History*, 91, 109.

33 Allen, interview by author.

34 Cook, interview by author.

35 Allen, interview by author.

36 Gendron, interview by author; Cook, interview by author; Starowicz, *Making History*, 274.

37 Gordon Henderson, quoted in "Step by Step: One Story, Many Perspectives," CBC series website, http://www.cbc.ca/history/BTSCONTSE3EP1 CH1PA1LE.html (viewed June 2018).

38 Starowicz, *Making History*, 149.

39 Gendron and Henderson to production team, n.d., Hubert Gendron private papers.

40 The CBC also advertised *War at Sea* as a "people's history," stating that the use of actors gave voice to regular people and that to be without it "would be to disenfranchise most of the ordinary people who fought the war." See Soles, "War at Sea Briefing Notes," 27 September 1995, 7; Jim Byrd to Janet H. Watt, 27 September 1995. Both in CBCRL, Production File "War at Sea."

41 Starowicz, *Making History*, 108.

42 See Green, "Engaging in People's History," in *Presenting the Past*, esp. 339–50.

43 Porter Benson, Brier, and Rosenzweig, "Introduction," in *Presenting the Past*, xvii.

44 [Starowicz] to "the directors, the editors and the cameramen in the first wave," [1999], Hubert Gendron private papers.

45 Cook suggested that, with *Culloden*, Peter Watkins was successful in creating an "alternative 'people's history.'" Cook, "Making the Past Present," 225.

46 Dick, "Saving the Nation through National History."

47 Patrice Groulx has made a similar observation about the predetermined quality of the narrative. See Groulx, "La meilleure histoire du monde," 412.

48 See Dick, "Saving the Nation through National History," 207; and Edgerton, "Ken Burns' Rebirth of a Nation," 129–30, for a similar practice in *The Civil War*.

49 Mark Starowicz quoted in Clark, "Engaging the Field," cited in Olivier Côté, *Construire la nation*, 84n17.

50 Gendron, interview by author.

51 Allen, interview by author; Starowicz in Friesen, "Canada," 189.

52 Henderson quoted in Friesen, "Canada," 190.

53 Henderson quoted in [CBC], "Telling the Story: Reconstructing History," at http://www.cbc.ca/history/BTSCONTSE3EP1CH1PA6LE.html (viewed June 2018).

54 Starowicz, *Making History*, 121; quoted in Anon. [Bell Globe Media], "Montcalm and Wolfe Haunt Series," *Globe and Mail*, 20 February 1997.

55 Knelman, "Charge of the CBC Marketing Brigade," *Toronto Star*, 15 October 2000.

56 CBC press release, "Comprehensive Educational Package to Accompany Canada: A People's History," n.d., CBCRL, Production File "Canada: A People's History." According to David Frank, this package cost two thousand dollars per educational institution. See Frank, "Public History and the *People's History*," 121.

57 CBC press release, 8 August 2001, CBCRL, Production File "People's History (Season 2)."

58 Noted by Ian McKay, personal communication.

59 Starowicz, *Making History*, 156.

60 Starowicz quoted in Gray, "History Wars," 36.

61 Gray, "History Wars," 36, also noted by Starowicz, *Making History*, 180.

62 Starowicz, *Making History*, 156–7.

63 Friesen, "Canada," 192.

64 Peter Watkins, e-mail communication with author.

65 [Starowicz] to "the directors, the editors and the cameramen in the first wave," Hubert Gendron private papers. See also Friesen, "'Canada,'" 187–9.

66 Michael Sweeney quoted in "Through a Journalistic Lens," CBC press release, CBCRL, Production File "Canada: A People's History."

67 Starowicz, *Making History*, 120–1.

68 Starowicz quoted in Friesen, "Canada," 187n5.

69 Jonathan Vance, "A Land of Poor Visibility," *National Post*, 23 October 2000. See *The Garland Library of Narratives of North American Indian Captivities*, vol. 28, Cornell University Library, which contains both the Jewitt and Alsop versions.

70 See, for example, Côté, *Construire la nation au petit écran*; and West, "Selling Canada to Canadians."

71 Zinn, *People's History of the United States*, 8.

72 For example Friesen, "Canada"; and Gray, "History Wars."

73 Gray, "History Wars," 34.

74 Gendron, interview by author.

75 Ibid.

76 Michael Posner, "CBC's Take on History Strikes Gold," *Globe and Mail*, 1 November 2000; Alan Hustak, "History in the Making," *Gazette* (Montreal), 21 October 2000.

77 Dan Brown reported that adding up the figures from multiple broadcasts in order to get one large number was not a common practice in the industry. Dan Brown, "2.9 Million Saw CBC's People's History, Just Not All at Once," *National Post*, 22 November 2000; and Michael Posner, "CBC's Take on History Strikes Gold." Both in CBCRL, Production File "Canada: A People's History." Allen noted that the average viewership for episodes in the first season, when added up like this, was 2 million. He also explained that, while 364,000 for Radio-Canada seems a relatively respectable number, it is low for what is considered to be popular programming in Quebec. Allen, "Professionals and the Public," 381, 390.

78 The two in the *Daily News* were Michael Cross and Ken Dewar. See Marla Cranston, "TV History Lesson Dull Complain Local Profs,"

Daily News, 24 October 2000, 29, CBCRL, Production File "Canada: A People's History." Those interviewed by the *Vancouver Sun* were Mark Leier, Tina Loo, and Jack Little. See Chad Skelton, "Historians Give CBC Series a Low Grade," 16 October 2000, A3, CBCRL, Production File "Canada: A People's History."

79 Jack Granatstein, "Slow and Stately," *National Post*, 30 October 2000; Jack Granatstein, "A Nation Born in Battle," *National Post*, 13 November 2000; Jack Granatstein, "History without the People," *National Post*, 29 January 2001; Jonathan Vance, "A Land of Poor Visibility," *National Post*, 23 October 2000, and "Through a Traditional Lens," *National Post*, 15 January 2001; Michael Bliss, "No Blood, No Screams," *National Post*, 1 November 2000; Michael Bliss, "Canada's History Multiplies," *National Post*, 8 January 2001; David Bercuson, "A Nation's Fate in the Balance," *National Post*, 6 November 2000; and David Bercuson, "A Superficial Look at Confederation," *National Post*, 22 January 2001.

80 Jack Granatstein, "History without the People," *National Post*, 29 January 2001.

81 Muise, "Media and Public History."

82 In "Through a Journalistic Lens," CBCRL, Production File "Canada: A People's History."

83 Marie Natanson, "Aide Memoire: War at Sea," 20 February 1995, CULSC, P112/G6, box HA 1346, file "CBC, Politics of Post Valour Films."

84 Veronica (Nikki) Strong-Boag to Gene Allen, 29 July 2000, 6, CTASC, F0293, file 2003-021/001 (9); Gendron, interview by author.

85 Strong-Boag to Allen, 29 July 2000, 6, CTASC, F0293, file 2003-021/ 001 (9).

86 Cook to Allen, 23 May 2001, CTASC, F0293, file 2003-021/001 (13).

87 Starowicz quoted in [CBC], "Telling the Story: Reconstructing History," at http://www.cbc.ca/history/BTSCONTSE3EP1CH1PA6LE.html (viewed June 2018).

88 James Elliott, "Canada as You've Never Seen It," *Hamilton Spectator*, 6 September 2000, online edition, www.hamiltonspectator.com/reports/284365.

89 Allen, "Professionals and the Public," 386.

90 Alan Hustak, "History in the Making," *Gazette* (Montreal), 21 October 2000.

91 Starowicz quoted in Friesen, "Canada," 200n76.

92 Conrad, "My Canada Includes the Atlantic Provinces," 394–8. See also Conrad, "To Have and Have Not," *Globe and Mail*, 7 March 2001, A11, CBCRL, Production File "'People's History' (Season 2)." In episode

2 the narrator mentions that a French presence was founded "first at Port Royal" before moving to the St Lawrence.

93 Bumsted, "Island Resistance." For more on the Prince Edward Island situation, see Robertson, *Tenant League of Prince Edward Island*. The Red River Resistance and the later North-West Resistance were featured in *A People's History* in from "Sea to Sea" and "Taking the West."

94 Conrad "My Canada Includes the Atlantic Provinces," 396–7.

95 Frank, "Public History and *The People's History*," 130.

96 Allen, interview by author, also noted by Gendron, interview by author.

97 Allen in Friesen, "Canada," 194; Allen, interview by author.

98 Gray, "History Wars," 42.

99 Gendron, interview by author.

100 Hubert Gendron, [comments on Gillmor Chapters], 2 December 1999, Hubert Gendron private papers.

101 Starowicz, *Making History*, 276–9; Christian Dufour, "Où est passée la Proclamation royale de 1763?," *Le Devoir*, 11 November 2000; Nathalie Petrowski, "Recherche désespérément Mel Gibson," *La Presse*, 16 January 2001; Franco Nuovo, "Le Canada: Historie plate," *Journal de Montréal*, 11 January 2001. All cited in Allen, "Professionals and the Public," 390n22 and 390n23.

102 Allen, "Professionals and the Public," 390.

103 Gendron, interview by author.

104 Starowicz, speech given at the History Teachers Conference at the University of Guelph, Ontario, 23 April 2004.

105 Allen, interview by author.

CONCLUSION

1 "Educational Broadcasting Draft," 2 January 1968, 7, LAC, RG 41, vol. 865, file PG 4-3-1.

2 Arthur Laird to Vincent Tovell, 19 May 1961, LAC, RG 41, vol. 484, file 11-18-11-108.

3 McKay, "CBC and the Public," 113–14, 196.

4 Knowlton Nash, interview by author.

5 The quote and summary below: McArthur, *Television and History*, 47.

6 Quoted in Friesen, "Canada," 190.

7 See Lowenthal, *Heritage Crusade and the Spoils of History*, regarding this penchant for detail on the part of heritage specialists.

8 Cited in Gray, "History Wars," 36.

9 The CBC/NFB co-productions *Canada's Sweetheart* and *The King Chronicle* were both well regarded series recognized as docudrama.

10 Dick, "Saving the Nation through National History," 192.

11 Koch, interview by author.

12 Cook, interview by author.

13 Jack Saywell, "Documentary Dramas – Broadcast on CBCTV 1960–1966," CTASC, F0402, file 2004-015/001 (02); Jack Saywell, interview by author.

14 Cook, *Craft of History*, 39, 136.

15 Groulx, "La meilleure histoire du monde," 408.

16 Including historian John English and Indigenous arts and curatorial studies scholar Gerald McMaster. See CBC Media Centre, "CBC's *Canada: The Story of Us* Brings a Nation's History to Life Starting March 26," 7 March 2017, at http://www.cbc.ca/mediacentre/press-release/cbcs-canada-the-story-of-us-brings-a-nations-history-to-life-starting-march (viewed May 2018); "Set Visit: *Canada: The Story of Us*," 12 August 2016, at http://bristowglobalmedia.com/set-visit-canada-the-story-of-us/ (viewed March 2018).

17 In Bill Brioux, "CBC's *Story of Us* Gives Canadians Fresh Take on 150 Years of History," *Star*, 27 March 2017, https://www.thestar.com/entertainment/television/2017/03/27/cbcs-story-of-us-gives-canadians-fresh-take-on-150-years-of-history.html (viewed May 2018).

Bibliography

NOTE ON SOURCES

This book is based on textual and audio-visual records housed in a variety of Canadian repositories, staffed by librarians and archivists whose assistance has been invaluable throughout the research process. A useful collection for any work about the CBC is the CBC corporate files at Library and Archives Canada (LAC). LAC also preserves copies of all of the pre-1990 television broadcasts reviewed in this book. LAC and other institutions hold important private archival collections as well. Especially pertinent for this study were the papers of the following individuals: Donald Creighton, Frank Underhill, J. Alphonse Ouimet, and Timothy Findley (all at LAC); Pierre Berton (McMaster University Mills Library: William Ready Division of Archives and Research Collections); Arthur Lower (Queen's University Archives); Brian McKenna (Concordia University Library, Special Collections); and Eric Koch, Jack Saywell, and Ramsay Cook (all at York University Libraries, Clara Thomas Archives and Special Collections).

The policy and production files at the CBC Reference Library are an essential source for internal policy records and reports, general production documents, and newspaper clippings and other published material such as the CBC Times. The CBC Times, published until 1969, is an excellent source of information on CBC radio and television programming, with articles on production matters as well as excerpts from interviews with production team members. The focus of this book is on the production side of CBC television programming, but newspaper reviews, found in library and archive collections and archived online, were helpful in providing a means to also make assessments of the professional reviews and public reaction to the programs.

TELEVISION PRODUCTIONS

Canada: A People's History. Parts 1–17. Exec. prod. Mark Starowicz. CBC. 2000–01.

CBC *Newsworld.* Host: Brian Johnson. Panel: Brian McKenna, Lionel Hastings, Don Elliot. 28 March 1992, 8:00 p.m., CBC Newsworld Collection, Carleton University MacOdrum Library (CUML).

A Conversation with Professor Donald Creighton. Prod. Larry Zolf. CBC. 1970. Ref. No. 354884. LAC.

"The Craft of History." *Images of Canada.* Prod. George Robertson. CBC. 1972. Ref. No. 54887. LAC.

The Days before Yesterday: Struggle for Nationhood. Parts 1–7. Prod. Cameron Graham. CBC. 1973. Ref. Nos. 54792–54796, 54888, 56408. LAC.

Durham's Canada. Parts 1–3. *Explorations.* Prod. Vincent Tovell. CBC. 1960. Ref. Nos. 287105–287107. LAC.

"The Fall of Quebec: A Battle for Historians." *Explorations.* Prod. Roger Racine. CBC. 1959. Ref. No. 86146. LAC.

"Folly on the Hill." *Images of Canada.* Prod. Vincent Tovell. CBC. 1973. Ref. No. 54782. LAC.

The Fourteenth Colony. Parts 1–3. *Explorations.* Prod. Eric Koch. CBC. 1962. Ref. Nos. 61775, 61788, 61803. LAC.

"Heroic Beginnings." *Images of Canada.* Prod. George Robertson. CBC. 1972. Ref. No. 54783. LAC.

"John A. Macdonald: The Impossible Idea." *The History Makers: Prelude to Confederation.* [*The Formative Years (Explorations)*]. Prod. Julian Biggs. NFB. 1961. Ref. No. 324842. LAC.

"Joseph Howe: The Tribune of Nova Scotia." *The History Makers: The Struggle for Self-Government.* [*Explorations.*] Prod. Julian Biggs. NFB. 1962. Ref. No. 324970. LAC.

"Journey without Arrival: A Personal Point of View with Northrop Frye." *Images of Canada.* Prod. Vincent Tovell. CBC. 1975. Ref. No. 299170. LAC.

"A Long View of Canadian History: An Interview with Donald Creighton." *Explorations.* Prod. Cliff Solway. CBC. 1959. Ref. No. 86144. LAC.

"A Long View of Canadian History, with Professor Frank Underhill." *Explorations.* Prod. Cliff Solway. CBC. 1960. Ref. No. 86138. LAC.

The National Dream: Building the Impossible Dream. Parts 1–8. Prod. James Murray. CBC. 1974. Ref. Nos. 54805–54812. LAC.

Portraits of the Thirties. Parts 1–4. *Explorations.* Prod. James Murray. CBC. 1962. Ref. Nos. 61628, 61630, 61686, 61688. LAC.

"Spirit in a Landscape: The People Beyond." *Images of Canada.* Prod. Carol Myers. CBC. 1976. Ref. No. 54790. LAC.

The Tenth Decade. Parts 1–8. Prod. Cameron Graham. CBC. 1971. Ref. Nos. 62–8, 74. LAC.

The Valour and the Horror. Parts 1–3. Prod. Galafilm, NFB, CBC. 1992.

A War for Survival. Parts 1–4. *The Formative Years [Explorations].* Prod. Melwyn Breen. CBC. 1962. Ref. Nos. 86042, 86057, 86074, 286986. LAC.

The Whitecomers. [Images of Canada]. Parts 1–5. Prod. Carol Myers/Vincent Tovell. CBC. 1973–75. Ref. Nos. 54784–54787, 56411. LAC.

"Winnipeg General Strike 1919." *Explorations.* Prod. Felix Lazarus. CBC. 1959. Ref. No. 214897. LAC.

ARCHIVAL COLLECTIONS

CBC *Reference Library (CBCRL)*
Production Files
CBC unpublished reports

Library and Archives Canada (LAC)
MG 30 D 204: Frank Underhill Fonds
MG 30 E 481: J. Alphonse Ouimet Fonds
MG 31 D 77: Donald Creighton Fonds
MG 31 D 196: Timothy Findley and William Whitehead Fonds
RG 41: Records of the Canadian Broadcasting Corporation

Concordia University Library, Special Collections (CULSC)
P112: Brian McKenna Fonds

McMaster University Mills Library. William Ready Division of Archives and Research Collections (WRDARC)
Pierre Berton Fonds

Queen's University Archives (QUA)
A.R.M. Lower Fonds

York University Libraries. Clara Thomas Archives and Special Collections (CTASC)
F0293: Ramsay Cook Fonds
F0402: John Tupper Saywell Fonds
F0472: Eric Koch Fonds

Private Collections
Hubert Gendron private papers
Ramsay Cook private papers

INTERVIEWS AND PERSONAL COMMUNICATION

Allen, Gene. Interview by author. Toronto, ON, 21 September 2006.
Cook, Ramsay. Interview by author. Toronto, ON, 22 September 2006.
Gendron, Hubert. Interview by author. Montreal, QC, 12 September 2006.
Koch, Eric. Interview by author. Toronto, ON, 21 September 2006.
Nash, Knowlton. Interview by author. Toronto, ON, 22 September 2006.
Robertson, George. E-mail communication, 14 October 2006; telephone
  communication, 17 October 2006.
Saywell, Jack. Interview by author. Toronto, ON, 21 September 2006.
Tovell, Vincent. Telephone interview by author. 14 October 2006.
Watkins, Peter. E-mail communication, 4 June 2007.

BOOKS, ARTICLES, REPORTS

Allen, Gene. "The Professionals and the Public: Responses to *Canada: A Peo-
  ple's History.*" *Histoire sociale/Social History* 34, 68 (2001): 381–91.
Anderson, Benedict. *Imagined Communities: Reflections on the Origin and
  Spread of Nationalism*, rev. ed. London: Verso, 2006.
Armstrong, Frederick H. "Maurice Careless." In *Old Ontario: Essays in
  Honour of J.M.S. Careless*, eds. David Keane and Colin Read, 12–35.
  Toronto: Dundurn, 1990.
Beck, J. Murray. *The Government of Nova Scotia.* Toronto: University of
  Toronto Press, 1957.
Bell, Erin. "Beyond the Witness: The Layering of Historical Testimonies on
  British Television." In *Televising History: Mediating the Past in Postwar
  Europe*, eds. Erin Bell and Ann Gray, 77–92. Basingstoke, UK: Palgrave
  MacMillan, 2010.
Bercuson, David J. "The Valour and the Horror: A Historical Analysis." In
  The Valour and the Horror Revisited, eds. David J. Bercuson and S.F. Wise,
  31–58. Montreal and Kingston: McGill-Queen's University Press, 1994.
Bercuson, David J., and S.F. Wise, eds. *The Valour and the Horror Revisited.*
  Montreal and Kingston: McGill-Queen's University Press, 1994.
Berger, Carl. "William Morton: The Delicate Balance of Region and Nation."
  In *The West and the Nation: Essays in Honour of W.L. Morton*, eds. Carl
  Berger and Ramsay Cook, 9–32. Toronto: McClelland and Stewart, 1976.
– *The Writing of Canadian History: Aspects of English-Canadian Historical
  Writing since 1900.* Toronto: University of Toronto Press, 1986.
Berton, Pierre. *My Times: Living with History, 1947–1995.* Toronto: Double-
  day Canada, 1995.
Bilodeau, Charles. "L'Histoire Nationale." In *Royal Commission Studies:
  A Selection of Essays.* Prepared for the Royal Commission on National

Development in the Arts, Letters and Sciences, Canada, 217–30. Ottawa: Edmond Cloutier, 1951.

Bomber Harris Trust. *A Battle for Truth*. Agincourt, ON: Ramsay Business Systems, 1994.

Bremner, Ian. "History without Archives: Simon Schama's *A History of Britain*." In *The Historian, Television and Television History*, eds. Graham Roberts and Philip Taylor, 63–75. Luton: University of Luton Press, 2001.

Breuilly, John. "Nationalism and the Making of National Pasts." In *Nations and Their Histories: Constructions and Representations*, eds. Susana Carvalho and François Gemenne, 7–28. London: Palgrave Macmillan, 2009.

Brook, Glen. "Picturing an Experience of the Past: The Case of *Canada: A People's History*." PhD diss. Concordia University, 2009.

Bumsted, J.M. "Island Resistance: Two Popular Movements for Political Change in the Era of Confederation." *Acadiensis* 27, 2 (1998): 135–41.

Bushnell, E.L. "Report on Television by Director General of Programmes of the Canadian Broadcasting Corporation on a Visit to The United Kingdom from May 20th to June 14th – 1949." 1949. CBCRL.

Canada. *Broadcasting Act*. 1991. https://laws-lois.justice.gc.ca/eng/acts/B-9.01/20120316/P1TT3xt3.html.

– Committee on Broadcasting. *Report of the Committee on Broadcasting*. Ottawa: Queen's Printer, 1965.

– *Debates of the Senate*. 34th Parliament, 3rd Session, 134, no. 84, 18 June 1992.

– Federal Cultural Policy Review Committee. *Report of the Federal Cultural Policy Review Committee*. Ottawa: Department of Communications, 1982.

– Mandate Review Committee, CBC, NFB, Telefilm (Canada). *Making Our Voices Heard: Canadian Broadcasting and Film for the 21st Century*. Ottawa: Supply and Services Canada, 1996.

– Parliament. House of Commons. *Debates*. Ottawa: King's Printer, [Various dates].

– Parliament. House of Commons. Standing Committee on Broadcasting, Films, and Assistance to the Arts. *An Act to Implement a Broadcasting Policy for Canada*... Ottawa: Queen's Printer, 1967–68.

– Parliament. House of Commons. Standing Committee on Broadcasting. *Minutes of the Proceedings and Evidence*, No. 3, 20 February 1961. Cited in Ryan Edwardson, *Canadian Content Culture and the Quest for Nationhood* (Toronto: University of Toronto Press, 2008).

– Parliament. House of Commons. Standing Committee on Canadian Heritage. *Our Cultural Sovereignty: The Second Century of Canadian Broadcasting*. Ottawa: Communication Canada, 2003.

– Parliament. Senate. *Production and Distribution of the National Film Board Production 'The Kid Who Couldn't Miss': Report of the Standing*

Committee on Social Affairs, Science and Technology. Ottawa: Supply and Services Canada, 1986.

– Parliament. Senate. Standing Senate Committee on Social Affairs, Science and Technology. *Proceedings of the Standing Senate Subcommittee on Veterans Affairs.* 34th Parliament, 3rd Session. [Issue nos. 1–10 and various dates between 25 June 1992 and 4 February 1993].

– Parliament. Senate. Standing Committee on Transport and Communications. *An Act Respecting Broadcasting.* Ottawa: Queen's Printer, 1958.

– *Report of the Royal Commission on Radio Broadcasting.* Ottawa: F.A. Acland, 1929.

– Royal Commission on Broadcasting. *Report of the Royal Committee on Broadcasting.* Ottawa: Queen's Printer, 1957.

– Royal Commission on National Development in the Arts, Letters and Sciences. *Report of the Royal Commission on National Development in the Arts, Letters and Sciences, 1949–1951.* Ottawa: Edmond Cloutier, 1951.

– Royal Commission on National Development in the Arts, Letters and Sciences. *Royal Commission Studies: A Selection of Essays ...* Ottawa: Edmond Cloutier, 1951.

– Task Force on Broadcasting Policy. *Report of the Task Force on Broadcasting Policy: Recommendations.* Ottawa: Supply and Services Canada, 1986.

Canadian Broadcasting Corporation. *Annual Report.* Ottawa: CBC [various dates].

– "CBC Television: Celebrating Fifty Years." 2002. In General File "CBC History," CBCRL.

– *CBC Times.* Ottawa: CBC [various dates].

– "CBC-TV Network 1962–63: 10 Years of Canadian Television." 1963, CBCRL.

– *Journalistic Policy/Politique Journalistique*, rev. ed. Montreal: CBC, 1988.

– "Material in Support of CBC Applications for Renewal of Network Licenses: English Language Television." November 1973, CBCRL.

– "Mission, Values, Goals and Objectives." October 1990, CBCRL.

– "A New Commitment" [Submission to the Parliamentary Standing Committee on Canadian Heritage]. 1 November 1994, CBCRL.

– Publications Branch. *A Long View of Canadian History.* The Text of Two Half-Hour Programs Originally Presented on the CBC Television Network, June 16th and 30th, 1959. Toronto: CBC, 1959.

– Publications Branch. *The Radical Tradition: A Second View of Canadian History.* The text of two half-hour programs by Frank H. Underhill and Paul Fox, as originally presented on the CBC Television Network in the program "Explorations," June 8th and 15th, 1960. Toronto: CBC, 1960.

– "Report of the Joint Study Group on Multicultural Broadcasting." 27 February 1973, CBCRL.

– Research Department. "What the Canadian Public Thinks of Television and of the Television Services Provided by the CBC." February 1974, CBCRL.

Careless, J.M.S. "'Limited Identities' in Canada." *Canadian Historical Review* 50, 1 (March 1969): 1–10.

Carr, Graham. "Rules of Engagement: Public History and the Drama of Legitimation." *Canadian Historical Review* 86, 2 (2005): 317–54.

Carvalho, Susana, and François Gemenne. "Introduction." In *Nations and Their Histories: Constructions and Representations*, eds. Susana Carvalho and François Gemenne, 1–3. London: Palgrave Macmillan, 2009.

Charland, Maurice. "Technological Nationalism." *Canadian Journal of Political and Social Theory/Revue canadienne de théorie politique et sociale* 10, 1–2 (1986): 196–220.

Clark, Penney. "Engaging the Field – A Conversation with Mark Starowicz." *Canadian Social Studies*, 36, 2 (2002), https://canadian-social-studies-jour nal.educ.ualberta.ca/content/articles-2000-2010#ARengaging_the_field119.

Conrad, Margaret. "My Canada Includes the Atlantic Provinces." *Histoire sociale/Social History* 34, 68 (2001): 392–402.

Cook, John R. "Making the Past Present: Peter Watkins's Culloden," in *Documenting the Documentary: Close Readings of Documentary Film and Video*, eds. Barry Keith Grant and Jeannette Sloniowski, 217–36. Detroit: Wayne State University Press, 2014.

Cook, Ramsay. "Canadian Centennial Cerebrations." *International Journal* 22, 4 (1967): 659–63.

– *The Craft of History*. Edited by Eleanor Cook with an introduction by Ramsay Cook. Toronto: CBC, 1973.

Cormier, Ronald, ed. *J'ai vécu la guerre: Témoignages de soldats acadiens, 1939–1945*. Moncton: Éditions D'Acadie, 1988. (The book exists in an English edition as: Cormier Ronald, ed. *Forgotten Soldiers: Stories from Acadian Veterans of the Second World War* [Fredericton: New Ireland Press, 1992].)

Côté, Olivier. *Construire la nation au petit écran : le Canada, une histoire populaire de CBC/Radio-Canada, 1995–2002*. Quebec: Septentrion, 2014.

Craig, G.M., ed. *Lord Durham's Report: An Abridgement of Report on the Affairs of British North America, by Lord Durham* [John George Lambton, Earl of Durham]. Montreal and Kingston: McGill-Queen's University Press, 2007.

Crosby, John. "The United Nations Gets Pushed Around." *New York Herald Tribune*, 11 February 1951.

Curtin, Michael. *Redeeming the Wasteland: Television Documentary and Cold War Politics*. New Brunswick, NJ: Rutgers University Press, 1995.

Daly, Christopher. *Covering America: A Narrative History of a Nation's Journalism*. Amherst and Boston: University of Massachusetts Press, 2012.

Daschuk, James. *Clearing the Plains: Disease, Politics of Starvation, and the Loss of Aboriginal Life*. Regina: University of Regina Press, 2013.

Deuze, Mark. "What Is Journalism: Professional Identity and Ideology of Journalists Reconsidered." *Journalism* 6, 4 (2005): 442–64.

Dick, Ernest J. "History on Television: A Critical Archival Examination of *The Valour and the Horror*." *Archivaria* 34 (Summer 1992): 199–216.

Dick, Lyle. "Saving the Nation through National History: The Case of *Canada: A People's History*." In *Settling and Unsettling Memories: Essays in Canadian Public History*, eds. Nicole Neatby and Peter Hodgins, 188–214. Toronto: University of Toronto Press, 2012.

Edgerton, Gary R. "Ken Burns' Rebirth of a Nation: Television, Narrative, and Popular History." *Film and History* 22, 4 (1992): 119–33.

– "Mediating *Thomas Jefferson*: Ken Burns as Popular Historian." In *Television Histories: Shaping Collective Memory in the Media Age*, eds. Gary R. Edgerton and Peter C. Rollins, 169–90. Lexington: University Press of Kentucky, 2001.

Edwardson, Ryan. *Canadian Content: Culture and the Quest for Nationhood*. Toronto: University of Toronto Press, 2008.

Evans, Gary. *In the National Interest: A Chronicle of the National Film Board of Canada from 1949 to 1989*. Toronto: University of Toronto Press, 1991.

Forbes, E.R. "In Search of a Post-Confederation Maritime Historiography, 1900–1967." *Acadiensis* 8, 1 (1978): 3–21.

Francis, Daniel. *National Dreams: Myth, Memory, and Canadian History*. Vancouver: Arsenal Pulp Press, 1997.

Francis, R. Douglas. *Frank H. Underhill: Intellectual Provocateur*. Toronto: University of Toronto Press, 1986.

Frank, David. "Public History and the *People's History*: A View from Atlantic Canada." *Acadiensis* 32, 2 (2003): 120–33.

Friesen, Joe. "'Canada: A People's History' as 'Journalists' History.'" *History Workshop Journal* 56, 1 (2003): 184–203.

Frisch, Michael H. *A Shared Authority: Essays on the Craft and Meaning of Oral and Public History*. Albany: State University of New York Press, 1990.

Fulford, Robert. "Canadian Cultural Nationalism." In *1974 Britannica Book of the Year*. Toronto: Encyclopedia Britannica, 1974.

Garland Library of Narratives of North American Indian Captivities. Vol. 28. [Containing John Jewitt, *A Journal Kept at Nootka Sound*, 1807; and Richard Alsop, ed., *A Narrative of the Adventures and Sufferings of John R. Jewitt*, ... [1815]. New York: Garland, 1976.

Golding, Peter, and Graham Murdock. "Culture, Communications, and Political Economy." In *Mass Media and Society*, eds. James Curran and Michael Gurevitch, 70–92, 3rd ed. London: Arnold, 2000.

Gordon, Alan. *The Hero and the Historians: Historiography and the Uses of Jacques Cartier*. Vancouver: UBC Press, 2010.

Granatstein, Jack L. *Who Killed Canadian History?* Toronto: HarperCollins, 1998.

Gray, Charlotte. "History Wars." *Saturday Night* 21 (October 2000): 34–42.

Green, James R. "Engaging in People's History: The Massachusetts History Workshop." In *Presenting the Past: Essays on History and the Public*, eds. Susan Porter Benson, Stephen Brier, and Roy Rosenzweig, 339–59. Philadelphia: Temple University Press, 1986.

Groulx, Patrice. "La meilleure histoire du monde." *Histoire sociale/Social History* 34, 68 (2001): 403–14.

Hall, Stuart. "Television and Culture." *Sight and Sound* 45, 4 (1976): 246–52.

Hardin, Herschel. *Closed Circuits: The Sellout of Canadian Television*. Vancouver: Douglas and McIntyre, 1985.

Harris, Arthur. *Bomber Offensive*. New York: Macmillan, 1947.

Hodgins, Peter. "The Canadian Dream-Work: History, Myth and Nostalgia in the Heritage Minutes." PhD diss. Carleton University, 2003.

Hogarth, David. *Documentary Television in Canada: From National Public Service to Global Marketplace*. Montreal and Kingston: McGill-Queen's University Press, 2002.

– "Public Service Broadcasting as a Modern Project: A Case Study of Early Public-Affairs Broadcasting in Canada." *Canadian Journal of Communication* 26, 3 (2001): 351–65.

Igartua, José E. *The Other Quiet Revolution: National Identities in English Canada, 1945–1971*. Vancouver: UBC Press, 2005.

John Grierson Project. *John Grierson and the NFB*. Toronto: ECW Press, 1984.

Johnson, A.W. "Broadcasting Priorities for the 1980s." 1978. [CBC], CBCRL.

Kealey, Greg. "1919: The Canadian Labour Revolt." *Labour/Le Travail*, 13 (Spring 1984): 11–44.

Kellner, Douglas. "Overcoming the Divide: Cultural Studies and Political Economy. In *Cultural Studies in Question*, eds. Marjorie Ferguson and Peter Golding, 102–20. London: Sage, 1997.

Kenter, Peter. *TV North: Everything You Wanted to Know about Canadian Television*. Vancouver: Whitecap, 2001.

Killan, Gerald. *Preserving Ontario's Heritage: A History of the Ontario Historical Society*. Willowdale, ON: Ontario Historical Society, 1976.

Klinck, Carl F., ed. *The Literary History of Canada*. Toronto: University of Toronto Press, 1965.

Knowlton, Steven R. "Into the 1960s – and into the Crucible." In *Fair and Balanced: A History of Journalistic Objectivity*, eds. Steven R. Knowlton and Karen L. Freeman, 221–35. Northport, AL: Vision Press, 2005.

Koch, Eric, and Vincent Tovell, with Jack Saywell. *Success of a Mission: Lord Durham in Canada – A Play for Television*. Toronto: Clarke Irwin, 1961.

Korneski, Kurt. "Prairie Fire: The Winnipeg General Strike." *Labour/Le Travail* 45 (Spring 2000): 259–66.

Kristmanson, Mark. *Plateaus of Freedom: Nationality, Culture, and State Security in Canada, 1940–1960*. New York: Oxford University Press, 2003.

Kuffert, L.B. *A Great Duty: Canadian Responses to Modern Life and Mass Culture in Canada, 1939–1967*. Montreal and Kingston: McGill-Queen's University Press, 2003.

Leach, Jim. "For the Record: Canadian Dramatic Anthology Series." http://www.museum.tv/archives/etv/F/htmlF/fortherecor/fortherecor.htm (viewed August 2018).

Lewis, Robert. "Pierre Juneau's Spectacular Leap of Faith." *Saturday Night* (August 1974): 11–16.

Linenthal, Edward T. "Anatomy of a Controversy." In *History Wars: The Enola Gay and Other Battles for the American Past*, eds. Edward Linenthal and Tom Engelhardt, 9–62. New York: Holt, 1996.

Litt, Paul. *The Muses, The Masses and the Massey Commission*. Toronto: University of Toronto Press, 1992.

Lockerbie, Ian. "Grierson and Realism." In *John Grierson and the NFB*, ed. The John Grierson Project, 86–101. Toronto: ECW Press, 1984.

Lowenthal, David. *The Heritage Crusade and the Spoils of History*. Cambridge: Cambridge University Press, 1998.

Lower, Arthur. *History and Myth: Arthur Lower and the Making of Canadian Nationalism*, ed. Welf H. Heick. Vancouver: UBC Press, 1975.

– *My First Seventy-Five Years*. Toronto: Macmillan of Canada, 1967.

Lytle, D.E., and Pierre Juneau. "Draft Report on Study of CBC/NFB Relations." 1 March 1966. LAC.

MacKinnon, Frank. *The Government of Prince Edward Island*. Toronto: University of Toronto Press, 1951.

MacLennan, Anne. "American Network Broadcasting, the CBC, and Canadian Radio Stations during the 1930s: A Content Analysis." *Journal of Radio Studies* 12, 1 (2005): 85–103.

MacNutt, William. *The Atlantic Provinces: The Emergence of Colonial Society, 1712–1857*. Toronto: McClelland and Stewart, 1965.

– *New Brunswick: A History, 1784–1867*. Toronto: Macmillan of Canada, 1963.

Mann, Susan. *The Dream of Nation: A Social and Intellectual History of Quebec*, 2nd ed. Montreal and Kingston: McGill-Queen's University Press, 2002.

Martin, Ged. *Past Futures: The Impossible Necessity of History*. Toronto: University of Toronto Press, 2004.

Matheson, Donald. "The Watchdog's New Bark: Changing Forms of Investigative Reporting." In *The Routledge Companion to News and Journalism*, ed. Stuart Allan, 82–92. Rev. ed. New York: Routledge, 2010.

McArthur, Colin. *Television and History*. London: BFI, 1978.

McKay, Bruce. "The CBC and the Public: Management Decision Making in the English Television Service of the Canadian Broadcasting Corporation, 1970–1974." PhD diss., Stanford University, 1976.

McKay, Ian. *In the Province of History: The Making of the Public Past in Twentieth-Century Nova Scotia*. Montreal and Kingston: McGill-Queen's University Press, 2010.

– *The Quest of the Folk: Antimodernism and Cultural Selection in Twentieth-Century Nova Scotia*. Montreal and Kingston: McGill-Queen's University Press, 1994.

– "Strikes in the Maritimes, 1901–1914." *Acadiensis* 13, 1 (1983): 3–46.

McKillop, A.B. *Pierre Berton: A Biography*. Toronto: McClelland and Stewart, 2008.

McNaught, Kenneth. *Conscience and History: A Memoir*. Toronto: University of Toronto Press, 1999.

Middlebrook, Martin. *The Berlin Raids: R.A.F. Bomber Command Winter, 1943–44*. New York: Viking, 1988.

– *The Nuremberg Raid: 30–31 March 1944*. New York: William Morrow and Co., 1974.

Mindich, David T.Z. *Just the Facts: How "Objectivity" Came to Define American Journalism*. New York: New York University Press, 1998.

Moore, Christopher. "Coffee with Mark Starowicz." *The Beaver* 81, 3 (2001): 54–5.

Morgan, William. "Report on *The Valour and the Horror*." 6 November 1992. CBCRL.

Morton, William. "Historical Societies and Museums." In *Royal Commission Studies, Canada*, 249–60. Ottawa: Edmond Cloutier, 1951.

Muise, Del. "Media and Public History: Canada: A People's History." https://web.archive.org/web/20050525222501o/http://www.cshc.ubc.ca/open_muise.php (viewed March 2019).

Murdock, Graham. "Base Notes: The Conditions of Cultural Practice." In *Cultural Studies in Question*, eds. Marjorie Ferguson and Peter Golding, 86–101. London: Sage, 1997.

Nash, Knowlton. *The Microphone Wars: A History of Triumph and Betrayal at the CBC*. Toronto: McClelland and Stewart, 1994.

– *Prime Time at Ten: Behind-the-Camera Battles of Canadian TV Journalism*. Toronto: McClelland and Stewart, 1987.

National Film Board. *Annual Report*. Ottawa: NFB, [various dates].

Neatby, Hilda. "National History." In *Royal Commission Studies, Canada*, 205–16. Ottawa: Edmond Cloutier, 1951.

Neatby, Nicole, and Peter Hodgins. "Introduction." In *Settling and Unsettling Memories: Essays in Canadian Public History*, 3–25. Toronto: University of Toronto Press, 2012.

Nelles, H.V. *The Art of Nation-Building: Pageantry and Spectacle at Quebec's Tercentenary*. Toronto: University of Toronto Press, 1999.

– "The Ties That Bind: Berton's CPR." *Canadian Forum* 50 (November–December 1970): 270–2.

Neillands, Robin. *The Bomber War: The Allied Air Offensive against Nazi Germany*. Woodstock and New York: Overlook Press, 2001.

Nichols, Bill. *Introduction to Documentary*. Bloomington: Indiana University Press, 2010.

Pearce, Donald. *Journal of a War: North-West Europe 1944–1945*. Toronto: Macmillan of Canada, 1965.

Peers, Frank. *The Public Eye: Television and the Politics of Canadian Broadcasting, 1952–1968*. Toronto: University of Toronto Press, 1979.

Porter Benson, Susan, Stephen Brier, and Roy Rosenzweig. "Introduction." In *Presenting the Past: Essays on History and the Public*, ed. Susan Porter Benson, Stephen Brier, and Roy Rosenzweig, xv–xxiv. Philadelphia: Temple University Press, 1986.

Portelli, Alessandro. *The Death of Luigi Trastulli and Other Stories: Form and Meaning in Oral History*. New York: State University of New York Press, 1991.

Posner, Michael. "The CRTC Gong Show Presents ... The CBC!" *Maclean's*, 23 October 1978, 20–33.

Raboy, Marc. *Missed Opportunities: The Story of Canada's Broadcasting Policy*. Montreal and Kingston: McGill-Queen's University Press, 1990.

Reid, John G. "Writing about Regions." In *Writing about Canada: A Handbook for Modern Canadian History*, ed. John Schultz, 71–96. Scarborough, ON: Prentice-Hall, 1990.

Reilly, Nolan. "The General Strike in Amherst, Nova Scotia, 1919." *Acadiensis* 9, 2 (1980): 56–77.

Robertson, Ian Ross. *The Tenant League of Prince Edward Island, 1864–1867: Leasehold Tenure in the New World*. Toronto: University of Toronto Press, 1996.

Rudin, Ronald. *Making History in Twentieth-Century Quebec*. Toronto: University of Toronto Press, 1997.

Rutherford, Paul. *When Television Was Young: Primetime Canada, 1952–1967*. Toronto: University of Toronto Press, 1990.

Schudson, Michael. *The Power of News*. Cambridge: Harvard University Press, 1995.

Sheppard, Gordon. "A Special Report on the Cultural Policy and Activities of the Government of Canada, 1965–66, volume 2." May 1966. LAC.

Sloniowski, Jeannette. "Popularizing History: *The Valour and the Horror*," in *Slippery Pastimes: Reading the Popular in Canadian Culture*, eds. Joan Nicks and Jeannette Sloniowski, 159–74. Waterloo, ON: Wilfrid Laurier University Press, 2002.

Smith, Anthony D. *Nationalism: Theory, Ideology, History*. 2nd ed. Cambridge: Polity Press, 2010.

Stacey, Charles P. "Canadian Archives." In *Royal Commission Studies, Canada*, 231–48. Ottawa: Edmond Cloutier, 1951.

– *A Date with History: Memoirs of a Canadian Historian*. Ottawa: Deneau, 1982.

Starowicz, Mark. *Making History: The Remarkable Story Behind Canada: A People's History*. Toronto: McClelland and Stewart, 2003.

Stewart, Andrew, and William H.N. Hull. *Canadian Television Policy and the Board of Broadcast Governors, 1958–68*. Edmonton: University of Alberta Press, 1994.

Swan, Susan. "Educative Activities of the Canadian Broadcasting System and The National Film Board of Canada." Paper no. 8 in the New Technologies in Canadian Education series. Toronto: Ontario Educational Communications Authority, 1984.

Thorburn, Hugh. *Politics in New Brunswick*. Toronto: University of Toronto Press, 1961.

Taras, David. "The Struggle over *The Valour and the Horror*: Media Power and the Portrayal of War." *Canadian Journal of Political Science* 28, 4 (1995): 725–48.

Taylor, C.J. *Negotiating the Past: The Making of Canada's National Historic Parks and Sites*. Montreal and Kingston: McGill-Queen's University Press, 1990.

Television Committee of the University of Toronto. "A Brief to the Royal Commission on Broadcasting." 10 April 1956. University of Toronto Robarts Library.

Trouillot, Michel-Rolph. *Silencing the Past: Power and the Production of History*. Boston: Beacon Press, 1995.

Vance, Jonathan. *Death so Noble: Memory, Meaning, and the First World War*. Vancouver: UBC Press, 1997.

Veilleux, Gérard. "Repositioning: A Report to the Staff of the CBC." 1992. CBCRL.

Vipond, Mary. "The Beginnings of Public Broadcasting in Canada: The CRBC, 1932–1936." *Canadian Journal of Communication* 19, 2 (1994): 151–71.

– "Financing Canadian Public Broadcasting: Licence Fees and the 'Culture of Caution.'" *Historical Journal of Film, Radio and Television* 15, 2 (1995): 285–300.

– *Listening In: The First Decade of Broadcasting in Canada, 1922–1932*. Montreal and Kingston: McGill-Queen's University Press, 1992.

Vos, Tim P., and Teri Finneman. "The Early Historical Construction of Journalism's Gatekeeping Role." *Journalism* 18, 3 (2017): 265–80.

West, Emily. "Selling Canada to Canadians: Collective Memory, National Identity and Popular Culture." *Critical Studies in Media Communication* 19, 2 (2002): 212–29.

White, Hayden. *Metahistory: The Historical Imagination in Nineteenth-Century Europe.* Baltimore: Johns Hopkins University Press, 1973.

Wise, S.F. "The Valour and the Horror: A Report for the CBC Ombudsman." In *The Valour and the Horror Revisited*, eds. David J. Bercuson and S.F. Wise, 13–30. Montreal and Kingston: McGill-Queen's University Press, 1994.

Wise, S.F, and David J. Bercuson. "Introduction." In *The Valour and the Horror Revisited*, eds. David J. Bercuson and S.F. Wise, 3–11. Montreal and Kingston: McGill-Queen's University Press, 1994.

Wright, Donald. *Donald Creighton: A Life in History.* Toronto: University of Toronto Press, 2015.

– "Donald Creighton, John Gray, and the Making of Macdonald." *Historical Perspectives on Canadian Publishing.* McMaster University Library, n.d. http://hpcanpub.mcmaster.ca/case-study/donald-creighton-john-gray-and-making-macdonald (viewed December 2018).

– "Creighton, Donald Grant." *Dictionary of Canadian Biography* http://www.biographi.ca/en/bio/creighton_donald_grant_20E.html (viewed January 2015).

– *The Professionalization of History in English Canada.* Toronto: University of Toronto Press, 2005.

Zinn, Howard. *A People's History of the United States.* New York: Harper Perennial, 2005.

Index